DATE DUE FOR RETURN

30. JUN 93 24

30. JUN 93

30. JUN 93 9 2640

This book may be recalled
before the above date

90014

Philoponus
On Aristotle on the Intellect

Philoponus
On Aristotle on the Intellect
(*de Anima* 3.4–8)

Translated by
William Charlton

with the assistance of
Fernand Bossier

Duckworth

First published in 1991 by
Gerald Duckworth & Co. Ltd.
The Old Piano Factory,
48 Hoxton Square, London N1 6PB

Introduction and Translation © 1991 by William Charlton
Preface and Appendix © 1991 by Richard Sorabji

ISBN 0 7156 2245 5

British Library Cataloguing in Publication Data
Philoponus, John *6th cent.*
On Aristotle on the intellect: (On the soul 3.4–8).
1. Humans. Intelligence. Theories
I. Title   II. Charlton, W. (William) *1935–*   III. Bossier,
Fernand   IV. Aristotle *384–322 B.C. De anima*
153.9092

ISBN 0–7156–2245–5

Phototypeset by Intype, London
Printed in Great Britain by
Redwood Press Ltd., Melksham

Contents

Preface

Richard Sorabji

This is a special volume. In 1989, William Charlton completed a very skilful translation which made the best possible sense of Latin that was often unintelligible. He equipped it with an introduction which brought out the unique views of Philoponus on sense perception, imagination and thinking and revealed how far Philoponus diverged from Aristotle. He also offered an up to date verdict on vexed questions of authenticity. That was already a notable achievement.

At that point Fernand Bossier spotted that there was something wrong with the Latin. The Greek original of Philoponus is lost. What survives is the Latin translation made in the thirteenth century by William of Moerbeke. Where the Latin translation reads, unintelligibly and ungrammatically, 'if not' (*si non*), William of Moerbeke must have had before his eyes a Greek text that read 'if not' (*ei mê*). That is equally unintelligible and ungrammatical. But it can easily be explained as a corruption of the Greek word *eidê* – the Platonic Forms – which makes perfect sense. Bossier's detective work pierces through the unintelligible Latin to the original Greek. On the basis of such conjectures and others that take account, for example, of William of Moerbeke's own idiosyncratic habits of abbreviation, Bossier suggested a new text at many points. Charlton had sometimes anticipated, sometimes accepted and sometimes dissented from the suggestions. The resulting agreed emendations are listed at the end and explanations are incorporated into the footnotes. The emended passages are retranslated by Charlton, and the indexes include Greek-Latin equivalences.

The result is much more than a translation of one of the most interesting ancient commentaries on Aristotle. In addition, we see a medieval translator at work and we have the basis of a new text, so that we may often know for the first time what Philoponus originally said. Finally, Charlton's philosophically sensitive introduction reveals the theories that Philoponus developed in Philosophy of Mind and how foreign they appear when attributed, as they are by Philoponus, to Aristotle.

The present translations have been made possible by generous and imaginative funding from the following sources: the National

vii

Endowment for the Humanities, Division of Research Programs, an independent federal agency of the USA; the Leverhulme Trust; the British Academy; the Jowett Copyright Trustees; the Royal Society (UK); Centro Internazionale A. Beltrame di Storia dello Spazio e del Tempo (Padua); Mario Mignucci; Liverpool University.

I should like to thank the following for their very helpful comments on the translation: Charles Burnett, Bernard Dod, Jill Kraye, Lars Mortensen, Vivian Nutton and Koenraad Verrycken.

Introduction

1. Text, authorship and translation

Text

The work here translated into English is a thirteenth-century translation into Latin from a Greek commentary on a portion of Aristotle's *de Anima* (*On the Soul*) known as the *de Intellectu* (*On the Intellect: de Anima* 3.4–8). The Greek original is now lost, although excerpts from it are embedded in a surviving Greek paraphrase of Aristotle's *de Anima* put together by Sophonias at the end of the thirteenth or the beginning of the fourteenth century (edited by Michael Hayduck, Berlin 1883). The Latin translation is preserved in three manuscripts, Toledo Cathedral Library 95.13, Vatican Library Lat. 2438, and Biblioteca Casanatense 957. These manuscripts are referred to hereafter as T, V and C. More than half the text is also preserved in Henry Bate's *Speculum divinorum et quorundam naturalium*, referred to as Bate or B. I am grateful to the Vatican Library and the Biblioteca Casanatense for sending me photocopies of their manuscripts and to the librarian of the Cathedral Library at Toledo for making me welcome for a week to study the codices 95.13 and 47.12 there.

The Latin translation was executed by the Belgian Dominican William de Moerbeke with a celerity which leaves his present namesake gasping. He finished translating Ammonius' commentary on the *de Interpretatione* on 12 September 1268 and he had got through this commentary on the *de Intellectu* (according to a note at the end of T) by 17 December. Not only was the work done at high speed, but Moerbeke says, 'Let the reader be warned that the Greek original was destroyed in many places by water so that I was completely unable to read it'. Roger Bacon, admittedly a member of a rival religious order, raises a doubt about his competence. William the Fleming, he says, 'had neither the knowledge of philosophy nor the knowledge of Greek on which he presumed'. Bacon reaches the conclusion that his translations are 'altogether erroneous and to be shunned' (quoted by Verbeke in his edition of Moerbeke's translation of Themistius' commentary on the *de Anima*, Leiden 1973, lxxiv). That verdict is too harsh, and for someone working, presumably, without dictionaries or grammar books Moerbeke did a creditable job. But it is not surprising under the circumstances that the

1

present Latin text has been found difficult by those who have worked on it. Marcel de Corte, who has none of Bacon's *animus*, is nevertheless compelled to say:

> The literal transcription of Greek into Latin, William de Moerbeke's invariable method, is inevitably bound to create obscurity. This is all the more so when it is a matter of passing from a style which is already tolerably convoluted like that of Philoponus to a scholastic vocabulary which, for all its effectiveness, bristles with stiffness in every phrase when compared with something of a diametrically opposite character which he has to translate nevertheless. (*Le commentaire de Jean Philopon sur le troisième livre du 'Traité de l'âme' d'Aristote*, Liège-Paris 1934, xviii.)

It is, in fact, Moerbeke's method to translate each Greek word as it comes into the nearest Latin equivalent, and this produces two sorts of mistake in particular. Pronouns and adjectives are translated as still agreeing in gender with the Greek nouns on which they depend even when the corresponding Latin nouns are different in gender; and verbs with neuter plural subjects, which are regularly singular in Greek, are rendered by singular verbs in Latin. These mistakes are so common in the text of the *de Intellectu* that the reader learns to discount them and I shall not always mention them in the notes.

De Corte published the first edition of Moerbeke's translation in 1934. In 1947 in *Mélanges Auguste Pelzer* Augustin Mansion published an article on de Corte's text in which he corrected some errors but confessed himself defeated by 'a series of passages which we have tried to reconstruct in vain' (p. 345). He, like de Corte, worked only from V and C but Gerard Verbeke inspected T, a superior manuscript written within twelve years of the original translation, and on the basis of this and Bate's *Speculum* produced a new edition in 1966 (Publications Universitaires de Louvain, Éditions Béatrice Nauwelaerts, Paris). It is this edition which I have used here and to which page and line numbers refer. Unfortunately Verbeke does not seem to have shared Moerbeke's optimistic hope that 'he who reads this will have more light than before on Aristotle's treatise' (120,69–70); at any rate he has often been content to print more or less untranslatable nonsense when considerable improvements could have been gained simply by changing the punctuation.

In codex 47.12 of the Cathedral Library at Toledo, in the margin of Moerbeke's translation of Themistius' commentary on the *de Anima*, there is a translation of the first six pages of our *de Intellectu* (1,1–6,35), apparently executed by Moerbeke in 1267. Verbeke conjectures plausibly enough that this passage was in the margin of the Greek manuscript of Themistius which Moerbeke was using. But there remains a puzzle. There are small discrepancies between the two versions (Verbeke prints them side by side as an appendix) but there is also a good deal of word-for-word identity. How can we account for this identity without supposing that Moerbeke had the 1267 translation beside him in the autumn of 1268? But if he had, how can we explain the discrepancies? There is no easy answer but perhaps it is least difficult to suppose he was extremely consistent as a translator and was also able to draw on some unconscious memories.

De Corte remarks that we have no sure way of distinguishing faults of copying from faults of translation. I think our manuscripts give us a pretty good idea of Moerbeke's original translation, but it is certainly hard to distinguish between his mistranslations, his misreadings of the Greek text in front of him, and copyists' mistakes in that. For this series of translations it seems most desirable to try to get back to Philoponus, and I have been very fortunate in obtaining the help of Fernand Bossier to whom many years of work on Moerbeke's translations have given an almost uncanny ability to divine the Greek that lies behind them. I have appended on pp. 135–9 a list of the suggestions I have accepted from him about how the Latin text or our understanding of it may be improved. A few are fairly obvious and I had arrived at them independently, but the vast majority solve problems which had defeated not only me but other scholars I had consulted. I have not included emendations which make no difference to the translation or changes of punctuation which are primarily cosmetic; but I have put in repunctuations which are not obvious and which will affect the reader's understanding of Philoponus' train of thought. I have also added his name in brackets to notes in which I am indebted to him. (My translation and notes have also benefited from comments by scholars whose aid the General Editor invoked,* and perhaps I may here acknowledge in passing an unquantifiable debt to Professor Sorabji himself who must surely be the most patient, painstaking and diplomatic of editors.)

C and V use larger letters to indicate lemmas and underlining for both lemmas and quotations. T uses underlining and, instead of larger letters, small horizontal strokes in the margin. (Verbeke may not have grasped the significance of these strokes; he says that T does not employ different handwriting to indicate lemmas, p. cxviii.) The scribes differ slightly in which passages they mark, they do not always distinguish clearly between genuine lemmas,

---

* Charles Burnett, Bernard Dod, Jill Kraye, Lars Mortensen, Vivian Nutton and Koenraad Verrycken – Ed.

i.e. passages taken from Aristotle for commentary, and quotations, i.e. passages of Aristotle used in commenting on these, and still less do they distinguish clearly between major lemmas, such as might introduce a general *theoria* of the subject matter, and lesser lemmas taken for detailed commentary on pieces of text (for this distinction see below pp. 6–7). Verbeke says, 'I have reckoned as lemmas all texts of Aristotle which without obliging us to break the continuity of a sentence in the commentary, allow us to reconstruct the text of *de Anima* 3.4–9' (p. cxviii). If, as appears to be the case, he uses capitals to indicate lemmas and italics to indicate passages of Aristotle which are not lemmas, I am not sure how consistently and correctly he has been able to follow this policy. A result of it, however, is that he has attached no special significance to the testimony of the scribes. The important question is how Philoponus regarded the various bits of Aristotle that enter into this work, and I think the guidance of the scribes, though not to be followed blindly, is not to be scorned. I have respected their consensus when it is not obviously mistaken. I use quotation marks for quotations. It does not seem to me that there is a firm distinction to be drawn between major and minor lemmas, but guided by the scribes I have refrained from separating some relatively minor lemmas from the commentary. Major lemmas are separated from the commentary and preceded by Bekker numbers in bold type. Minor lemmas appear within the text in bold type.

Authorship of the work translated by Moerbeke

Moerbeke attributes the work he translates to Philoponus. However, although a commentary in Greek on the *de Anima* under the name of Philoponus has come down to us (edited by Michael Hayduck, *CAG* 15, Berlin 1887), the commentary on Book 3 is plainly not what Moerbeke is translating, and there is no surviving Greek text corresponding to his Latin. The commentary on Book 3 in Hayduck, however, is very different in style and content from the commentary on the first two books. The general opinion of scholars is that the work Moerbeke translates originally stood in the place of the present commentary on Book 3. How the present commentary came to be substituted for it is a mystery which no one has any persuasive suggestion for resolving. I agree, however, that the work Moerbeke translates is by Philoponus. The chief arguments for its authenticity are as follows:

(1) Codex 47.12 of the Cathedral Library in Toledo contains not only the beginning of our *de Intellectu* but also, in the margin of 6v–7v, a translation by Moerbeke of a passage in the commentary

on Book 1 which we possess (Hayduck 115,31–120,33). It looks as if the Greek text of Themistius once belonged to someone who had a commentary containing both Hayduck's commentary on Book 1 and Moerbeke's commentary on Book 3. If we refer to the authors of Hayduck's commentaries as G1–3 and the author of Moerbeke's as L, then L = G1.

(2) De Corte offers a series of 27 arguments in the introduction to his edition, pp. ix–xv. He notes the following parallels in thought, expression or both:

2,27–31 with Hayduck's 266,4–7, 39,19–20. The words 'as we said earlier' (2,27) 'incontestably' refer back to one or the other of these passages.
4,70–72 with 10,1–3, 159,9–10.
4,78–80 with 159,32–3.
6,27–32 with 237,29–33.
13,96–8 with 160,32–4.
48,42 with 6,29.
91,62–92,65 with 3,17–23.
96,98–97, 00 with 379,11–14.
115–42 with 5,38–6,9, a passage to which L may be referring at 13,1 and 61,73–5.

To these we might add 20,77–81, parallel with 4,30–5, and 89,96–9, parallel with 2,13–16. G's rhetorical questions at 194,12–18 are echoed by L at 4,75–6, 45,66–7 and 60,55–60. 119,42–9 is partly parallel to 45,15–46,6, though here there is also a discrepancy (see my note ad loc.)

(3) There are many distinctive expressions common to L and G1–2; most of the following are noted by de Corte:
aliter, meaning 'besides': *allôs* (passim).
autoenergeia (53,60; 84,69): 35,1.
characterizare (52,31 etc.): 10,13 etc.
conditor intellectus (4,73 etc.): *dêmiourgikos nous*, 58,9.
eikonice (83,45): 126,31.
semper motus (45,47): *aeikinêtos*, 18,29 etc. (The point here is that *aeikinêtos* and *autokinêtos* are alternative readings at Plato, *Phaedrus* 245C5, a passage which the commentators will have had in mind: it looks as if G1 and L shared the reading *aeikinêtos*.)
simplices adiectiones (67,15 etc.): *haplai epibolai*, 2,7 etc.
supersalire (70,78): *huperbibazein*, 64,26 etc.

(4) G1–2 and L have the same style: both are discursive, both

favour long sentences of recapitulation and so on. There are no disagreements in doctrine between them and there are substantial agreements about intellect, thought (*dianoia*) and imagination. The same cannot, as I shall show in a moment, be said of L and G3. Étienne Évrard in his unpublished thesis *L'école d'Olympiodore et la composition du Commentaire à la Physique* (University of Liège 1957), p. 184 adds that L, like G1–2, is sparing of references by name to other commentators, but he overlooks the reference to Themistius at 78,14.

The Greek commentary on Book 3

If L is indeed Philoponus, who is G3? Subsequent discussions refer back to the opening paragraph of Hayduck's preface. Hayduck suggests that G3 is not Philoponus but Stephanus of Alexandria, the author of a surviving commentary on the *de Interpretatione*. In some 150 words of pregnant Latin he makes at least five points:

(1) G1 and G2 have the painstaking verbosity, the 'verbosa industria' of Philoponus, whereas G3 exhibits a conciseness, a 'ieiuna brevitas' which would be abhorrent to him.

(2) Two manuscripts, one of them the authoritative twelfth-century Parisinus 1914, have annotations attributing the commentary on Book 3 to a certain Stephanus. The codex Vaticanus gr. 241 f. 6 notes that among Greek commentaries on Aristotle there *was* one by Stephanus on the *de Anima*.

(3) G3 divides his commentary into *praxeis* (lessons). This is a device found in Stephanus' commentary on the *de Interpretatione* and 'nowhere else'.

(4) Certain (unspecified) locutions are favoured by both G3 and Stephanus.

(5) G3 declares (543,9) that he himself has said certain things in a commentary on the *de Interpretatione*; these things are found in Stephanus' commentary.

As they stand, Hayduck's points are not decisive.

(1) Hayduck does not specify any stylistic differences in detail, and G3 is not fairly described as jejune; it runs to 162 pages.

(2) This is significant but not decisive.

(3) G3 and Stephanus do indeed divide their commentaries into *praxeis*. A *praxis* appears to have been a single lecture or lesson consisting of two parts. The first, known as the *theôria*, is an overall critical account of a convenient chunk of text, sometimes about the length of a chapter in our edition of Aristotle, sometimes less. G3

gives four *praxeis* to the chapter on imagination: *de Anima* 3.3. The second part of the *praxis* is a detailed commentary on particular phrases or sentences in the text. The *praxeis* themselves are grouped into divisions, *tmêmata*. This system, however, is not peculiar to G3 and Stephanus. Raymond Vancourt in *Les derniers commentateurs d'Aristote: l'école d'Olympiodore* (Lille 1941) finds it in Olympiodorus, Elias and David, and suggests it is distinctive of the school of Olympiodorus. He claims that there is 'no trace' of it in Philoponus (pp. 11, 46), and infers that G3 is not Philoponus but Stephanus whom he takes to be a direct or, more probably, an indirect pupil of Olympiodorus. Olympiodorus refers to an astronomical event which took place in 564, but he was a pupil of Ammonius son of Hermeias, who was teaching in the 480s. Vancourt is inclined to identify G3 with a Stephanus who was appointed to a chair in Constantinople in 618 (p. 27).

Vancourt himself betrays the weakness of this argument in a footnote on p. 49. He there admits that there *is* a trace of a *praxis* in L whom he identifies with Philoponus. Étienne Évrard in his unpublished thesis *L'école d'Olympiodore et la composition du 'Commentaire à la Physique' de Jean Philopon* argues forcefully that not only is L's commentary on *de Anima* 3.5 a *praxis* but a systematic division into *praxeis* is found in Philoponus' commentary on the *Physics*. Contrary to what Vancourt says, there are also traces of it in G1–2. 271,10–273,6, 301,1–302,3 and 310,10–313,12 are *theôriai* followed by detailed commentaries, and at 302,19 there is a phrase which must mean 'as we said earlier in the *theôria*'. R. Beutler on Plutarch of Athens, P.W. col. 968 and Évrard, op. cit., p. 176 refer also to a long *theôria* at 407,17–422,10, followed by a detailed commentary containing at 424,4 a reference to the *protheôria*.

(4) is faulted by Évrard, op. cit., p. 191, on the ground that the resemblances of style are not specified.

(5) Hayduck says G3 speaks of things '*disputata a se*' and Vancourt, who accepts this argument, translates G3 as saying 'as we have taught' in the *de Interpretatione*. But what G3 actually says is *hôs emathomen* which means not 'as we have taught' but (as Évrard correctly has it, p. 192) 'as we have learnt' or simply 'read'. G3 makes no claim to have written any commentary on the *de Interpretatione*, and in any case the doctrine he has in mind, sc. that a term is a 'simple word' (*phônê*), is not peculiar to Stephanus' commentary but occurs in the *de Interpretatione* itself.

The indecisiveness of Hayduck's arguments has allowed Évrard (op. cit., p. 188) to claim that G3 may after all be Philoponus. He even suggests that Gennadius may be correct in saying that Aquinas' commentary on the *de Anima* is a translation from Philoponus.

We must say of Évrard what he himself says of Hayduck: 'He ventures to express this opinion only with reservations' (p. 174). Wolfgang Bernard, however (in Richard Sorabji (ed.) *Philoponus and the Rejection of Aristotelian Science* (London, Duckworth 1987), 154–5), says definitely that he believes G3 to be Philoponus. The opposite view is taken by Henry Blumenthal in 'John Philoponus and Stephanus of Alexandria', in D. J. O'Meara (ed.) *Neoplatonism and Christian Thought* (University of New York Press 1982).

Gennadius makes his claim in a note to his translation of Aquinas' commentary into Greek (Codex Laurentianus 19, Plut. 86): he says that Aquinas 'stole' (*hêrpaxen*) this commentary from Philoponus. Unlike Évrard I have been able to verify that Gennadius' translation is in fact a translation of the commentary by Aquinas which we possess. I do not think anyone could seriously maintain that that commentary is a translation from Philoponus, and the extent to which it could have been influenced by Philoponus is limited. Direct influence would be hardly possible, for how could Aquinas have seen a translation? He normally used Moerbeke's translations. But Verbeke has argued with some plausibility that he could not have used Moerbeke's translation of L because he parted from Moerbeke before it was finished; whence his reliance on Themistius rather than Philoponus in his controversy with the Averroists (*Revue Philosophique de Louvain* 49, 1951, 222ff.)

Richard Sorabji has pointed out to me that there are indirect ways in which Aquinas could have been influenced by Philoponus, for instance through Averroes and Michael of Ephesus, and puts it that Aquinas' commentary on Aristotle's treatment of sense-perception in Book 2 is in the Philoponus tradition. So far as *de Intellectu* goes, however, I find little in Aquinas that is distinctive of Philoponus. There is no polemic against Alexander, no Platonic theory of soul that exists before birth and descends into the physical world, none of the other idiosyncratic doctrines sketched below, and on many smaller points of interpretation, such as the references to future discussions at 430a5–6 and 431b17–19 or the number of kinds of indivisibility distinguished in Chapter 6, the two commentators go their own ways regardless of one another.

It would not be appropriate for me here to say positively who G3 is, though a cursory comparison with our Stephanus commentary on the *de Interpretatione* does confirm the stylistic resemblance. I shall try, however, to show that G3 is not identical with L or, therefore, with Philoponus.

Évrard says that it will be correct to attribute two different commentaries on the same work to the same author only if they agree in content, and that Vancourt (in his pp. 48–58) 'sufficiently shows' that the Greek and Latin commentaries on the *de Intellectu* satisfy this condition (pp. 187–8). I think a commentator should be allowed to change his mind on at least some matters in the course of time, but Vancourt does not in fact demonstrate that G3 and L are in general agreement. His main argument is that both discuss the same four rival interpretations of Aristotle's theory of the active intellect and reach the same conclusion: L 43,18–45,59 and ff. is parallel to G 535,1–19 and ff. So much is true; but for the rest Vancourt says only: 'If we compare the other parts to the text we arrive at the same conclusion: the doctrine expressed on each of the two sides is identical' (p. 58). This claim is false, and the only justification Vancourt offers for it – that G3 and L both reject the theory of Alexander – is quite inadequate.

G3 and L disagree on a matter of such central importance that on this account alone it is very difficult to believe they are the same person. L holds we are born with dispositional knowledge: it is hard to get at, but it is there. He endeavours to explain away Aristotle's image of the tabula rasa (36,70–40,43) and says that our intellects existed before 'descending' into our bodies. G3 discusses this interpretation, which he attributes to Plutarch, and rejects it (520,1–12). Whereas L wants to reconcile Plato and Aristotle, G3 insists on the difference between them (cf. also 565,1–2). Apparently following Ammonius G3 distinguishes (i) the child who actually has intellect but who is merely capable of acquiring knowledge; (ii) the adult who has acquired knowledge but is not exercising it; (iii) the adult who is exercising it and therefore has intellect simultaneously *kath' hexin kai kat' energeian*, in disposition and in act.

There are two other substantial differences of content. First L puts much emphasis on the part played by human beings, 'teachers', in causing intellect to become actual; G3 says nothing about teachers. Secondly G3 is interested (see e.g. 547,26, 548,24, 550,6–7, 553,27) in *dianoia* (discursive thinking) and has an elaborate theory (545,12–546,12) of it. *Dianoia* is sharply distinguished from *nous* (intellectual intuition) from the beginning of his commentary: 446,9, 486,1, 546,27, 556,32. In the last of these passages he says it is not genuinely *nous* at all and adds (lines 32–4): 'Do not think that *nous* is the same as *dianoia* in subject but different in account, as was said in the *theôria*; for *nous* differs from *dianoia* in subject also.' I do not find that G3 actually does say in the *theôria* that *nous* and *dianoia* are the same in subject, but he perhaps thinks that was Aristotle's view. He himself, in contrast, believes that *dianoia* is a capacity for discursive thought as distinct from intellectual intuition and he perhaps assigns it to the living organism, soul and body together. L does not make *dianoia* a separate faculty or part of the soul from *nous*. In 19,65–20,72 he denies that it belongs to body and soul together. '*Dianoia*', he says, 'is indeed intellect, but intellect impeded by the body' i.e. the two *are* the same in subject (cf. also 104,00). No doubt thinking, *dianoeisthai*, is discursive rather than intuitive, but L does not emphasise the difference, and his treatment is in line with G1: see 2,2–3, 155,4–16.

Besides these major differences there are a number of minor discrepancies between G3 and L:

429a27–9: L construes: 'soul is not actually but *dunamei* (potentially) the place of forms'; G3 construes: 'forms are present in the soul not actually but *dunamei* (potentially).'

429b7: G3 says it is difficult to think in old age: L says that the intellect improves (13,98; cf G1: 160,34).

429b10–13: G3 construes: 'being flesh is the same as flesh'; L correctly takes *t'auto* (the same) with what precedes.

429b13–14: G3 takes this to favour the view that intellect thinks material and non-material things with different parts; L takes it to support the distinction between water and being water etc.

429b22–5: L is quite certain that intelligibles which are separate from matter are all intellects (35,19–21); G3 is dubious both for theological reasons and because universals are not intellects (528,4–6).

430a5–6: G3 says that Aristotle does not solve the problem he raises here, though 'we have' (534,10); L says 'Aristotle does not as some have thought, omit to provide a solution; he gives it later' (42,72–3; see also below on 430a23–5).

430a10–11: G3 takes *hapasa phusis* to be every genus, e.g. animal, and *hekaston genos* to be every species, e.g. man, horse (539, 20–4); L takes *hapasa phusis* to be the whole world of generable and corruptible things (54,86–90).

430a23–5: L says Aristotle here solves the problem raised at a5–6 (61,67); G3 attributes this interpretation to Plutarch (541,20–1).

430a26ff: L says Aristotle is now addressing himself to the third problem raised at the beginning of Ch. 4, viz. 'How does thinking come about?' (64,48–50); G3 thinks this question is answered in Ch. 4 (525,9–10).

430b4–5: G3 takes Aristotle to be saying that if what is predicated is false of the subject at all, it is false at all times; L takes him to be contrasting falsity arising from what is predicated with falsity arising from the tense. Underlying this difference may be different ways of understanding the example: G3 perhaps thinks (naturally enough for an Alexandrian) that Aristotle is talking about Europeans and negroes, L that he is talking about pale men and sunburnt men.

430b9: G3's text of Aristotle apparently omitted the words *tôi mêkei* (549,22–5), whereas L's text was non-defective (72,32).

430b19–20: L takes the unifying factors to be point-like (80,54–6) G3 thinks they are forms (551,33).

430b23–4: According to G3 (552,28–9) the discussion of divine knowledge starts at *dei de dunamei*; according to L, this sentence relates to the human intellect (82,25) and the discussion of divine cognition starts at *ei de tini*.

430b26–431b12: G3 interprets this whole passage as a systematic drawing of distinctions concerning *nous*; L has no synoptic view and there is little correspondence between his dividing up of the passage and G3's. L takes 430b26–30 to be about the apprehension of separate forms whereas G3 takes it to be about the difference between *nous* and *dianoia*.

431a24-b1: L's interpretation is obscure, but I cannot think that any clarification would make it similar to G3's.

431b12–432a14: determined to find unity in this passage G3 interprets it as a discussion of whether we have knowledge in this life of non-material things. L has no synoptic view here either.

Even if we allow for a commentator's changing his mind, it seems impossible that G3 and L should be identical. On the other hand there are points of agreement between the two that cannot be coincidental. Vancourt calls attention to the similarity of their treatment of Aristotle's chapter on the active intellect and of current interpretations of that chapter. We may add that they both identify imagination with passive intellect (G 523,29 etc., L 61,72–5 etc.), something de Corte describes as a 'very salient trait' of Philoponus; both argue that the imagination is indivisible on the ground that images do not obliterate each other (G 551,10–11, L 77,78–82) and they share some examples: the Trojan War for the significance of tense (G 545,24, 548,7, L 69,62), and water for something potentially undivided (G 549,7, L 72,22). For these similarities I am happy to accept Vancourt's explanation (p. 49): G3 and L are both direct or indirect pupils of Ammonius.

Évrard is unwilling to attach great significance to differences in style and mode of presentation, partly because he thinks our actual texts may be the work not of G3 or L themselves, but of students who took notes of their (or his) lectures (pp. 182, 187). It seems to me, however, that differences emerge between the personalities responsible for the two commentaries which cannot be ignored. G3 has a taste for order, neatness and enumeration. He imposes order on such recalcitrant chapters as 3.6 and 7; he makes lists of points (534,20ff.), distinctions (553,22ff.), and arguments (*sunêgoriai*, 563,22ff.) and offers a highly ingenious classification of kinds of indivisible (544,5ff.). No such love of tidiness, much less ability to achieve it, appears in L. G3 is not only a model of lucidity but an

experienced teacher; when a point is difficult he repeats it:
527,18–22, 546,27–30. L makes no such concessions to student
weakness and we cannot blame all his obscurities on Moerbeke's
inexpertise and bad manuscript. G3 has a vivid device of addressing
in the second person singular not just the reader but people he is
discussing such as Empedocles, Alexander and Aristotle himself
(e.g. 487,25, 518,7–8, 563,27–30). This freshness and directness
seem to be quite alien to L. On the other hand L is more interested
than G3 in the state of the text. He reports variant readings at
430a22, 430b14–15, 430b23–4, 430b27–9, 431b15–16; G3 notes a
variant only at 431a2.

As for the division into *praxeis*, the Greek commentary is entitled
'Notes by Philoponus from the classes of Ammonius with some
personal observations' (*epistaseis*) (1,1–3). In L we find the traces
of *praxeis* being interrupted by long excursuses on topics which are
known to have interested Philoponus such as personal immortality
and infinity (15,49–16,96, 36,70–40,43 etc.) This well fits the
description at G 1,1–3. I suggest, then, that Ammonius' lectures
had a division into *praxeis*. Philoponus was not interested in this
but it survives where he does not depart greatly from Ammonius;
G3 preserved and perhaps refined it.

This translation

The Latin text is dominated by two triads of cognate terms: *intellectus, intelligere* and *intelligibile*, which translate *nous, noein,
noêton*, and *sensus, sentire, sensibile*, which translate *aisthêsis, ais-
thanesthai* and *aisthêton*. Taken by themselves the first three might
be rendered 'mind', 'to think' or 'to understand' and 'object of
thought' and the second 'sense' (i.e. a sense-faculty or, occasionally,
actual perceiving), 'to perceive' and 'object of perception'. I hope I
have made it easier for the modern reader to follow L's thought by
using the triads 'intellect', 'understand' and 'intelligible' and 'sense',
'to perceive' or 'to sense' and 'sensible', even if that gives my translation a slightly eighteenth-century flavour –

> See Physic beg the Stagyrite's defence!
> See Metaphysic call for aid on sense!

2. Philoponus' theory of the intellect

Commentators on Aristotle are inclined to try to attribute to him
doctrines which they themselves think sound. Philoponus believed
that the human soul is a non-material substance which exists before
its entry into the body in the womb. As a result his commentary

on the *de Intellectu* contains many things which a modern reader may think neither sound nor Aristotelian.

Sense-perception

It is necessary to start with this because Aristotle approaches intellect by comparing and contrasting it with sense. Aristotle holds that when we perceive, some part of the body, a sense-organ, takes on a quality which is its proper sense-object; when we see something, for example, the eye takes on its colour. This cannot be the whole story since cloth does not perceive the colour it is dyed, neither does a cinema screen see the film which is projected onto it. What more Aristotle thinks there is to perceiving I have discussed in my papers 'Aristotle's definition of Soul' (*Phronesis* 25, 1980) and 'Telling the difference between Sweet and Pale' (*Apeiron* 15, 1981). Philoponus holds that the quality which is a proper object is received 'cognitively' (*cognoscibiliter*) (32,57–8, similarly G 303,4–5, 309,25, 432,38, 437,10–11). The inadequacy of this becomes clear when we realise that all Philoponus can tell us about 'cognitive reception' is that when it befalls sensible things they are perceived and when thinkable things, they are thought.

Philoponus' views on perception, however, are by no means exhausted by a perhaps unconscious tautology. He believes that our soul has three kinds of body: a solid one of flesh and bone, a pneumatic one which is composed chiefly of air (G 17,19–23) and a heavenly one of the same form as light and the stars (G 18,26–8). Whereas the vegetative soul attaches to the solid body, the super-vegetative but sub-rational soul, which includes the senses we exercise in our present life, attaches to the pneumatic. The pneumatic body, though it survives death to be purged in Purgatory (G 17,26–18,8) can eventually be shed; but the heavenly body is eternal; and this, as we learn at 24,60–5, has senses of its own, superior to those of the sub-rational soul, which are immune to perceptual illusion and enable the soul to know sensible things even when it is completely separated from the other two bodies.

Imagination

The capacity to imagine belongs to the subrational soul; it is lodged in the pneumatic body (G 158,16–17) and incapable of a completely incorporeal existence. That being so, it is disturbing to Philoponus that Aristotle says that it is impossible to think without exercising it (403a8–9, 431a16–17, 432a8–9). Philoponus tries to explain away these texts by saying that we *rarely* think without imagining (61,79–81), and that imagining is necessary for practical thinking and the mathematical sciences (97,13–15, 118,36–119,42); it is not, however, necessary for logic (98,39–42), still less for theology (61,85–62,87, 116,82–3, cf. G 3,3–4).

In ordinary thinking it plays the following role. 'Imagination receives impressions through sense of sensible things, just as sense receives impressions from sensible things, and judges them as sense does: like sayings [sc. utterances of a single term] when it receives an image simply of, say, heat, like affirmations or denials when the soul receives them in itself as pleasant or distressing. Intellect sees these forms in the imagination, and when it sees the simple imprint of the sensible thing it has a simple concept of it. . . . When, in contrast, it judges one of these things as good or bad for the animal there is a composite conceiving . . . , and from this comes pursuit or avoidance' (96,80–90). To confine ourselves for the moment to the case where intellect sees a simple imprint, it does not by any Lockean or other process abstract a universal from this, neither does it use the image as a general representative or stand-in for images of other things of the same sort as Aristotle anticipates Locke and Berkeley by suggesting at *de Memoria* 450a1–7. Intellect 'finds' (115,44) or 'recurs to universal accounts' of the imagined particulars 'which are already present in itself' (23,51–2; 116,85–6).

Philoponus' proximate source for the notion of an imprint may be Stoicism (so Verbeke, pp. liii–liv of his edition) though the notion is prominent in Alexander and goes back to Aristotle (e.g. 423b17–21) and even to Plato (*Theaetetus* 191D and ff.) How are imprints transmitted to the imagination? Aristotle envisages a physiological process which terminates at the centre of the perceptual system, and Philoponus occasionally uses language suggestive of that: at G 158,18–19 images are *enkataleimmata*, 'things left behind by the sensory apprehension'. But at G 5,38–6,1 imagination 'taking from the senses the imprints of the sensible remodels (*anaplattei*) them in itself', and I think that Philoponus' personal view is that imagination is a power to produce non-physical images *like* the sensory imprints.

Imagination is a mixed blessing. It is a blessing in the literal sense that it is given to us by Providence in order that we may act in the physical world (98,33–4) and it enables us to act because it stores images of beneficial and harmful things (96,43–7), images without which the appetitive powers of 'spirit' and 'desire' (G 6,20–4) would be unable (cf. 95,57) to function. It is a 'vehicle' to the geometer (61,83, 62,03, 119,49), perhaps because intellect, as it were taking its seat in it (cf. Plato, *Timaeus* 41D-E), can see on the one hand (by a kind of natural television) sensible things and on the other (by reflective intuition) its own universal accounts. In an extremely opaque passage (63,18–23) Philoponus calls it a servant or squire (*opados*) of intellect. But at the same time it impedes the proper operations of intellect (62,00–1) by being a source of absurd or bizarre (*allokotoi*) opinions (33,90) and mental stupor or fog (63,17).

Philoponus identifies imagination with 'passive intellect' (13,3, 61,73–4). In this he perhaps follows Alexandrian orthodoxy – G3 does the same – and his motivation is patent. Aristotle says that the passive intellect, the '*nous* which undergoes', is destructible (430a24–5). Since Philoponus holds that intellect in general is inde-structible, and that this goes for what Aristotle at 430a14–15 calls 'intellect which becomes all things', he must make 'passive intellect' different from 'intellect which becomes' and identical with the whole or some part of the sub-rational soul. This generates an awkward-ness, however, in the commentary since it is clear that Aristotle himself takes the passive intellect and the intellect which becomes to be identical.

Aristotle introduces his distinction between the *nous* which becomes and the *nous* which makes in such a way that I think he must have conceived it as a matter-form distinction. Philoponus does not find this puzzling because his own theory of the body-soul relationship is dualistic. Aristotle, however, explains it as the relationship between the matter and the form of a living thing, that is, he explains our psychological concepts as concepts of living things in their formal aspect, and it is therefore surprising to find him trying to apply a form-matter distinction *within* the realm of the psychological. Modern commentators generally, though not invariably, attribute to him the idea that the lower psychological concepts are matter-concepts relatively to the higher. As bricks and beams are form relatively to clay and wood but matter relatively to a house, so the concept of a perceiver is a form-concept relatively to that of flesh or even that of a self-nourisher, but a matter-concept relatively to that of a thinker. It is consistent with this line of interpretation to explain the difference between the two intellects in terms of a difference between powers. The passive intellect would be either a second-rate intellectual capacity, owners of which are matter for a capacity which is more creative, or some or all of the sub-intellectual capacities, among which that of imagining would be prominent. The passive intellect would be destructible if a thing could not have these powers without having a body. If Philoponus wanted to take this line he could still maintain that Aristotle allows for personal immortality if he maintained two further theses: first, that Aristotle does not really hold that all thought involves imagin-ation, and secondly that Aristotle rejects a principle advocated by Bernard Williams (*Problems of the Self*, Cambridge 1973, ch. 5), namely that whatever is at any time composed of material is essen-

tially material. Philoponus actually does maintain the first of these
theses. He would not maintain the second because, being a dualist,
he holds that that which thinks is at no time composed of material.

Theory of thought

Philoponus holds that the rational soul or intellect has three cognitive powers, for judgment or opinion (*doxa*), for reasoning (*dianoia*)
and for intuitive thought (*nous*) (G 1,14–15). The first receives an
occasional mention in our commentary, for instance, 1,7–8, but no
extensive treatment. We exercise it in holding general opinions
which might be proved (such as that the soul is immortal) without
having the proof (G 1,17–20). The capacity for reasoning, which he
calls '*dianoia*', is chiefly discussed at 20,71–82, a discussion in line
with the fuller treatment in G 155 and 258–60. Philoponus is insist-
ent that it is the same intellect which intuits and which reasons,
and that these are simply different uses of its power, reasoning
being a use to which it is driven by its union with the pneumatic,
and through that with the solid, body. In separation it operates by
simple intuition, *simplex adiectio*, and this forerunner of Descartes'
pure intellection is also used in looking at mental images.

These modes of cognition are not prominent in Aristotle. Instead
we find the puzzling claims that knowing, like perceiving, comes
about through receiving form without matter (429a13–16), that to
acquire knowledge of something is to become like it or even identical with it (429a6, 431b26–8), and that knowledge and the thing
known are identical (430a4–5, a19–20, 431a31–2). It is reasonable
for Aristotle to say that when we perceive something, a sense-organ
takes on its perceptible form. The optic lens projects coloured slides
onto the retina, and the ossicles of the ear reproduce the vibrations
of the violin string. But whatever objects of knowledge Aristotle
may have in mind (his examples are drawn from biochemistry and
mathematics) it is plain that the ornithologist does not become
a bird, the geometer a triangle or the moral philosopher (unless
'incidentally') virtuous. It is a big problem, then, how Aristotle
could have thought that intellectual cognition can be explained in
terms of receiving forms in the same sort of way as sense-perception.

As to the identity of knowledge and the thing known, the word
'knowledge' is used in two ways. Sometimes by a man's 'knowledge'
we mean precisely the things he knows. Truths or propositions he
knows are 'pieces of knowledge'. But 'knowledge' is also used for a
psychological state or activity, for a man's dispositional grasp of
items of knowledge or for his actual contemplation of them. To say
that knowledge in the first sense is identical with the thing known

is trivially true; to say that knowledge in the second is identical with what is known is a monstrous paradox.

Has Philoponus any light to throw on these problems (as Moerbeke claims, 120,69–70)? We saw that he gives a vacuous account of Aristotle's theory of sense-perception: the perceiver receives perceived forms 'cognitively'. At 9,11–12 he says similarly: 'intellect is said to become the things understood in that it receives accounts of them cognitively'. There is, however, some explanation of this at 83,37–48: intellect does not become the intelligibles 'in substance':

> It does not, when it understands God, become God, or when it understands heaven or earth, become any of these things. But since the accounts of all things are in the soul, the accounts of the better things which are superior to it in the form of representations (*eikonice*), the accounts of less good things which are posterior to it as exemplars, when it actually produces the accounts which are in it it actually becomes what they are either in a representative or in an exemplary way, as we say that the image of Socrates becomes what Socrates is or that the account in the art of building [or perhaps, in the builder] becomes what the house is.

This explanation depends heavily on the notion of representation. It will not do to say that a thinker becomes like the things known in that he becomes a knower of them, since the problem is precisely to see how coming to have knowledge of *x* or to conceive *x* *is* coming to be *x*-like. A representation, however, (or so I have argued in 'The Art of Appelles', *Aristotelian Society, Supplementary Volume* 53, 1979) must have some resemblance to things of the sort it represents. Philoponus, then, must insist that an intellect which knows *x*es really is a kind of representation of *x*es.

The trouble with this line of interpretation is that knowledge, whether of superhuman objects like the theologian's or of subhuman objects like the civil engineer's, cannot easily be explained in terms of representation. A representation (if I may slip into Philoponese) is a sensible particular. Supernatural objects are not, strictly speaking, representable at all, and although physical objects are representable, knowledge is not itself a representation but at best an intellectual capacity with regard to representations.

Let us proceed to the doctrine that knowledge is identical with the thing known. At 21,95 Philoponus says that knowledge (presumably dispositional knowledge) is 'theorems which are not actualised'. At 59,6–8 actual knowledge is 'actualised theorem' and at 113,95–6 and 113,4–7 it is the collection of scientific accounts. These passages by themselves might suggest that Philoponus is taking knowledge in the first of the two ways I distinguished, as items of knowledge. In 91,58–92,72, however, commenting on 431a1–4, he offers an

account which suggests a more interesting interpretation. He equa-
tes the claim 'actual knowledge is identical with the thing known'
with 'actual intellect is identical with the intelligible, the thing
understood'. He then offers two explanations of the identity of intellect with the intelligible. The first is that intellect receives the
form which is understood (91,60–1). He is here drawing on his
representative theory of intellect's assimilation to the intelligibles.
I think he draws on it also at 92,66–7 when he asks, 'What else is
actual intellect but thoughts and concepts?': actual intellect is seen
as a kind of representation of the things known, analogous to the
image of Socrates at 83,46–7. This explanation, then, applies to the
paradoxical, not to the trivial, version of the doctrine that knowledge is identical with the thing known. And so does his second
explanation, which is that intellect *qua* actual is itself intelligible or
an object of consciousness (91,61–2). But to understand this second
explanation we must look at Philoponus' handling of a further point
in Aristotle's theory of thought.

The puzzling remarks we have been considering have juxtaposed
to them in Aristotle's Chapter 4 a problem about self-knowledge
(429b22–430a9). How is a thinker aware of himself? If he is aware
of himself by virtue of having some property other than that of
being a thinker, that contradicts statements that he has no such
property (429a21–2, 429b31–430a1) but is 'simple and unmixed'
(429b23–4, b28–9). If, however, he is an object of awareness to
himself simply because he is a thinker, if being a thinker is what
makes him a thing of which he is aware, shall we not have to say
that anything else of which we are aware is a thinker too, and
hence that all things think (429b27)?

Philoponus firmly grasps the second horn of this dilemma. 'It is
not false' he says (33,96–7) 'that every intelligible is an intellect, but
true and necessary.' Why? In 35,19–27 he argues that if intelligibles
which are separated from matter (and any intelligible which is *not*
so separated is not an actual but only a potential object of intellect)
are not intellects they will have no activity, since the only possible
activity for non-material things is thought. But nothing can exist
which does not have some activity. 'Of necessity, then, separate
intelligible things will also be intellects.' This argument applies
only to intelligible objects which exist apart from matter, and
although Plato may have thought that Forms are such entities yet
do not think, a Christian like Philoponus might readily suppose
that the only such entities are angels and God. But what about
more mundane objects of intellectual thought? Will they too, when
actually thought of, themselves think? Commenting on 429b6 Philoponus offers an account of self-knowledge which is relevant here.
Since, he says, understanding things is becoming them, in under-

standing them intellect understands itself (20,91–21,93, 21,8–10). Something other than God or an angel, a horse, say, or a triangle, is actually thought of only when intellect represents it; the object of actual thought, then, is strictly speaking not the physical triangle or the form of the real, live horse (if any such horse or triangle exists) but the form which the intellect has assumed; and this is the actually operating intellect itself.

This is an ingenious and internally consistent interpretation of some very obscure Aristotelian doctrine. No doubt Philoponus owes something to his predecessors. The identification of knowledge with theorems, for instance, is developed by Themistius (Verbeke's edition 217,55–63) and it is clear that Philoponus has read Alexander's *de Anima* with much attention. Alexander's 86,14–29 has close parallels in L 21,7–10 and 85,82–95. I think also that Philoponus' identification of intelligibles with intellects as I have reconstructed it could well have been inspired by Alexander's speculations especially at 87,28–88,5. On the other hand he is no slavish follower of Alexander and he has developed his theory in his own distinctive way, mixing into it a dualism which I find absent from Alexander.

His interpretation, then, is a creditable achievement. As I said earlier, however, a commentator will be reluctant to attribute to Aristotle a doctrine which he himself finds radically unsound. I do not think that thought can be explained in terms of representation (though some distinguished philosophers today seem to think it can) or that a thinker can be viewed as a representation of the things he thinks of in the way Philoponus proposes. Anything which represents in this way must be a material object and so must any subject it represents. There is the further objection that Philoponus (even if unconsciously) is using our visual perception of material objects as a model for our intuition of these non-material representations. But is there any other way of understanding Aristotle? I suggest an alternative line of interpretation in my paper 'Aristotle and the place of mind in nature' in Allan Gotthelf and James G. Lennox (eds), *Philosophical Issues in Aristotle's Biology* (Cambridge 1987). I cannot claim to have proved that this interpretation is correct, but it may be worthwhile to describe it as an alternative to the kind of interpretation favoured by Philoponus and his predecessors.

Its fundamental idea is that our philosophically puzzling concepts of mental activities and states, of knowledge, self-knowledge, thinking etc., are not (as Descartes and Locke thought) further concepts coordinate with our concepts of physical properties and changes which we apply in the same way; rather thinking that a person knows or desires something or is conscious is making a special use of ordinary concepts; it is applying concepts of ordinary objects to the thinker in a special way.

Ordinary objects are conceived as having a certain practical significance; they are such as to benefit us in some ways and in some circumstances and such as to cause harm or damage in other ways and in other circumstances; and we have more or less technical knowledge of how to derive benefits and prevent or remedy harms. We apply technical knowledge in acting for reasons which make our action technically right, that is, effective or preventive of change we want to effect or prevent; and we apply practical knowledge in acting for reasons which render our action practically right: that is, advantageous, necessary to prevent harm, morally obligatory or whatnot. We think that others have knowledge or desires and are conscious of things in understanding their behaviour as being for certain reasons and purposes. But in doing this we do not apply special psychological concepts, concepts of knowledge etc. We make a special, psychological use of concepts of those things which, if we understand an agent's behaviour correctly, he is aware of. Suppose that on a picnic I see you move a bar of chocolate into the shadow of a wall; and I think you do this because the sun has come out and in order that the bar may not melt and lose its shape and texture. Then I attribute to you 'actual' knowledge of a way in which the sun can cause harm, of how the harm can be prevented and so on. I do not, however, apply to you the paraphysical concepts of a knower and a desirer. Rather I make a special use of my own knowledge of the sun, of chocolate, of shadows. I apply this knowledge, however, not straightforwardly in moving the bar myself, but in a special way, in understanding your action and perhaps in encouraging or impeding it. To be a thinker, to have intellect, is to be a thing to which knowledge of other things can be applied in this peculiar way. As for self-knowledge, I have suggested (in 'Knowing what we think', *Philosophical Quarterly* 36, 1986) that we are aware of ourselves as causal and purposive agents in grasping the technical and practical reasons for our own behaviour. You are aware of yourself as a thinker and as intelligent or stupid not by applying to yourself the concept of intellect but in understanding why you moved the bar of chocolate; and you do this by making a further use of your concepts of the bar, the sun and the wall.

Immortality and pre-existence of the soul

Aristotle says that the 'intellect which makes' is 'separable, unaffected and unmixed' and 'when separated, it is just what it is (or perhaps, it is this alone which exists) and it is not the case that it sometimes thinks and sometimes not' (430a17–22). Modern commentators mostly refuse to read this as a confirmation of popular ideas about personal immortality such as we find in the *Odyssey*. Philoponus, however, not only asserts with an almost obsessional repetitiveness that Aristotle makes 'the rational soul in us' immortal; he also argues (16,83–96, 38,84–9) that it exists before birth. Readers may judge for themselves how good a case Philoponus makes for his interpretation of Aristotle and how strong the reasons are which he gives for holding that we shall survive death. But a word may be said about the doctrine of pre-existence.

Although this doctrine is in Plato it is hardly Christian orthodoxy. Partly for this reason A. Gudeman in his article on Philoponus in Pauly-Wissowa suggests that when Philoponus composed this commentary – indeed throughout the phase of his career in which he was producing commentaries on Aristotle – he was still a pagan, i.e. a Platonist, and that he became a Christian only later. This view has been energetically assailed by Évrard in 'Les convictions religieuses de Jean Philopon' (*Bulletin de l'academie royale de Belgique, classe des lettres* 5, 1953, 299–357) and H. D. Saffrey in 'Le chrétien Jean Philopon' (*Revue des études grecques* 67, 1954, 396–410). They argue that Philoponus was a Christian all his life, a conclusion I find persuasive, and explain his acceptance of the pre-existence of the soul by saying that Christians were freer to hold unorthodox views in sixth-century Egypt than they were in sixteenth-century England or Spain. They give Origen as an example; Origen too held that souls exist before becoming incarnate. This explanation could be correct, but it admits of supplementation.

Philoponus has two arguments for pre-existence. The first is that whatever is generable is corruptible, so if the soul is immortal, it must have existed from all eternity (16,94–6, 38,85–9). If the principle invoked here is sound, the orthodox Christian doctrine is in difficulty, but that whatever is incorruptible must be ungenerated is less than self-evident and Philoponus himself does not maintain it without qualification: see Richard Sorabji (ed.), *Philoponus and the Rejection of Aristotelian Science*, pp. 33, 177–96. The second may be formulated as follows. The universe has existed for an infinite length of time and has always been much as it is now; it has always contained men. There must, therefore, have been infinitely many human beings. But if each man has his own soul created at birth, and these souls are immortal, there will now be infinitely many (Gogolian) souls. But there cannot be an actual infinite. So the same souls must be used again and again (38,90–6). Now we know that Philoponus not only held that there cannot be an actual infinite but in 529 argued that if there cannot be an actual infinite it follows that the universe cannot have existed for an infinitely long time. If Philoponus came to reject the Aristotelian doctrine that the universe has existed for an infinitely long time, he could hold that there have been only a finite number of men, and each could then have had a soul created at his conception. When he wrote the *de Intellectu* Philoponus might not have yet decided that the universe could not have existed for an infinite time. It has to be said, however, that the development of Philoponus' thought is the subject of much controversy at present and to advance any hypothesis otherwise than very tentatively is to ask for trouble.

Contemplative and practical thought

Although Aristotle does not make the sharp distinction Philoponus makes between opinion, reason and intuitive thought, he does distinguish between practical and theoretical or contemplative *nous*. Philoponus too recognises this distinction. We saw that he attributes reason and intuitive thought to the same subject and makes them the same faculty employed in different ways. His treatment of contemplative and practical thought is largely similar. They are the same 'in subject' (G 194,20–1). He quotes Aristotle's statement at 433a14 that they differ 'in end' and comments: 'When intellect directs itself up towards things above it, it becomes contemplative, enquiring into the nature of the universe; when it directs itself towards inferior things it is practical' (G 194,22–4). Not that all thought about things inferior to intellect is practical; presumably there is non-practical *dianoia*. But at G 241,7–9 we are told that intellect is practical only 'from its relation to the body; which is why, after its release from the body, it is exclusively contemplative'.

There is some superficial tension between these passages and G 5,24–32. Philoponus there says that the rational soul has two practical powers, wish (*boulêsis*) and choice (*proairesis*). The second belongs to it in its incarnate state, but the first belongs to it on its own, 'for when the soul is outside the realm of becoming it operates solely in accordance with wish' and aims solely at the good. Presumably in the later passages he is identifying practical intellect with intellect which chooses, not with intellect which wishes, but why is that? Perhaps because the good which is the object of wish is truth and the exercise of the intellect's intuitive powers. At 107,51–4 he says that the true is the good apart from action, and that it is good absolutely, not just for a particular kind of organism.

In the chapters covered by our commentary Aristotle does not deal explicitly with the relationship between contemplative and practical thinking. He discusses the relationship between perceiving on the one hand and on the other, experiencing pleasure and pain and appetition (431a8–16); and having said that for the rational soul images or appearances take the place of perceptions he adds the difficult sentence which I translate as follows: 'And that which does not involve action, the true and the false, belong to the same genus as the good and the bad: they differ in that the one is absolute, the other relative.' Philoponus understands this second passage in the way I have just indicated: he takes Aristotle to mean that the true and the practicable good are two species of good (107,45–57). The first passage he interprets as follows: Sometimes a sentient organism perceives an object of perception simply as having a certain temperature, flavour or the like, but at other times it perceives it in relation to itself as a source of pleasure or pain. These modes of perceiving differ as merely uttering a word or conceiving something differs from saying or thinking something true or false. When the organism perceives in the second way there 'immediately follows' pursuit or avoidance (94,22–38).

I find it difficult to accept the doctrines Philoponus attributes to Aristotle as Aristotelian. I have discussed 431a8–16 in *Weakness of Will* (Blackwell, Oxford, 1988), ch. 3 and elsewhere. On Philoponus' interpretation, perceiving a perceptible quality, perceiving something as pleasant and reaching for it are three logically independent episodes, and the first two appear to be mutually exclusive alternatives. On my interpretation they are three aspects of a single piece of psychological activity which we distinguish only in thought. Contemplative and practical thinking differ 'in end' not because they are used to deal with different sorts of object but because a single piece of thinking can be assessed for its truth, in which case it is viewed as contemplative, or for its conduciveness to the thinker's well-being, in which case it is viewed as practical. Philoponus takes *boulêsis* to function chiefly when the soul is separated from the body and to be directed (if my surmise is right) solely towards cognising truth. It is hardly controversial that Aristotle considers *boulêsis* to be appetition for what, upon rational deliberation, appears to be the best practicable objective, and he sees it at work in an adult's practical life. Finally, Philoponus' interpretation is bound up with the idea of the soul's 'descent' from a pre-incarnate existence; in 'Aristotle and the place of mind in nature' I emphasise those Aristotelian texts which suggest that we acquire intellectual powers as we grow up.

Having said so much I should acknowledge that many scholars may think that my interpretation, here and at other points noted earlier, is less true to Aristotle than that of Philoponus. And even if it is truer I should not wish to belittle Philoponus as a commentator. I hardly expect anyone to be studying my comments on Aristotle fifteen hundred years hence; though a translation into Futurese of a twentieth-century translation into English of a lost thirteenth-century translation into Latin of a lost sixth-century commentary in Greek on three pages of the third book of Aristotle's *de Anima* would be proof indeed that the torch of pure scholarship is unextinguishable.

Philoponus

On Aristotle on the Intellect

Translation

The Commentary of John the Grammarian on the Chapter concerning the Intellect in the Third Book of Aristotle's *De Anima*

CHAPTER 4

429a10 Concerning that part of the soul by which the soul gets to know things and is prudent, whether it is separate, or inseparable in magnitude but separate in account, we must consider: what are its differentiating features, and how does understanding ever come about?

Having spoken about the vegetative soul and the sensitive and that 5 which imagines – to put it simply, about the non-rational soul – Aristotle passes to his teaching about the rational soul. But first he discusses judgment, I mean that which opines and thinks. For that the present discussion is not about the contemplative intellect or about what is called the 'dispositional' intellect, is implied by his 10 saying 'by which the soul gets to know things and is prudent'. Being prudent occurs over things that are *done*, for prudence is concerned with these; and the contemplative intellect does not occupy itself with things that are done.

Aristotle proposes to make three enquiries here. One is whether 2 the rational soul is separate from the body or inseparable. The 15 second is how it differs from sense. [He raises this question] even though he has already distinguished them from one another in saying that all animals have sense but not even all men have intellect.[1] But now[2] having first spoken of the resemblance of intellect[3] and sense in order to show[4] the need to investigate the difference between them, he later speaks of a different and real separ- 20 ation of them. For earlier, as I have said, he distinguished intellect

* In what follows 'read' introduces readings found in one or more Latin MSS but not accepted by Verbeke; 'conjecture' introduces readings not found in the MSS which, it is suggested, restore Moerbeke's original Latin; 'understand' introduces words corresponding, it is suggested, to words in Philoponus' original Greek which were not in Moerbeke's manuscript or which he misread or misunderstood. Words enclosed in single square brackets are inserted by me to help the reader; those in double square brackets translate words in the MSS which probably do not go back to Philoponus.

[1] 427a19-b14.

[2] Conjecturing *nunc* for *ideo* at 2,17 (Bossier).

[3] Understanding *ipsius*, as in 1267, for *ipsorum* at 2,18 (Bossier).

[4] So the MSS *ostenderet*; if we read *ostendat* with 1267 the clause should be taken with 'he later speaks', not with 'having spoken'.

from sense by the fact that intellect is not found in all [animals]
while sense is. But now he derives the distinction from the very
nature of the two powers; and considering both in the same animal,
he distinguishes intellect, and moreover in those very points in
25 which intellect seems to be at one with sense he shows the difference
between them and distinguishes them. After this he enquires
thirdly[5] how understanding comes about in us. We said earlier[6] that
when he was discussing the non-rational powers of the soul he first
discussed the objects of these powers because they were easier to
grasp. Here in contrast he has first discussed the intellect and
30 afterwards the objects, that is, the intelligibles. That is because the
intelligibles are less well known and less easy to grasp than the
intellect. Hence once again with the same plan he starts with what
is more easily grasped.

Aristotle here uses 'intellect' indiscriminately for any rational
substance, and he says that intellect in this sense is a part of soul.
35 That is an abuse of the word ['part'].[7] For the rational substance is
not a part of the whole soul; if it were, either the whole soul would
be immortal or the whole would be mortal, since a part is of one
substance with the whole.[8] Neither consequence is acceptable, and
he himself says earlier of this intellect that 'it seems that this is a
different kind of soul, and that this alone can be separated, in the
40 way in which the everlasting is separated from the corruptible.'[9]
He says, then, that the rational soul is a part of the whole inasmuch
as it is one thing signified by 'soul' when said equivocally of the
3 non-rational and the rational soul; just as one might speak of[10] the
sun equivocally so called. For we use 'the sun' both for the celestial
body itself and for the light produced in the air; we are in the habit
45 of calling an illuminated[11] place 'the sun'.[12] If we called the light
'part of the sun' we should say this not because it is a part of one
substance with the whole (the one thing, the body, is the cause
whereas the other is the thing caused), but because it too is a part
of the whole [extension] of the equivocal term; that too is the way
in which Aristotle here says the intellect is part of the soul. We
might say likewise that part of [the extension of] the equivocal
word 'Ajax' is Ajax son of Telamon, but in that he is one thing
50 signified, not because he is of one substance with the other Ajaxes.

[5] 1267 has *primo*, 'first'.
[6] G 264–6.
[7] Supplied in 1267.
[8] Aristotle's use of 'part' here led Plutarch to hold that all souls are 'one in
substance with many powers' (G 517,34–5).
[9] 413a25–7.
[10] Or perhaps 'of one meaning of'; 1267 has *et solis aequivoce dicti*.
[11] 1267 has *inferiorem*, 'lower'.
[12] e.g. 'He sat in the sun'.

For he is not identical with Ajax son of Oileus[13] just through being
a thing signified by 'Ajax' but it is as if someone were to say that
the angelic substance is part of all things that are, or that the pilot
is part of the ship.[14]

Aristotle says that intellect is threefold, not in essence but in   55
manner of being. There is intellect in potentiality, which is present
in children.[15] Secondly there is 'dispositional' intellect: that is present in people who know but who are not using their knowledge,
like a geometer who is asleep or in general anyone who does not
have his theorems on display. Thirdly there is intellect in actuality
having its operations already[16] on display – there being another   60/4
contemplative intellect distinct from these, in which there is no
potentiality in respect of anything, but which is actuality without
potentiality. It is from this that the intellect in potentiality derives
principles of the sciences and this which he says is genuinely in
actuality. (For as to the intellect which ratiocinates, even when it
comes to be in actuality Aristotle says it is still in potentiality in
a way,[17] because it does not have its activity all at once but passes
from earlier things to subsequent.) And this intellect all make   65
immortal. They[18] call it 'rational substance', and they show that
Aristotle agrees with them[19] even in what is said here. For he
outright[20] declares this part of the soul 'separate' and 'unaffected'
and 'not mixed' with the body.

Alexander is not able to contradict the things said here. But   70
believing that the rational soul too is immortal, and wishing to
drag Aristotle too over to his opinion, he says that Aristotle is here
speaking of the creative intellect,[21] and that it is this which is said
to be separate and not mixed and unaffected. This is not an intelligent suggestion. In the first place it would be a waste of time to   75
offer a proof of this concerning the creative intellect; for who would
ever doubt that that is separate? Moreover earlier on when speaking
about the intellect Aristotle says that 'it seems to come into being
in us and not to be destroyed; for it would be likeliest to be destroyed

---

[13] The MSS have *Troiano*, 'the Trojan Ajax', but no Trojan Ajax is known to legend,
and Moerbeke probably read *Iliadei*, 'Trojan' for *Oiliadei*, 'son of Oileus' (Bossier).

[14] Probably an allusion to 413a8–9.

[15] Moerbeke's *omnibus*, 'everybody', translates *pasi*, but Sophonias 132,30 has
paisi, 'children', which is probably correct.

[16] Reading *iam* after *actum* at 3,59 with CV (Bossier).

[17] 429b8.

[18] Bossier prefers to read *dico* with 1267 for *dicunt* and punctuate to give 'this
intellect, I mean rational substance, all make . . .'

[19] Or, less well, 'is consistent with himself'.

[20] Taking *econtra* to translate *antikrus*, as often (Bossier). The reference is to
430a18, cf. 429a15, 24–5.

[21] i.e. God. See Alexander, *de Anima* 89,4–18, cf. G 10,1–3; 159,9–17; 194,12–19.

by the weakness that occurs in old age.'[22] Who would ever suspect
80   that it is of the creative intellect that he says that it comes into
being at all in us and having come into being is not destroyed? How
5   could he say of it:[23] 'If it were destroyed it would be likeliest to be
destroyed by the weakness which occurs in old age', as if anyone
could ever doubt that the creative intellect is indestructible? But
that by intellect in actuality which he also says[24] is separate and
85   not mixed he means none other than the one which is in us in
potentiality, and which,[25] having been brought to perfection,
becomes the intellect in actuality, is clear in the first place from
Aristotle's very words. It is also clear from the sequence of the
sense. It would be irrational to say that that which is intellect in
potentiality in us is not the same as that which by being perfected
is brought to actuality; for there is nothing which is always in
90   potentiality and never brought to actuality. But if it is brought to
actuality, and it is the intellect in actuality which he says is separate, then it is the intellect in us which he says is separate.

What led Alexander to suspect that Aristotle is talking of the
creative intellect, is the Philosopher's saying that it 'makes all
things'.[26] In what way this is said by him, however, we shall say
95   when we get to the passage;[27] we shall then show that Aristotle's
remarks do not at all fit the creative intellect; and the words 'But
what part the intellect will hold together and how, it is hard even
to imagine',[28] being said of intellect in actuality, show that Aristotle
is not speaking of the divine intellect.[29]
00   Some other people[30] say that Aristotle is here talking not indeed
of the creative intellect, but of some other intellect lower than the
creative but higher than ours, for example some angelic intellect.

---

[22] 408b18–20. Aristotle actually says: 'Intellect seems to come to be in us *as a kind
of substance.*'
[23] Omitting *primo* with 1267 at 5,81 (Bossier).
[24] Reading *et ait* after *quem* at 5,84 with 1267 (Bossier).
[25] The construction of the sentence is unclear. 1267 has a second *potentia*, suggesting a few words may have dropped out.
[26] 430a12.
[27] See 50,82–51,99.
[28] 411b18–19. I translate the text of the *de Anima*. In Greek 'what part' is neuter
(see below 6,11–12) and can therefore be taken (as the sense demands) as the object
of 'will hold together'. Moerbeke has the nominative *qualis pars* for 'what part',
making the sentence untranslatable. He may have had the correct Greek before him
(as at 12,90) and mistranslated.
[29] I find 5,96–8 difficult. In my translation (which follows a suggestion by K.
Verrycken) *hoc dictum ostendens* is a hanging nominative; *ostendit* for *ostendens*
would improve the grammar. Keeping the MSS *hic* for *hoc* at 5,97 and deleting
dictum would give the sense 'shows that Aristotle is speaking *here*, sc. at 430a12,
of intellect in actuality, not of the divine intellect.'
[30] Marinus, a pupil of Proclus at Athens, according to G 535–7.

The truth, however, it is neither this[31] nor the former but what we have said: he is speaking of that intellect which is in us when it has been perfected and attained its proper activity, since he says it is a part of our soul; and we shall prove this when we come to his words.[32]

Concerning that part of the soul by which the soul gets to   5
know things and is prudent. By 'gets to know' he refers to the cognitive powers of the soul, and by 'is prudent' to the practical, for the powers of the soul fall into these two divisions, the contempla-   **6**
tive and the practical. Prudence is concerned with [practical things,][33] things which are done, for this is what we usually mean by 'prudence', conducting oneself well in relation to things which   10
are capable of being otherwise.

It should be noted here that he calls the intellect a part of the soul in the neuter. [For the Greek word for a part is neuter.][33a] After he has said many things in between[34] about the intellect using a masculine noun for it, he finally says by way of conclusion about the intellect: 'Knowledge which is in actuality is identical with the thing [known]. Knowledge which is in potentiality is prior   15
in time in the individual but overall it is not prior even in time. But it is not the case that sometimes [the intellect] understands and sometimes not. When it is separated, it is that only which truly is, and this alone is immortal and everlasting.'[35] When he says 'this alone' he no longer uses the masculine, as though referring to the intellect, but the neuter, referring back to his words here, I mean   20
'that *morion*' (in the neuter) [i.e. part] 'of the soul by which the soul gets to know and is prudent';[36] clearly it is this alone[37] of the parts of the soul that he declares to be immortal and everlasting.

[31] Deleting *in* after *neque* in 5,2 (Bossier).

[32] Understanding *dicit* for *dicitur* and *siquidem* (1267) for *sive* (Greek *ei ge*) at 5,3, and punctuating *sortitum, siquidem partem . . . animae; et verbis . . .* (Bossier).

[33] The Greek was probably *praktika ê prakta* as variant readings (Bossier).

[33a] Words added by Moerbeke.

[34] Reading *intermedia* after *dixisset* at 6,12 with 1267 (Bossier).

[35] 430a19–23. The words 'Knowledge which is in actuality . . . even in time' also appear at 431a1–3 and Ross (1961) brackets them here, I think rightly. The sentence I translate 'When it is separated it is that alone which it truly is' reappears 60,42–3 as 'When it is separated it is just what it is' (similarly 1267 at the present place). Aristotle has *monon*, 'only' or 'alone', and *hoper esti*, 'just what it is' or 'just what is'. His sentence is difficult and though grammatically it is easiest to understand it as Philoponus does, I suspect Aristotle may wish to say that when separated the intellect is 'just what exists', i.e. it has existence of the primary kind which attaches to substances (*Metaphysics* 4, 1003b5–10).

[36] I follow Bossier's suggestion that we have a comma after *relationem* (6,19) and that the Greek which follows was something like *legô de morion (oudeterôs) tês psukhês hôi . . . .*

[37] Understanding *quam quidem solam*, translating *hoper monon* as in 1267 for *quia solam* at 6,21 (Bossier).

It is clear that he would not have called[38] the creative intellect or any other intellect which is superior to us and more honourable a
25   *part* of the soul. Most clearly, then, he has been proved to mean that the rational soul is immortal and everlasting.

429a11 Whether it is separate, or not separate in respect of magnitude but in respect of account.

There are different interpretations of this. He says **separate in respect of magnitude** either, as Timaeus[39] seems to say, because that which is spirited[40] is in one part, say the heart, that which is
30   desirous in another, say the liver, and that which reasons in a third, say the brain, the parts of the soul being distinguished from one another and not united; – either 'separate in respect of magnitude' means this, or, better, 'in respect of magnitude' should be understood as equivalent to 'from magnitude', that is, it is separated from
35   body and magnitude; or 'in respect of magnitude' is a substitute for 'in respect of essence and substance',[41] that being how magnitudes are said to be separated from one another, which is the same as the
7   second interpretation, that is, having a substance separated from body and magnitude. Whether, he says, intellect is separate in this way, or is not at all separate in this way but only in account, that
40   is, only in our understanding of it and in definition – just as that which touches is separated from that which moves from place to place only in account and not in magnitude – this, then, is the first of the problems: whether intellect is separate in essence or only in account. He has not, however, produced this problem as coordinate with the others,[42] which is why there seem to be [only the] two problems after this. He has brought this out not as one of the
45   problems but in the form of hypothetical alternatives: 'concerning that part of the soul' he says 'by which it gets to know and is prudent, whether it is separate or not'. Then he says what enquiries are made concerning this part: 'we must consider how it differs' from the others 'and how thinking comes about'. Two problems are
50   left: how the intellect is differentiated from sense or, in general,

[38] I accept Bossier's suggestion that *utique ... appellavit* translates a counterfactual Greek conditional.
[39] Or (cf. 15,48) 'the *Timaeus*' (the Greek will have been *ho Timaios*). The reference is to Plato, *Timaeus* 69C–70A.
[40] The Greek word is taken from *thumos* which primarily means 'anger' (a meaning preserved by Moerbeke's *irascitivum*) but Plato and Aristotle use it to cover motivations to compete, conquer or excel.
[41] Moerbeke preserves the Greek word *hupostasis*; this has the same connotations as 'substance'.
[42] Or, perhaps, 'in its place in order of treatment' (so Bossier).

how the rational powers are differentiated from one another; and how thinking comes about.

429a13 If, therefore, understanding is like perceiving, it will be either being affected in some way by the thing understood, or something similar to that.

From this he means to make clear how intellect and sense resemble one another, in order that in this way they may be distinguished. If, then, he says, understanding is like perceiving – they are alike 55 because they are both modes of cognition and discernment and because as sense occurs with the grasping of sensible things so intellect occurs with the grasping of intelligible things – if understanding is like sense, and sense is affected by the sensibles,[43] understanding too will be affected by the intelligibles. 60

But being affected is twofold: there is a way of being affected which makes for perfection and a way which makes for destruction, and the way of being affected which is most properly so called is **8** the latter. That is why, having said **it will be being affected** in some way by the thing understood he adds **or something else like that**. For the way of being affected which is called 'perfective', I mean the one that leads from potentialities to actuality, is not 65 thought by him to be properly called 'being affected', which is why not even perception consists in being affected, as he says in the preceding book.[44] Still less, then, does understanding consist in being affected. For sense or the power to perceive, even if it is not itself affected, nevertheless makes use of certain organs. On account of that, it seems to come about through being affected, for that which perceives is affected in some manner. But the intellect has 70 no need of organs for its functioning; hence understanding involves being affected less than perceiving. Nevertheless he says **it is being affected** in some way because it is when something happens that we understand (that is why we do not understand all the time); also the fact that it belongs to the intellect to understand different things at different times is an indication that it is being differently affected in some manner. Just, then, as in the case of the perceiving 75 soul it is from the things perceived and the soul's activity concerning them that he finds out the nature of the perceiving soul, so he proceeds here with the intellect: it is from the things understood that he finds out what the intellect is and conducts his enquiry.

429a15 It ought, then, to be unaffected, but receptive of form, and in potentiality such [as the form], but not it. 80

[43] Adding a comma after *sensibilibus* at 7,59 (Bossier).
[44] 417b18–418a5.

This is the conclusion from what has been said. He calls the intellect 'unaffected', that is, not having any affection or form of its own. Just as sense is potentially what the things perceived are [actually], but it is not actually any of these things, so too the intellect, if it

85 is to be receptive of all intelligible things, must not itself have the form of any intelligible thing. It is on this account that dyers, so

9 far as they can, get wool which is colourless, in order that it may be suitable for any colour they want; for if wool is coloured, the colour it already has impedes the colour that comes afterwards.

90 And when glass is already imbued with some colour, red, dark or what you will, it can no longer transmit colour, since the colour which already imbues it impedes the passage of the other colours. Hence a sense should not have the form of any sensible thing; and neither, then, should the intellect have the form of any intelligible thing, in order that it may be able to grasp all. But if it is none of the intelligible things in actuality, it must nevertheless be all of

95 them potentially, in order to receive them all. The line of thought running through the whole passage is this. If understanding is being affected in some way as perceiving is, then just as a sense is none of the sensible things, so the intellect must be none of the intelligible things. But if it is none of the intelligible things, then it will be unaffected, that is, without form, having the form of

00 nothing intelligible in order to be receptive of everything intelligible.

Someone might raise a doubt here about how the intellect gets to know itself. For if it ought not to have any of the forms it is going to get to know; and if, when[45] it gets to know things, in receiving their forms it becomes just what the thing known is: then

5 when the intellect understands itself it apparently receives the form of itself. It will turn out, then, that before it receives the form of itself, it is potentially such as itself but not actually; and that is awkward. But if it were actually such as itself, how could it come back to receive precisely the form it [already] actually had?[46]

I reply that if, indeed, the intellect in getting to know things

10 became such in substance as they are in substance, this doubt would have some appositeness. But if the intellect is said to become the things understood only because it receives accounts of them in a cognitive fashion,[47] it will be able to receive accounts of its own substance too, especially as it is a thing of such a nature, one apt by nature, I mean, to get to know itself. Moreover there is no

15 awkwardness in saying that the intellect, before it understands,

[45] Conjecturing *sique* for *si quae* at 9,3 (Bossier) and adding *quando*.
[46] Conjecturing *erat* for *erit* at 9,8 (Bossier).
[47] This is Philoponus' view, but I doubt if it is Aristotle's: see Introduction, pp. 16–20.

has its form potentially, not actually (for this very thing is also called intellect in potentiality, since it has not yet received its own perfection). First, then, it has its perfective form in potentiality, **10** and as soon as it is perfected, it gets to know itself. For its being perfected consists in this, that its operations have been perfected; **20** these are takings in of intelligible things; and it is itself an intelligible thing.

429a16 And as that which perceives stands to sensibles the intellect stands to intelligibles.

That is, just as a sense is none of the sensibles [actually] but is potentially like them, and is perfected by them and becomes actu- **25** ally similar, so too the intellect has no form of anything intelligible, but is a thing which is potentially they, and when perfected by them it becomes actually what the intelligible things truly are. We ought to note these very words, that the intellect is said to be brought to actuality in the same manner as a sense. Just as a sense, then, is first in potentiality and remaining the same later becomes a sense in actuality as well, and that which is in potentiality is not **30** other than that which is in actuality, so, plainly, Aristotle means that it is the same intellect which is first in potentiality and then in actuality. It is not as Alexander imagined: that the intellect in actuality by which intellect in potentiality is perfected is different [from it], the latter becoming not intellect in actuality but only dispositional intellect. That the intellect in potentiality is perfected by another intellect which is in actuality we too admit. But we do **35** not say this is the creative intellect. We say it is the intellect which is in the teacher, this being external to and other than the intellect which is perfected.

429a18 It is necessary, then, since it understands all things, that as Anaxagoras says it should not be mixed, in order that it may get possession,[48] that is, get to know.

Since the intellect [understands] all intelligible things, it is absol- **40** utely necessary that it should have no form in itself of those things it understands, but should not be mixed with them, that is, should have none of their forms mixed with its own substance. This is what Anaxagoras says, calling it not mixed but pure. According to him things consist of homeomerous components and all things are **45/11** in everything, but at the same time he says that intellect is pure

---

[48] Aristotle uses a stronger word, *kratei*, 'get control', which (see below) is used by Anaxagoras himself.

and not mixed.[49] There are no homeomerous components mixed into
it, but it is a single form. If it had homeomerous components (that
is, components with parts similar to themselves)[50] of different species, they would impede the cognition of things. In the first place it
50   could not receive as something other what it has in itself. Secondly
what it has in itself, sc. the form, would appear alongside and
thereby prevent or impede the exact cognition of other forms, just
as the colour in coloured glass impedes the passage through the
glass of other colours.

429a21 Hence neither does it have any nature of its own, not
55   one, except this, that it is possible.

That is, it cannot have any nature or form in itself, but must be
all forms in potentiality. But [it may be thought][51] if this is so, the
intellect will turn out to be matter,[52] if it is all things in potentiality,
but not at all in actuality. But we maintain that he says it has no
60   nature of anything it understands in the way in which sense is no
form of anything perceived. Whereas even if we say that matter is
no form or nature, of those, that is, which it is by nature such as
to receive, it is still something, viz. that very thing, over and above
all these, which is by nature such as to be transmuted.[53]

65   **429a22** That therefore which is called the 'intellect' of the soul
(by 'the intellect' I mean that by which the soul thinks and
judges) is no existent thing in actuality before it understands;
and hence it is not reasonable that it should be mixed with
the body.

70   'Think' here means thinking itself, and 'judge' means opinion. Hith-
erto he has used the word 'intellect' somewhat as a blanket term,
but now he rightly makes clear what sort of intellect he means,
namely that it is not that by which we imagine but that by which

---

[49] Diels-Kranz 59 B 12: 'Intellect is unlimited and autonomous and mixed with
nothing. . . . If it were mixed with anything it would have a share of everything.
For as I said earlier [cf. B 11], in all things there is a portion of everything. And
the things mixed with it would have impeded it so that it did not control anything.'

[50] This may be an insertion by Moerbeke (so Bossier) explaining the meaning of
'homeomerous'. We today might say that an object is homeomerous under description
'*d*' if it is divisible into parts to which '*d*' applies.

[51] Alexander thought (or was alleged to think: G 519,26) this.

[52] Punctuating *si hoc, accidet* at 11,57 (Bossier).

[53] Following Bossier's reconstruction of the Greek: *alla k'an tēn hulēn legōmen
mēden eidos einai mēde phusin mēdemian toutōn dēlonoti hōn pephuke hupodekhes-
thai esti goun ti dēlonoti para tauta panta auto touto to pephukos metaballesthai.*
Bossier calls for a comma after *harum* at 11,62 and deletes Verbeke's parentheses.
Philoponus contrasts intellect and matter in a similar way at 15,70–16,81.

we judge and think. This, he says, is nothing in actuality before it understands, but in potentiality it is all intelligible things. That **12** being the case, it is plain that it is not only incorporeal but separate from all body as well. 75

It must be incorporeal because sense, which is inferior to it, is incorporeal; for it does not belong to body to get to know things nor to that which is divisible to embrace different things at the same time.

It is necessary too that it should be separate and not mixed with the body. For if, being incorporeal, it is mixed with a body, it must either be mixed by composition[54] or it must be the form of the body 80 as sense is of that which perceives and digestion of that which digests. If it is mixed with the body by composition it will be of some quality, he says, such as cold or hot or the like. Now in the first place it is awkward for the intellect to be a thing of qualities; but it will have to be if it is mixed with the body by composition. And further if even sense has been shown to be no quality or 85 composition of the body, still less is intellect. Besides, if it is hot [say] in actuality, how will it get to know the other qualities? The one it already has will impede its cognition of the rest, as has been said more than once. But if it is mixed with the body as a form, in the same way as the non-rational and vegetative powers of the soul, 90 plainly it will make use of the body as an instrument, as do they. But 'what part the intellect will hold together and how', he says, 'it is difficult even to imagine.'[55] For we do not see the intellect making use of any organ in its intellective operations; on the contrary, it is impeded by the body, not only in situations like that of drunkenness but even when the body is well. That shows plainly 95/13 that the intellect is not in a body as its subject; if it were it ought to be at its best[56] with the body and suffer impairment at the same time. But in fact it is the other way round. When the body is at its best its operations are weaker, and as the body becomes enfeebled it shines out more clearly. There is no way, then, in which it is mixed with the body: it is separate and not mixed.

Why does he say **That which is called the 'intellect' of the** 00

---

[54] Moerbeke's word *complexio* could mean a kind of disposition, in which case the idea would be that if intellect is 'mixed' with the body it must be either as a non-essential or as an essential property. But the Greek word was probably either *sumplokê*, literally 'inverweaving' or *krasis* (so Sophonias 124,30). These words suggest a putting together of material components. If intellect is incorporeal it cannot be such a component; nevertheless if it were, the point that 'it would be of some quality' would hold, and on balance I think Philoponus' idea is: if intellect were mixed with the body it would have to be either as a component or as a form.

[55] 411b18–19. Moerbeke translates correctly here.

[56] *coalescere* here probably translates *sunakmazein* (cf. Sophonias 28,25–6) and *crescere* at 13,97 *akmazein* (cf. G 160,33) (Bossier).

soul? Either to distinguish it from the imagination, as I said just now.[57] For imagination is not strictly speaking intellect; it is not intellect without an added qualification;[58] with an added qualification it is called 'passive intellect' – which is as much as to say,[59] it is not intellect at all. For added qualifications, as we have said

5   more than once, destroy the original sense. Or alternatively [he says it] to differentiate it from the intellect in actuality – I mean the contemplative intellect – for that is what is primarily and above all intellect. For just as 'the hand', he says, 'is the instrument with which we use instruments', so too 'the intellect' in actuality 'is the form of forms'.[60] For just as the science of sciences is the one which contains all sciences within it, so the form of forms is the form

10   which contains all forms within it.

When he says **by which the soul thinks and judges, by which** does not mean 'by which as an instrument' but 'that by virtue of which it thinks'.[61] [[For the intellect is not the instrument of the soul; rather the reverse, the soul is the instrument of the intellect.]][62] It is as though someone were to say 'By soul we are people

15   who know', 'by soul we perceive', instead of 'by virtue of the soul', 'by virtue of sense'. In the same way 'by which the soul thinks' stands for 'by virtue of which it thinks'. For the intellect is not the instrument of the soul; rather the reverse, the soul is the instrument of the intellect. Hence in **that which is called the 'intellect' of the soul** he speaks as when calling it a part of the soul, or in the way in which one might call substance 'part' of what is.

20   It is plain from this too that he is talking about our intellect, for it would be quite out of place to say such things about the creative intellect. Even Alexander[63] admits they[64] are said about our intellect even though it would not be impossible for these things to be said about our creator;[65] but even, he says, if it is not mixed [with the body] in the manner in which bodies are mixed, it is still[66] not

---

[57] 11,71–2.

[58] Moerbeke's word *adiectio* is here used in its literal sense of 'an addition'. Elsewhere, however, he uses it to render the technical term *epibolê*, 'intuition'.

[59] Reading *idem* (with T as well as with CVB) for *id* at 13,3 (Bossier).

[60] Deleting *et* after *organorum* at 13,7 (Bossier). The reference is to 432a1–2.

[61] Reading **anima** *non ut per organum habet le quo, sed* for **anima**, *non ut: per organum neque le quo, sed* at 13,11–12 (Bossier).

[62] This sentence appears to have been moved here from below, 13,16–17, as a gloss.

[63] Verbeke refers us to Alexander *de Intellectu* 116,5–13, but I cannot trace this reference.

[64] Conjecturing *haec* at 13,21 for *hoc* ('it') (Bossier).

[65] So our MSS, but it is hard to believe they are right. Bossier suggests deleting *nostro*, 'our', before *conditore*, 'Creator', at 13,22. Alternatively we might delete *conditore* here and read it in place of *nostro* at 13,21. The sentence could then be translated: 'Alexander, however, says that these things too are said about the Creator, even though it is not impossible they should be said about our intellect.'

[66] *enim* at 14,24 probably translates *goun* (Bossier).

impossible that it should exist in [the body]. But we reply to him   25/14
nonetheless in the words of Aristotle that if though incorporeal it
exists in [the body] either it will have some quality or it will use a
corporeal instrument; and both are impossible.

429a27 They say well who say that the soul is the place of
forms. But this is true not of the whole soul but only of the
intellective soul, and the forms are not present in actuality
but only in potentiality.[67]

He here agrees with Plato[68] and anyone else who says that the soul   30
is the place of forms. 'Place', of course, is used metaphorically, on
the ground that as a place contains things in itself, so the soul
contains forms. He says, however, that not the whole soul is the
place of forms, but only the rational soul, and that it is not actually
but only potentially the place of forms before it understands. We
should be aware that Plato too calls only the rational soul the place
of forms. He says that a soul 'which does not at all' know being   35
would not attain to this shape,[69] that is, the human. Hence he says
that not every part of the soul knows being and neither, therefore,
does every part have forms. Only the rational soul knows being, so
only this is a place of forms.

And Plato too, just like Aristotle, says that forms are present in   40
the rational soul potentially, not actually. But Plato says they are
present in the second sense of 'potentially', present in the way in
which theorems are present in a sleeping geometer, when for the
ready use of these theorems all he needs is something to remove
this impediment. Aristotle, in contrast, says they are present in the
first sense of 'potentially', inasmuch as the intellect is by nature
able to receive them, but does not yet possess dispositional knowledge, and takes in the forms, as it appears,[70] from things which
are perceived. Seeing, as it might be, this or that white thing, we   45
recur to that which is white absolutely, and similarly from particular men we take in understanding of man simply, and so on. This   **15**
opinion, however, is refuted by Socrates in the *Phaedo*.[71]

I say, therefore, that it is not from things which are perceived
that we become knowers and have ideas of things. If it were from   50
sensible things that we took in understanding of forms, why should

[67] I prefer this translation to 'It is not actually but potentially the forms' (so Ross
1961, followed by Hamlyn 1965). Philoponus' comment steers a middle course.
[68] The nearest Plato comes to saying this in a surviving work is at *Parmenides*
132B.
[69] i.e. would not become incarnate as a human being: *Phaedrus* 249B.
[70] Philoponus considers this appearance deceptive: see p. 14.
[71] Philoponus may have in mind *Phaedo* 73–5, though the argument there does
not extend to forms like man and white, but only to forms like equal and just.

we reject sensible forms as not pure? I mean something like this: if we have our understanding of a circle, a sphere, beauty and the rest because we obtained it by abstraction from things perceived,
55 why do we reject perceived things as not exact,[72] and say that there is no exact circle in any artifact? Can it be judging with an eye to this [perceived thing] and not to some other form superior to this which is in us? In the same way we say that the beauty which is in matter is not genuine;[73] it is not exclusively beautiful because it is in a subject which is not beautiful but ugly, namely matter.
60 Indeed, if it were from perceived things that we had our understanding of beauty, we should never reject that which is perceived. But as it is, we judge by the standard of a different, more divine beauty; and that is how we reject perceived things. We come to a recollection of intellectual beauty led by the hand and awakened, so to speak, by things we perceive.
65 Alexander has claimed that Aristotle says the intellect exists only in potentiality, and not at all in actuality; and because Aristotle agrees with those who say that the soul is the place of forms Xenarchus (according to Alexander) was misled into making the ill-judged conjecture that Aristotle is saying the intellect is prime
70 matter. Ill-judged because even if there is some similarity between matter and intellect, still they are not the same. For matter, he
16 says, is not the place of the forms it receives, but is itself altered and transmuted and becomes in actuality what it was potentially. For the matter of a thing never becomes what it was potentially by
75 receiving something from outside; it is by virtue of the transmutation within itself that it becomes actually what it was potentially. Matter is a kind of subject. Hence when it receives form it becomes a body. The intellect, in contrast, is the place of forms in such a way that it is receptive of them not in being a subject for them or because it becomes these forms, but as a tablet is receptive of letters when nothing is yet written on it. Hence when matter receives
80 what it is able to receive it becomes a composite substance;[74] very different is that which is intellect in actuality.
I think it is perhaps from these and similar things that Aristotle might be judged to make the soul mortal. For how would it be possible for the forms to be in the soul potentially in the first sense,
85 if the soul is immortal and the world has always existed? For if there is not an actual infinity of immortal souls, but only a finite number, it is absolutely necessary that they should exist before the body and enter many bodies in succession. But that being so, how

---

[72] Bossier wishes to punctuate with a comma after *certus* in 15,55.

[73] Punctuating with a question mark after *nobis* at 15,57 and a semicolon after *sincera* at 15,8, and reading *similiter* for *consimiliter* with T at 15,57 (Bossier).

[74] I take Moerbeke to translate *sunamphoteros ousia* (cf. G 212,20)

could the forms be present [only] in the first sense of 'potentially'
in these souls which from all eternity have had understanding of   90
them?[75] It is absolutely necessary, then, if the universe is eternal
as Aristotle believes, either that the soul, if immortal, should have
the forms potentially not in the first but in the second sense of the
word, i.e. dispositionally, which is what Plato thinks; or else, if the
forms are present in the soul potentially in the first sense, that the
soul should be generable in time, and on that account should be   95
mortal – for they say that whatever is generable is destructible.

429a29 That the unaffectedness of that which understands is   **17**
not like the unaffectedness of that which perceives is clear in
the sense organs and in [the faculty of] sense.

Earlier he said what is common to intellect and sense, namely that
as sense is affected by sensible things so intellect is affected by   00
intelligible things; then, as if not altogether happy to call this 'being
affected' he added 'or something else like that';[76] and he drew the
conclusion that both that which perceives and that which understands ought to be unaffected, i.e. that they ought not to have any
form of those things by which they are said to be affected. For they
would not be affected by something wholly similar, if they were   5
already occupied by some one of the forms of which they are receptive.[77]

Now he makes a distinction between them, showing that the
unaffectedness of the intellect is not like that of sense: that is, that
it is not in the same way that each is said to be separate from every
form of the things of which it is receptive. At the same time he   10
shows by these words that the intellect is separate from the body
and not mixed. 'For sense', he says, when it has received greater
sensible things, cannot receive less. When we look at the sun,
immediately afterwards we cannot read, and when we have tasted
stronger and more penetrating flavours, we cannot perceive weaker
ones. But the greater the intelligible things which the intellect   15
perceives, the more easily it perceives lesser intelligibles. The cause
of this, he says, is that sense perceives sensible things in and
through the body, and hence even if it itself, being incorporeal, is
not affected, when the body is affected and still as it were preserves traces from the things perceived, it is in some manner

[75] Moerbeke has the neuter *ipsorum* instead of the feminine *ipsarum* (to agree
with *species*, 'form') because the Greek word for form, *eidos*, is neuter. This is a
frequent mistake in his translation.
[76] Quotation marks added.
[77] Understanding plural verbs for *dicitur*, 17,4, *pateretur*, 17,5, *susceptivum est*,
17,6; the subject is *sensitivum et intellectivum*.

20   affected along with the [body which is] subject, and cannot function
      in relation to the lesser things, since its operations are in and
      through the body. The intellect, however, neither being in the body
      nor operating through the body as an instrument, is all the more
      able to function in relation to lesser things the more it has func-
      tioned in relation to greater; for it undergoes no kind of being
25   affected by the latter, since it is truly pure and not mixed with
18   anything. He does well, then, to say that the unaffectedness of the
      intellect is not like that of sense. For though sense is unaffected,
      that is because it has no form of anything sensible. But because it
      has its being in the body and needs the body to function, when
30   its subject receives violent [stimulations] and is in some measure
      affected by them, on account of the powerfulness of the things
      perceived there remain traces of the affections caused by them in
      the sense organs[78] and, on account of this, in the senses[79] also, since
      it is in them [sc. the sense-organs] that they have their being. And
      thus it turns out that the senses, not being genuinely without
      mixture or unaffected, are impeded in their perceptual operations;[80]
35   the affection which remains gets in the way and impedes the sense's
      being affected by the lesser things. The unaffectedness of the intel-
      lect is different in character. Since it is in truth wholly pure and
      not mixed with the body, its unaffectedness is not affected at all by
      the reception of the greater intelligible things; on the contrary,
      aroused by the greater things it becomes all the more operative in
      grasping the lesser.

40   **429b5** When it becomes particular things as does one who
         knows, it is called that which is in actuality;[81] that happens
         directly it is able to function by itself. . . .

      Having spoken of that which is [intellect] in potentiality, he now
      speaks of that which is dispositional, in other words of intellect in
45   actuality, for disposition is the first kind of actuality. When, he
      says, the intellect which is in potentiality, having trained itself by
19   time and teaching, becomes as one who knows, so that it has no
      more need of teachers from outside but itself from itself brings forth
      forms and accounts of things, needing no teaching, then it becomes
      intellect in actuality.

      _____

      [78] Conjecturing *sensiteriis* (Greek *aisthêtêriois*) for *sensitivis* ('things which per-
      ceive') at 18,31 (Bossier).
      [79] Conjecturing *sensibus* for *sensibilibus* ('things perceived') at 18,32.
      [80] Inserting a comma after *operationes* at 18,34 (Bossier).
      [81] Punctuating *ut sciens, dicitur* with Verbeke. That this is how Philoponus con-
      strued the sentence is shown by 39,20 and 47,9. Aristotle's text, however, should be
      translated 'When it becomes each thing (*hekasta*, not *ta kath' hekasta*) as does one
      who is said to be a knower in actuality'.

He is careful, however, to put in the words 'particular things' and 'becomes', in order to distinguish this from the perfect and divine 50 intellect.[82] That does not understand particulars one by one. It understands all things together in a non-discursive way by a single operation. Our intellect, on the other hand, even when it comes to be in actuality still understands each thing separately and passes from one thing to another, not able to understand several things under one. Hence the perfect intellect does not *come to be*, but *is*, in actuality; or rather it is itself actuality without potentiality, having cognition that remains steady and exists always in the same 55 way. Our intellect *comes to be* in actuality and is not all at once, but both understands and expounds through particular intelligible things.

429b8 And indeed in the same way it is even then in potentiality in a way; not, however, in the same way as before it
learnt and found out.

There are two ways of being in potentiality and two of being in actuality, as has been observed more than once. Even, he says, 60 when it [the intellect] becomes actually able to bring out theorems from itself which it wants, even then it is in potentiality in a way, namely in the second sense of 'in potentiality', that is, disposition-ally. It is not, however, in potentiality as it was originally, sc. in the sense of being by nature capable.

This is an appropriate point at which to enquire how it is that in 65 an earlier passage[83] he claimed that *dianoia*, [[that is, mind or thinking, or reasoning]][84] belongs not to the soul alone but to the two together, that is, to the animal, for when separated from the **20** body the soul does not think or reason,[84a] but confronts things face to face; but here, in contrast, he says that *dianoia* [[that is mind 70 or thinking]][84b] is intellect in potentiality and separate from the body.

The reply must be that *dianoia* is indeed intellect, but intellect impeded by the body. It is not that *dianoia* is a product of body and intellect, but *dianoia* is intellect impeded by body; so *dianoia* does not occur without body, but it is not *from* body. For the body does 75 not cooperate with the intellect, but rather hinders its natural

[82] Reading *ad distinctionem perfecti et divini intellectus* with T supported by Sophonias for *ad distinctionem et differentiam perfecti intellectus* ('to distinguish and differentiate this from the perfect intellect') at 19,49–50 (Bossier).

[83] 408b13–15 (cf. G 155,4–35).

[84] The bracketed words are probably insertions by Moerbeke (Bossier). On *dianoia* (discursive thought) see Introduction pp. 9–10, 16.

[84a] These two words may translate the one word *dianoeisthai* (Bossier).

[84b] See n. 84.

operations, as ash does those of a burning coal; that, he thinks, is why it is, and is called, *dianoia*. Just as if a burning coal is not functioning in accordance with its nature because it is buried in ash, and someone says that it is a burning coal in potentiality, that is, dispositionally, and that such a thing does not exist without ash,

80 he says this not because such a burning coal is composed of burning coal and ash, but because it is only by ash that it is hindered from functioning perfectly; in the same way if *dianoia* should be said to be not without body, this is how we will interpret the saying. When intellect which already has dispositional knowledge is impeded by the body, it is said to be dispositional intellect. When it is no longer

85 in any way impeded by the body, either because it is perfectly removed from the body or because some superior illumination has come its way, and it is lifted up away from the state of being affected along with the body, then it is said to be that intellect in actuality which is most perfect, and which contemplates things intuitively; and on account of this it is termed 'contemplative'.

429b9 And it is then able to understand itself.[85]

90 For if just as sense[86] in actuality is nothing other than immaterial sensible forms, so intellect, having become actual, is intelligible forms, then it is natural that when it becomes actual it has under-

21 standing of itself too. For in understanding them it understands itself. The intellect in actuality is the intelligibles in the way in

95 which sense in actuality is the things perceived; for knowledge is not something other than the things known. Knowledge is theorems which are not actualised, and the dispositional intellect is intelligible things which are not understood but, so to speak, laid up. When, therefore, intellect takes each intelligible thing separately and as it were actualises it,[87] it is intellect in actuality (for it is not

00 possible to understand a plurality of things all at once). But when it takes intelligible things all at once and without their being active, it is dispositional intellect. If, therefore, the intellect is identical with the things understood, rightly whenever it understands it understands itself.

But if the intellect in understanding intelligible things understands itself, will not opposite things belong at the same time to

5 the same thing and in relation to the same? The same thing will be at once making and affected. But things which are relative are

---

[85] So Aristotle's MSS. His editors amend to *di' hautou*, 'understand *through* itself', but Philoponus clearly had the unemended text.

[86] Deleting the comma after *sensus* at 20,90 (Bossier).

[87] Punctuating *actuans hoc, est* for *actuans, hoc est* at 21,98 (so Bossier, who suggests Moerbeke read *energoun touto* instead of the correct *energounta*).

relative to one another, not to themselves. The reply must be that
even if it [that which understands] is the same *qua* subject [as that
which is understood] it differs in the manner it is both. Intellect
insofar as it is intellect is primarily something which understands
intelligible things. But because for it to understand is for it to
become those things which it understands, on that account in understanding them it understands itself. It is incidentally, then, that it   10
understands itself. So just as there is no obstacle to the same thing's
being at rest and moving at the same time, so long as it is in one
respect that it is at rest and in another that it moves (it is at rest
in itself and moves incidentally, like a man at rest in a ship which
is moving); in the same way the intellect understands of itself, but   15
it is understood by itself because it befalls it to be assimilated to
that which at the time it understands. Hence the intellect understands itself not insofar as it is intellect but insofar as it is a thing
understood.

429b10 But because a magnitude is one thing and being a   **22**
magnitude another, and water is one thing and being water   20
another . . .

Some things are simple and some composite.[88] Immaterial things
are simple, for instance soul, intellect, God; indeed, these are the
separated forms themselves[89] without the matter. Things which
consist of matter and form are composite, for instance, fire, water
and, in a word, all bodies. In composite things the form is one thing,   25
the two together another. For instance fire itself is one thing, I
mean the composite, and what it is to be fire another, I mean the
form by virtue of which something is fire. Similarly in the *Categor-*   **23**
ies[90] he says that animal is one thing, what it is to be animal
another, and man is one thing, what it is to be man another.   30
   Since, then, the form is one thing and the two together another
but we get to know both of them, both the composite and the form,
he now asks whether we get to know the composite and the simple
with the same part of the soul, or one with one part and one with
another, or whether we get to know both with the same part, but
with that part differently disposed. His reply is that both are understood by the same thing differently disposed. The same intellect, he   35
says, understands both simple things and composite, standing to

---

[88] 22,19–25,4 looks like a *theoria*; a detailed commentary on the same passage
runs down to 29,44.
[89] Understanding *ipsae separatae* for *ipsa separata* at 22,23 (Bossier): Moerbeke is
again thrown by the fact that the Greek word for form is neuter.
[90] This does not appear to be a quotation from the *Categories*, but the distinction
is implicit at 3a17–20. For *Praedicamento* at 23,28 we should probably understand
Praedicamentis (Bossier).

itself in understanding both as a bent line to one that is not bent.
It is not without sense that it gets to know the composite; but
40   sense gets to know a particular instance of fire and informs the
imagination, and then the intellect, being supplied from this, has
cognition not just of the particular but also of the universal composite thing, for it belongs to the intellect to get to know universals,
and it attains to understanding of them from particulars which it
receives through sense. In its cognition of the composite, then, it
45   resembles a bent line. A bent line differs from one that is not bent
in having a certain inflection backwards which the other lacks.
Since, then, it is not by virtue of itself and by simple intuition that
the intellect gets to know something composite, but it stands in
need of sense and imagination, and so has a kind of doubling over
50   of itself and an admixture, on that account Aristotle compares it to
a crooked line. It first, so to speak, extends outside itself to the
imagination, and then turns back to itself and recurs from particulars to the universal accounts which are in it.[91]

For sense is not receptive of intellectual things and neither is
intellect receptive of sensible things, but when it understands sen-
55   sible things it does so *using* sense. When it has separated itself
from body and sensible things and applied itself to intelligible
things alone, it has no grasping of sensible things. For the operation
24   which is proper and natural to it is grasping of intelligible things.
But when it understands sensible things, it is not without body or
sense that it understands them. It does so in conjunction with sense
60   and through sense, not only when it is in this body here but after
the removal of the body as well. For plainly the body which is
always attached to it[92] and which is of luminous form,[93] [[that is, of
the same form as itself,]] being much better than this body here
and everlasting, uses better and purer senses, and therefore does
not drag down the intellect, being removed from all mortal trouble-
65   someness but rather the reverse: it does not draw the intellect to
itself but is drawn by it.[94] Since intellect, then, does not understand
sensible things apart from sense, on that account he says that when
it understands them it is like a curved line. But when it looks at
forms themselves, not using sense but setting in motion the

[91] Philoponus' interpretation of the analogy with the line is ingenious but (pace
Philoponus ad loc., 27,53–7) Aristotle himself compares our apprehension of the
composite with the line when straight and our apprehension of the form with the
line when bent back (429b16–18).
[92] *ipsius appensum* probably translates *autou exêrtêmenon* (see marginal note in
T), literally 'hanging from it' (Bossier). For the doctrine see Introduction p. 13.
[93] Moerbeke appears to have read (or misread) *autoeides* for *augoeides*. Philoponus
uses *augoeides* of our celestial bodies at G 18,27, cf. 138,9. The words 'of the same
form as itself' may be Moerbeke's attempt to explain *autoeides*.
[94] *illius* at 24,65 probably translates *hup' ekeinou* (Bossier).

accounts which are in itself, such as the account of heat or of man, or, indeed, of soul or angel, then it resembles a line that is not 70 curved, for it has a single mode of operation[95] and is in no need of sense. It is, then, one[96] and the same intellect that gets to know composite things and forms, but when it gets to know composite things it does so in conjunction with sense, whereas it gets to know simple things by virtue of itself by direct intuition without sense.

It is the same, he says, with mathematical things which he calls 75 'abstract',[97] for in these, even though they are abstracted from matter, there is again this doubling over. Straight is one thing, what it is to be straight another, curved one thing and what it is to be curved another. Here too something is subject and matter- **25** like, namely continuum; this takes the place of matter in objects of mathematics, as he says in the *Physics*.[98] Straightness, curvature, 80 roundness is the form, straight, curved or circular the composite. For the circular arises out of continuum (as matter) and roundness (as form), and similarly with the rest. Again, therefore, when intellect understands a circle or curved or straight, i.e. something composite, it does so disposed analogously to a bent line. Along with 85 the sense it is, so to speak, bent back on itself from the sensible things. When, however, making no use of sensible things or, consequently, of sense, it understands the bare forms, sc. curvature, straightness, on their own, it is analogous to a line that is not curved; for it does not need external things or sense, but brings 90 forward accounts of forms within itself. As a bent line, then, differs from one that is stretched out, being the same subject but different in the way in which it is disposed, for when the curved line is stretched out it does not take in anything additional to the account of its essence, so the intellect which understands that which is composite differs from the intellect which understands the simple: it differs in the way in which it is disposed only, not in essence. And again, as the form in composite things stands to the composite, 95 so the intellect which gets to know a form by itself[98a] stands to the intellect which gets to know a composite. Since, then, the form which is in composites is not separated from the composite except by thinking alone (it is by thinking alone even that the fiery form is separated from fire), in the same way the intellect which gets to 00 know the composite is [differentiated as] other than the intellect which gets to know form only by thinking and by the way in which

[95] Reading *operans* with the MSS for *operationis* at 24,71 (Bossier).

[96] Understanding *unus* (Greek *heis*, as in Sophonias 126,34) for *si*, Greek *ei*: see Verbeke's note ad loc.

[97] Literally 'in the abstract', *en aphairesei*, 429b18.

[98] Verbeke refers to *Phys.* 2, 193b23–194a12, but the passage Philoponus has in mind may be rather *Metaphysics* 7.10–11.

[98a] Understanding *ipsam* (so B) for *ipsum* at 25,96.

it is disposed, while *qua* subject it is the same. When it gets to
know the composite it is thought of in relation to the senses; when
it gets to know forms, it is without relation to them. It is the same
thing, differing in its mode of operation.

5   **429b11** [. . . and similarly in other cases, but not in all],⁹⁹ for
         in some they are the same.

For in the case of immaterial things there is not, on the one hand,
form, on the other, the composite, for there, indeed, there is no
matter or composite thing; but intellect is the same as being intellect, angel as being angel, soul as being soul.

26/10   **429b12** . . . It judges flesh and being flesh either with different
          things or with the same thing differently disposed.

By 'being flesh' he means the form of flesh, by 'flesh', the composite;
and here he reaches his conclusion.¹⁰⁰ After having said 'Since magnitude is one thing and being a magnitude another, and water is
one thing and being water another', and then said some other things
in between, he now draws his conclusion and says: 'It distinguishes
15   flesh and being flesh either with different things or with the same
thing differently disposed'; that is, either one is distinguished by
one part and the other by another, or they are distinguished by the
same part disposed now one way and now another.

          429b13 For flesh is not without matter, but it is like snub-
          nosed,¹⁰¹ this definite thing in this definite thing.

20   This too is a proof of what he has said above. After having said 'A
magnitude is one thing and being a magnitude another, and water
is one thing and being water another' he continues by way of proof:
For flesh is not without matter. That is indicated also by the
word **for**, which is a conjunction assigning a cause. In saying 'For
flesh is not without matter' he leaves it to us to understand that

---

⁹⁹ I supply the words in brackets from Aristotle's text.
¹⁰⁰ i.e. the conclusion or main clause (apodosis) of the sentence beginning 'Because
a magnitude . . .' at 429b10.
¹⁰¹ Aristotle wrote *to simon*. This could be translated as the abstract noun 'snubnosedness' but I think it is more likely that *to* is used to show that the adjective *simon*
is being mentioned and not merely used. Aristotle often contrasts it with words like
'spherical' and 'hollow'. In 'The Sun is spherical' 'spherical' signifies simply a certain
shape. But in 'Socrates is snubnosed' 'snubnosed' signifies not just a certain shape,
hollowness, but that shape in a definite thing, the nose. Aristotle claims that all
words for natural kinds are like 'snubnosed', not like 'hollow' (*Met.* 6, 1025a30–10,
26a3). He would not say that 'snubnosedness' (as Philoponus at 28,68) but only that
hollowness is a word for a form.

'being flesh' *is* without matter; hence if the one is with matter and the other without it, it follows that flesh is not the same as being flesh.[102] That 'flesh is not without matter' is shown by the illus- 25 tration **but it is like snubnosed, this definite thing in this definite thing**. For snubnosedness means a certain sort of curvature in the nose, and 'snubnosedness' signifies this curvature with the nose, 'this in this' [[nose]].[103]

429b14 With that which perceives it distinguishes cold and hot and the things of which flesh is a certain ratio.

He now says what he had undertaken to make clear, whether it 30 [sc. the soul] distinguishes what is simple and what is complex with the same thing or with two different things. He says it is with the same thing, but differently disposed. It distinguishes the composite, he says, i.e. flesh, with the part which senses, for the things of which flesh is composed are distinguished by sense. These are this particular hot, this particular cold and the other things in a certain 35 ratio and balanced mixture of which flesh has its being. He means 27 the wet and the dry; not that flesh is simply a balanced mixture of these things or the proportion in which they are mixed, but flesh does not exist unless they are mixed in a certain proportion. If, he says, the cognitive part by which we get to know these[104] is perceptive ('it is by that which perceives', he says, and it is of these things 40 that flesh consists) then we get to know flesh too by that which perceives. He calls it 'that which perceives' not because we use that which perceives alone, but because we do not dispense with that which perceives. But it gets to know the form by the bare intellect, with no assistance from sense. It is plain that when the intellect distinguishes hot and cold by sense it distinguishes each as something composite. For the hot is one thing, being hot another. The 45 hot is a body which participates in heat, while being hot is the form of heat itself. Similarly with cold, dry and the rest.

429b16 It is with something else, either something separate or something related to it as a crooked line is related to itself

---

[102] Reading *subintelligendum* after *nobis* at 26,23 and *est; quare si hoc quidem cum materia, hoc autem sine materia*, after *materia* at 26,24 (Bossier).

[103] Deleting *nare* ('nose') at 26,27.

[104] Reading *haec* for *hoc* ('this') at 27,39 with Bossier. Bossier wishes to continue: *ait, sensitivo* [[*cognoscitivo*]] *cognoscimus* [['sensitivo' *autem dicit*]], *ex his autem caro, et carnem . . .* , 'if, he says, we get to know these by that which perceives, and it is of these that flesh consists, then we get to know flesh too . . .'; this is certainly an improvement.

when it has been straightened out, that it distinguishes being flesh.

50   Reordering the sentence we should read: 'It is with something else that it distinguishes being flesh, something either separate . . .' He means separate not in place but in essence, in the way in which the good smell of an apple is separate from its sweetness or its rotundity. As a crooked line, then, stands to itself when straight-

55   ened out, when it receives a different disposition and is transmuted, so to speak, from being doubled over to simplicity, but without losing anything from its substance, so too the intellect which gets to know what is composite stands to that which gets to know what is simple; it merely receives a different disposition, since in the one case it operates along with sense, in the other by virtue of itself.

429b18 Again, in the case of abstract things, straight is like
60   **snubnosed; it is with continuum.**

By 'abstract things' he means objects of mathematics,[105] and he says there is a certain duplication considered here too. Straight is one thing, namely a kind of composite, and being straight is another. But here too in the same way intellect, while being one and the

28/65   same, will get to know the composite and the simple through being disposed now in one way and now in another. For with objects of mathematics, he says, continuum takes the place of subject. For the subject of every[106] shape is a continuum. The model for straight, something composite, is snubnosed; as snubnosed is composite (it is hollowness in the nose: the nose is subject, snubnosedness is the form, snubnosed is the two together)[107] so too is straight. It is 'with

70   continuum', he says; that is, it is in a continuum as subject.

429b19 But what it was to be, if being straight is different
from straight, is something else. For so there is duality.[108]
Hence it distinguishes it either with something different or
with the same thing differently disposed.

---

[105] Punctuating *In abstractione ait mathematica*; at 27,61 (Bossier).
[106] Reading *omni* at 28,66 for *omnis* (Bossier).
[107] Punctuating *cavitas . . . utrumque* (28,67–9) as a parenthesis (Bossier).
[108] Aristotle says 'Let it be duality'. His meaning seems to be that (because it has two terminal points, or for some such reason) a line might be defined as 'duality in a continuum'; 'duality' would then express the form. That the reading 'for so there is duality' (*sic* rather than *sit*) goes back to Philoponus is suggested by the commentary; but a similar interpretation is given for the correct text at G 532,1–4. At 28,78 the MSS have, not as at 28,72 *sic*, but *sicut* ('for as duality'). This is no improvement and merely illustrates the tendency of textual corruption to spread; I therefore read *sic*.

Reordering we should read: 'What it was to be is something else, if being straight is different from straight.' That is, the form is some- 75 thing else besides the composite if being straight (i.e. straightness itself) is one thing and the straight (the composite, straightness in a continuum) is another. The next words are 'For so there is duality'; that is, in objects of mathematics also we suppose that there are two things, on the one hand form, on the other the composite. If, therefore, in objects of mathematics too the form is something else 80 besides the composite, it [sc. the soul] will get to know the simple and the composite either with different parts or with the same part differently disposed, as has been made clear.

429b21 Altogether, then, in the way in which the things are separate from matter, so it is concerning the intellect.

Here he gives his final answer along with the proof.[109] It is reason- 85 able, he says, that as the form stands to the composite, so the intellect which gets to know the simple should stand to that which gets to know the composite. Just as the form is separated from the composite only by thinking, so the intellect which gets to know the composite is separated from the intellect which gets to know the simple only by understanding. For as the intellect [which gets to 90 know the form] stands to the form, so the intellect [which gets to know the composite] stands to the composite. Hence as the form stands to the composite, so the one intellect stands to the other. If **29** the form is separated not in essence but only by understanding from the composite, so is the one intellect from the other. In essence, then, it is one and the same.

429b22 Someone may feel it a problem, if the intellect is 95 simple and unaffected and has nothing in common with any-thing as Anaxagoras says, how it will understand,[110] if to understand is to be affected in some way.

He expounds two problems here.[111] One is: if the intellect is unaffec-ted and not mixed, and unaffected in the way that has been said, how will it understand? For if to understand is to be affected in 00/30 some way as was said above (he said 'If understanding is like perceiving it will either be being affected in some way by the thing

---

[109] Bossier suggests that this paragraph contains two alternative drafts by Philo-ponus.

[110] Correcting *intellegeret* at 29,97 to *intelleget* (Bossier).

[111] Philoponus again uses the technique of double exposition; the passages to which he refers in this section receive further comment below.

understood or something else similar to that'),[112] how, not being affected, will it understand? The intellect ought to have a certain relationship to that which it understands and, as it were, touch it.
5 But if that is how it is, it will not be unaffected. Things which are affected seem to be affected by things which act upon them because they have something in common with them. Things which make and things which are affected seem to share a common matter. Hence if the intellect is affected by the intelligibles when it understands them, it will have something in common with the things
10 which it has understood and by which it is affected. But then it will not be without mixture or unaffected, neither will it have nothing in common with any of the things by which it is affected. Hence we have not spoken well, we and Anaxagoras, in pronouncing it to be without mixture and unaffected. That is one problem.

The second[113] is whether or not the intellect understands itself.
15 If it does not understand itself, that is contrary to the plain fact that it does. For what is it that pronounces on the intellect and says that it is incorporeal, unaffected, everlasting and so on, if it is not the intellect itself? But if it understands itself, either it understands and is understood by virtue of the same thing[114] (and it is the same thing for it to be intellect and to be thing understood), or
20 it will understand by virtue of one thing and be understood by virtue of another. If the first, to be intellect and to be thing understood will be the same for it and conversely. It will be a thing understood by virtue of being intellect, and hence intellect by virtue of being a thing understood. These will be so many words for the same referent
25 like 'sword' and 'brand' or 'corn' and 'grain'. But if that is so, all intelligibles will be intellects. But[115] since all forms are intelligible, so will be those of stone and wood. For it is not by sense that the form in the sense of substance[116] is graspable but by intellect. So there will be intellects in inanimate things, which is awkward. If,
31 on the other hand, the intellect is not both intellect and understood by virtue of the same thing, but it understands by virtue of one
30 thing and is understood by virtue of another, it will not be simple or without mixture, nor will it have nothing in common with other things. If it is not by virtue of being intellect that it is understood, along with being intellect it will have something else mixed with it in virtue of which it is understood. In this way, then, it will be

---

[112] 429a13–15, see above pp. 16–18.

[113] Stated in the next lemma.

[114] Understanding *idem* at 30,18 for *ipsum*, 'itself'; Moerbeke probably read *t' auton* as *tauton* (Bossier).

[115] Punctuating *erunt; igitur quoniam* at 30,25 after Sophonias (Bossier).

[116] Understanding *quae secundum essentiam* as at 76,33; Sophonias has *to kat' ousian eidos*. For the notion see on 65,64 below. The MSS have *species (hoc est substantia)*, 'form (that is substance)'.

neither simple nor without mixture; nor will it be a thing which
has nothing in common with other things. As each one of them is   35
intelligible, so will the intellect be. There is something in virtue of
which each of them is intelligible, and it will have this in the same
way as they[117] along with being intellect. These are the problems.

He solves the first problem by saying that 'to be affected' is
equivocal. A thing is said to be affected if it is subverted and   40
destroyed in respect of its substance. It is in this way that we say
that the elements are affected by one another: they destroy and
transmute one another. But things are also said[118] to be affected if
they are brought to what is in accordance with their nature and to
their proper perfection. In this way we say that sense is affected by
the things perceived when it is perfected by them and takes on the   45
operations which are in accordance with its nature; it is perfected
in receiving the forms of sensibles. According to the first meaning
of 'affection' – and this is being affected in the strict sense – intellect
is unaffected. But because of its being affected in the perfective way
and its reception of forms, which is how, in fact, it understands, we
say 'it is affected' using the word 'affection' equivocally. That is   50
why, after saying that understanding is being affected (in the words
'If understanding is like perceiving, it will be either being affected
in some way'), since the word 'affection' did not seem to him quite
appropriate here, he added 'or something else similar to that'.[119]
For this is how sense too[120] is said to be affected by the things
perceived: it is not destroyed by them but brought to perfection.   55/32
Just, then, as sense receives sensible forms, say white, without
being destroyed by them or made what they are, sight, for
instance,[121] being made white or black, but it receives the forms of
these things in a cognitive manner, so also intellect remains unaffected in respect of its substance but is affected by the intelligibles
in that it receives them in a cognitive manner. But it is affected in   60
a more lofty fashion, as was said above, than happens with sense.
For sense is destroyed by excess in the sensible things, whereas the
greater the things intellect grasps the more apt to grasp it becomes.
It is unaffected, then, according to the first meaning but affected
according to the second.

Of things which are affected, those share one matter with the   65
things that act which in being affected are brought to destruction
and not only that[122] but which in being affected also act upon what

---

[117] The MSS have *secundum illa*; Bossier suggests this translates *kat' ekeina*,
literally 'in accordance with them'.
[118] Understanding *dicuntur* for *dicitur* at 31,42 (so too Bossier).
[119] 429a13–15.
[120] Reading *et* after *enim* at 31,54 (Bossier).
[121] Reading *puta* before *albus* at 32,57 (Bossier).
[122] Conjecturing *hoc* for *haec*, 'these', at 32,66.

affects them – for the sublunary things which are affected by the heavenly bodies are not altogether of the same matter, and body which is affected by soul, a kind of affection which is not destructive

70 but perfective, has nothing in common with it in respect of substance. Hence even if the intellect is said to be affected by the intelligibles, it will not on this account have anything in common with them, since the mode of being affected which it undergoes is perfective, not destructive.

33 Why, then, is it said to be affected? Things which are affected in the strict sense, that is, destructively, when they receive the form

75 of the thing which acts, continue to exist for some time in it, as does air or wood when affected by fire; what becomes[123] fire remains some time in this state of reception of fire; and in the same way when intellect and sense receive forms they remain in the receipt of them, the difference being that the former change in substance[124] and the latter do not.

Further, sense does not continue to have the forms of sensible

80 things but quickly gets rid of them, while intellect continues. And intellect is self-moving and sometimes understands from its own resources, whereas sense needs the presence of sensible things. Also intellect is changed from intellect in potentiality to intellect in actuality not through taking in forms it did not already possess,

85 nor by changing from potentiality in the first sense, but like the sleeping geometer who at that time does not know the things he knows. He possesses the accounts, but is hindered from the cognition of what he possesses by sleep, and needs something to remove the impediment (I mean sleep); in the same way intellect needs something to remove the impediment. That will be intellect in actuality, either a teaching intellect or the universal intellect; and

90 the impediment is the absurd opinions which come from the connection with imagination and which it purges away by refutations to bring to light the treasure which has existed in it all along. Sense, in contrast, is changed from potentiality in the first sense, and receives forms it did not already possess.

95 In solution to the second problem he agrees to it and says that such a thing is not a problem; it is in truth[125] by virtue of the same thing that intellect is intellect and intelligible, and it is not false that every intelligible thing should be intellect but true and necessary. The intelligible [here], however, is the properly and actually

34 intelligible, and the actually intelligible is what is completely non-

00 material and separate. The forms in things perceived are not prop-

---

[123] Conjecturing *fit*, 'becomes', for *sit*, 'is', after Sophonias at 33,75 (Bossier).

[124] Taking *vertunt* as intransitive and *substantiam* as accusative of respect, after Sophonias.

[125] Deleting the colon after *veritatem* at 33,95 (Bossier).

erly intelligible, neither are they intelligible in actuality but only in potentiality. Hence they are intellects [only] when the intellect itself is on its own, separated from all matter.

We should notice how here too he plainly supposes that the rational soul is separate and non-material, and that it is on this account that it is at once intellect and thing understood. But if 5 it is separate from all matter, being at once intellect and thing understood, plainly it is also immortal. For there are two ways of destroying. One is that which dissolves a composite into the things of which it is composed. That is how all bodies which consist of matter and form are destroyed. The other affects those things which are incorporeal but have their existence in a body as subject.[126] 10 These too are destroyed, but not by being resolved into simple constituents (for they are not composites); when their subject is made unsuitable for supporting them their substance is necessarily extinguished, like the shape which was in wax when the wax is consumed. If anything, therefore, is completely separate from matter and incorporeal it will necessarily also be indestructible, since in 15 neither way will it have the nature of that which can be destroyed, neither the way of bodies, since it is incorporeal, nor the way of incorporeal things, since it does not have its existence in bodies but is separate in substance from all matter and established on its own.

<But that> intelligible things which are separate from matter **35** must be intellects is clear from this: if one is separate but not an 20 intellect it will not understand either, and hence will exist to no avail as a functionless thing. It was said in the <Introduction>,[127] however, that whatever things have their substance separate will have their mode of operating entirely separate too; hence whatever intelligibles are separate from matter will have separate functioning. What, then, will be their mode of operating except understand- 25 ing? it will not be sensing, or any other bodily operation. Of necessity, then, separate intelligible things will also be intellects.

429b26 And also, is it itself intelligible?

Here he expounds the second problem. 'Someone may feel it a prob- 30 lem' belongs to both. 'Also,' he says, 'someone may feel it a problem' whether the intellect is, at the same time, 'intelligible', and if so, whether it is by virtue of the same thing or of different things that it is intellect and intelligible.

429b27 For either intellect will be present in the other things,

---

[126] Reading *incorporeorum in subiecto autem corpore* after Sophonias for *incorporea in subiecto aut corpore* (Bossier).
[127] G 15,18–22.

if it is not by virtue of something else that the intellect is
intelligible, and the intelligible is one single thing in form; or
35   it will have something mixed which makes it intelligible like
the other things.

If, he says, it is not intellect by virtue of one thing and intelligible
by virtue of another, but it is both by virtue of the same thing, then
since the intelligible qua intelligible is one single thing in form,
40   the other intelligible things too will be intellects. And that is awkward, for then there will be intellect in inanimate things too. He
uses 'form' here for 'account': there is one single account of intelligible things insofar as they are intelligible, even if they differ in
form. If, on the other hand, the intellect is intellect by virtue of one
36   thing and intelligible by virtue of another, it will have something
45   mixed in with itself by virtue of which it is made to be intelligible.
And then it will be neither simple nor unmixed, but will have
something in common with the other intelligible things.

429b29 A[128] division has been made earlier about being
affected by virtue of something common.

This is the solution to the earlier problem, that 'be affected' is
50   equivocal: it means that which brings a thing to destruction and
that which brings it to perfection. He has spoken about this in the
preceding book.[129] Being, then, in potentiality what the intelligibles
are, when it comes to be in actuality the intellect is affected by
them, not in being destroyed, indeed, but perfected. In the other
meaning of 'affection' it is unaffected. The words **A division has**
55   **been made earlier** could be referring us to the place where he
says: 'Those things which have something common as subject act
and are affected in return at the same time.'[130] Hence not all things
which act and are affected, act and are affected by virtue of something common. Those things which are affected by a heavenly body
are not affected by virtue of anything common. So if the intellect
60   too does not act in return it will <not>[131] be affected by virtue of
anything in common. Hence it will remain unmixed. 'A division

---

[128] The lemma begins with *aut*, 'or', translating Aristotle's *ê*. Although *ê* often
means 'or', here it serves simply to introduce a solution tentatively and there is no
English equivalent.
[129] The reference is probably to 417b2–16.
[130] *de Gen. et Cor.* 1, 328a18–22, cf. 322b18–19. The word, however, which I
translate 'a division has been made' (and which is so understood by Philoponus)
could mean, more vaguely, 'a clarification has been made'.
[131] The MSS have: *Quare et intellectus si non contra agat, secundum commune
aliquid patietur utique*, 'So if the intellect too does not act in return it will be affected
by virtue of something in common'. I insert *neque* before *secundum*; a similar sense
can be obtained by putting *neque* in place of *et* (Bossier).

has been made earlier' could remind us also of what he has said about the intellect. He said it is unaffected and not affected in the place where he said that the unaffectedness of that which understands is not like the unaffectedness of that which perceives. We called it 'unaffected' there, he says, using 'unaffected' according to the undifferentiated meaning of 'be affected'. 'Affection' being 65 equivocal, 'unaffected' is equivocal too. The intellect, then, is unaffected according to one meaning of 'affection' which is, indeed, affection in the strict sense; and it is not unaffected according to the other meaning, inasmuch as it is none of the intelligible things in actuality, but all of them in potentiality.

He likens it to a tablet which has nothing written on it. Just as 70 on an uninscribed sheet all those things which can be written on 37 it are present in potentiality, on account of its suitability, but none of the things to be written is present in actuality before it is written, so too, the intellect, he says, is no intelligible thing in actuality, but all in potentiality. And just as something you write on when it is inscribed becomes a thing you write on in actuality, yet the form 75 the sheet had before is not destroyed, so too the intellect when it becomes the things understood in actuality is in no way changed from its proper nature. If, in changing from potentiality to actuality, the intellect were affected to some extent and subverted from its proper nature, there would be occasion to feel a problem. But as it is, being likened to an uninscribed thing you write on, plainly it continues unaffected. 80

We should notice here that in likening the rational soul to an uninscribed thing you write on, Aristotle places the forms of intelli- 38 gible things in the soul according to the first sort of potentiality – I mean by virtue of a suitability [to receive them] – not, as Plato does, by way of disposition. That being so he does not, like Plato, 85 think the soul pre-exists [birth], for if it is pre-existent it should possess accounts dispositionally. But if it is not pre-existent, it must have had a beginning to its existence. If it began to be, it is wholly necessary on the same account that it should have a limit. For everything which has a beginning in time has a limit in time. So 90 from these premises the soul is shown to be mortal. Further, if from what has been said here it is shown that a rational soul is never pre-existent but always has a beginning to its existence, and if, furthermore, Aristotle wants the universe to be eternal, one of two things must follow. Either rational souls are immortal, in which case infinitely many of them exist and come to be; for the past and the future are both infinite; or else, if an infinity is impossible, they 95 are mortal like everything else. In that case either the soul passes away into that which does not exist at all, if it is incorporeal; or it is resolved into matter, and then it is not incorporeal but a body.

But to this it may be replied that we ought to interpret what
39/00   Aristotle says here carefully and thoughtfully with regard to his
whole thought and to what he says everywhere about the intellect.
If we have shown a thousand times over, quoting Aristotelian texts,
that he wants the rational soul to be separate and immortal, it is
plain that even if he here likens it to an uninscribed thing we write
5   on he does not mean that it has forms in potentiality in the first
sense (the sense in which semen is a man in potentiality). But a
certain latitude must be recognised in both meanings of 'potentiality'. For we say that prime matter is in potentiality a man,
and also the elements and semen and all the things which are in
potentiality in the first sense, that is, by virtue of suitability; but
10   they are not in potentiality in the same way but some are closer to
the thing and some more remote. A similar latitude, then, must be
recognised in connection with potentiality in the second sense, i.e.
by way of disposition. Both the sleeping geometer and the one who
is awake are said to be [one who knows][132] in potentiality, but the
waking geometer is closer to the actuality; and the geometer who
15   is asleep or drunk because he is held down by sleep or intoxication,
resembles the man who does not have the disposition at all. So in
the same way even if he says the soul resembles an uninscribed
thing you write on, he calls it this because of the holding down of
cognition by the passions which makes it seem as if it did not have
forms at all.[133] And when it has already become a knower he still
20   calls it 'in potentiality'. For he says: When it becomes particular
things as one who knows in actuality is said to [even then it is in
potentiality in a way].[134]

That he means it to be everlasting and immortal he has said
plainly before more than once, and he now pronounces it to be
separate from all matter. And a little later he again plainly says
it is immortal. But these earlier words are sufficient: 'Concerning
25   the intellect and the contemplative capacity the position is not yet
clear; but this seems to be a different sort of soul, and it falls to
this alone to be separated as that which is everlasting from that

[132] cf. Aristotle *Met.* 9, 1048a34.

[133] Lines 39,16–18 make no sense as they stand. We should certainly read *cognitionis oppressionem* for *et cognitione oppressionem* at 39,17; Sophonias has *tês gnôseôs epiprosthêsin*. I am inclined to agree with Bossier that Moerbeke has mistranslated the rest of the sentence as it stands in Sophonias, and I therefore translate that.

[134] After 'When it becomes particular things' the MSS have *tunc dicitur qui secundum actum*, 'it is then said to be in actuality'. In Aristotle the word 'then' comes not here but before 'it is in potentiality in a way', the words we should expect Philoponus to quote. We could suppose that *tunc dicitur qui secundum actum* has somehow come to replace *et tunc potentia aliqualiter* or we could supply these words after *dicitur qui secundum actum* and excise the earlier *tunc*. My translation corresponds to doing the latter.

which is destructible.'[135] And later he says that just as the sun
makes colours which are in potentiality, i.e. colours at night, to be   **40**
colours in actuality, so intellect which is in actuality, i.e. the
teacher's intellect and the Divine Intellect, makes intellect in potentiality intellect in actuality. The Philosopher's meaning is plain   30
from the model itself. Just as the rising sun does not provide existence for the colours, but makes manifest colours which exist there
but are not evident, and does not make them to be colours (for they
were just as much colours during the night) but makes them visible,
so intellect which is in actuality perfects intellect which is in poten-   35
tiality and brings it to actuality not by putting into it forms which
are not there, but by bringing to light forms which are non-evident
and hidden because of the state of swoon which is the effect of birth.
And it is this that he calls 'potentiality' in the first sense. For there
is a difference between the geometer who is in a cataleptic swoon[136]
though he still possesses [knowledge] dispositionally, or who is
asleep, and one who is in none of these conditions but is not exercising the disposition;[137] the one has both the disposition and the   **40**
actuality hidden and is not capable of functioning; the other functions when he wants without being impeded by anything. The intellect which enters the world of becoming is like a person asleep or
delirious.[138]

430a2 And it is itself intelligible as are intelligible things.[139]

He passes to the solution of the second problem, which is how   45
intellect understands itself. Either it is in virtue of something else,
and then it will not be simple and without mixture, or it is in virtue
of the same thing, and then all intelligible things will be intellects.
He solves this in the way we have said above. It is in virtue of the
same thing that it is intellect and intelligible, and everything which
is properly and in actuality intelligible is also intellect. That, how-   50
ever, which is intelligible in potentiality is not the same as intellect,
since it is neither properly nor in actuality intelligible.

[135] 413b24–7.
[136] The Latin *qui in nubilo . . . aut qui occupatus* literally means 'who is in a fog or
preoccupied' but *nubilum* translates *karos* (Sophonias) and *occupatus kateilêmmenos*
(Bossier).
[137] Reading *a nihil horum habente, non exercente autem habitum*; at 40,39–40
(Bossier). Verbeke (following Mansion) alters the MSS *exercente* to *exercens* and
punctuates *a nihil horum habente. Non exercens autem habitum*, which he might
wish us to translate: '. . . one who is in neither of these conditions. When each is
not exercising the disposition, . . .'.
[138] Or, perhaps, 'swooning': T has *karoumeno* in the margin (Bossier).
[139] The MSS show this as a quotation rather than as a lemma.

41   **430a4 For contemplative knowledge and that which is known in this way are the same.**[140]

That is, that which[141] contemplates and 'that which is known in
55   this way' (i.e. that which is properly and in actuality intelligible)
are interchangeable. And besides, he says this in proof of this, that
what is intelligible without matter is straightaway intellect; but
what is intelligible without matter is actually intelligible, and
therefore in actuality.[142]

Contemplative knowledge (this in contradistinction to knowledge concerning things that are done, which is prudence) is there-
60   fore the same as the things known in this way, that is, contempla-
tively.[143] For what else is knowledge but theorems? But these are
precisely the things known − not, indeed, those which lie outside
[the soul]; it is the concept of a circle, not the sensible circle, that
is knowable. If that is so, however, and knowledge is a kind of
understanding and intellect, and knowable things are intelligible
65   things: then that which is in actuality intelligible and immaterial
is the same as intellect.

**430a5 But we should consider the cause of its not understand-
ing always.**

Aristotle here interposes another problem. If the intellect is both
intellect and intelligible thing, why does it not understand all the
70   time? Since the intelligibles are always in actuality,[144] how is it
that it does not understand them all the time? And if it[145] is both
42   intellect and intelligible thing, why does it not understand itself
all the time? Such is the problem or difficulty. Aristotle did not, as
some have thought, omit to provide a solution; he will give it later,

---

[140] The MSS do not show this sentence as a lemma.

[141] Deleting *intellectus* at 41,54 (Bossier).

[142] I find the sequence of thought in this sentence puzzling. I take it that Philoponus is saying that (a) 'Contemplative knowledge and what is known in this way are the same' is offered as a proof of (b) 'What is intelligible without matter is straightaway intellect', a paraphrase of the sentence which in fact precedes (a) in Aristotle's text; though it would be possible to interpret the Latin as saying that (b) is offered as a proof of (a). But does he think that (a)'s being intended as a proof of (b) confirms his interpretation that 'contemplative knowledge' in (a) means 'that which contem-plates', and is the last part of the sentence designed to show how it confirms it? The final words 'and therefore in actuality' could mean either 'and therefore intellect in actuality' or 'and therefore actual understanding'.

[143] Conjecturing *speculative* for *speculativis*.

[144] In place of 'are always in actuality' Sophonias (134,32) has 'are present to it'.

[145] Verbeke prints *idem*, 'the same', but T has *isdem*, an occasional mediaeval masculine for *idem*; the Greek was probably *autos* (so Sophonias), not *to auto* (Bossier).

as we shall make clear when we get there.[146] Let us now, however, return to our present concern.

430a6 But in things which have matter each of the intelli- 75
gibles is present only in potentiality.

In material things, he says, though there are forms, these forms are [separated from matter][147] in potentiality, not in actuality, that is, only by understanding.

430a7 But intellect is the potentiality without matter of such **things.**[148]

That is, of intelligible things. Hence if some are material and some 80 are without matter, intellect is not the same as the material intelligible things. But if anything intelligible is without matter it is also intellect. Plainly, then, he declares intellect to be separate from all matter.

---

[146] 61,67–63,23.

[147] So Sophonias 134,29–30.

[148] The MSS do not show this sentence as a lemma. Before it Aristotle has: 'Hence intellect will not be present in them' (sc. material objects). In calling intellect the 'potentiality' of intelligibles Aristotle probably meant it has the potentiality of becoming them (so D. W. Hamlyn, *Aristotle's De Anima Books II and III*, Oxford, Clarendon Press 1965, ad loc.).

CHAPTER 5

430a10 Throughout nature there is one thing which is matter for each kind (that which is capable of all of them) and another which is cause and maker, in that it makes all (which is what art does in relation to the material); so in the soul too there
90   must be these different elements.

In *Physics* 4 it is said that since there was uncertainty among past thinkers about place,[1] it was desirable to give an account of place such that all the things that belong to it according to a proper understanding of it would be entailed, the problems which are
95   raised about it would be solved, and the reason why past thinkers went astray concerning it would be made clear to us. We must
43   supply a similar exposition of the things Aristotle says here about the intellect which is in actuality: it must be consonant with what he says everywhere else about the intellect in actuality; it must resolve the problems which arise; and it must make clear to us the
00   reason why certain of his expositors have been led astray to alien expositions.
      Since, then, he is now speaking of the intellect, and proposes to reveal to us what he thinks about the whole of rational life, let us see what he says about that life. He says that there is intellect in
5   potentiality and intellect in actuality, and that intellect is not mixed or affected, that it is separate, simple and psychical, a word derived from *psukhê*.[2] For there is intellect in potentiality, he says, and intellect in actuality in the soul just as in every other kind of thing we find that which is in potentiality and that which is in actuality. Further, it is analogous in its making everything to art
10   and light; just as light makes colours which are potentially visible actually visible, and art makes forms which are present in the material potentially present in actuality, so the intellect in actuality perfects the intellect which is in potentiality; it makes it be in actuality, and makes it the same as the things [understood]. Aristotle makes these observations about the intellect, and every-
15   body with one voice agrees that the intellect in potentiality is none other but ours. Non-rational animals do not have it, since they are in no way equipped to understand anything, and neither do kinds

---

[1] The reference is to *Phys.* 4, 211a7–11. Bossier wishes to read *ratio* at 42,92, 'the account of place', for *ideo* which makes no contribution to the sense.
[2] Aristotle does not say explicitly that intellect is psychical (*animalis*); that is Philoponus' inference from his saying that the distinction between potential and actual intellect is found in the soul (430a13).

of being superior to us, since they exist in actuality with no potentiality.

But there is dispute about the intellect in actuality.[3] Some say
that by this he means the intellect which is universal, that is, divine   **44**
and creative. For the human intellect is not in essence actuality (for   20
it is sometimes in potentiality), nor does it make everything (our
intellect is not such as to make all things) nor does it understand
always (seeing that sometimes it is in potentiality). The intellect
in potentiality which is in us, they say, is perfected by an intellect
in actuality which is universal and external.

Others say that Aristotle is not here referring to the universal   25
and creative intellect. For the creative and divine intellect is not
psychical at all. There is another intellect, lower than that but
placed next above[4] ours, which irradiates our human souls and
perfects them. That is why he calls it 'psychical', because it stands
next above souls, whereas the creative intellect is more universal. It   30
is on this account, they say, that he calls it analogous to light. Just
as light has the middle rank between the cause of light and the
things which are illuminated (for it proceeds from the sun and illuminates other things) so the creative and wholly perfect intellect is
analogous to the Sun, and our intellect is to the things illuminated.   35
But there is a third intellect which is above us but ranked next to
us, and this perfects our intellect; it is inferior to the creative intellect and resembles light in that it proceeds thence to illuminate us.

According to others he says neither of these things. They do not   **45**
make the intellect transcend[5] the soul, since he himself says that   40
both the intellect in potentiality and the intellect in actuality are
in the soul; but they say our soul has two intellects, one which
is in actuality and one in potentiality. The intellect which is in
potentiality is always in the soul, and at a certain time is perfected
by the intellect in actuality, but the latter enters from outside. This
opinion has been defended by some ostensible Platonists. Plato   45
nowhere seems to have thought this, but they were led to this
conjecture because Plato says that the soul is always in a state of
change.[6] They say that if it is always in a state of change, clearly
it must always have intellect in actuality in order that it may
always be thus changed. For they thought Plato uses the word   50
'change' to refer to cognition. But [in fact] he is not referring to a
change consisting in cognition when he says it is always in a state

---

[3] The four interpretations Philoponus discusses are attributed at G 535 to Alexander, Marinus, Plotinus and Plutarch.

[4] Reading *superpositum* with T and Sophonias for *suppositum* at 44,28 (Bossier).

[5] Taking *ereptum* to translate *exêrêmenon* (Bossier).

[6] *Phaedrus* 245C (*semper motum* at 45,52 probably translates Plato's *aeikinêton*,
not *aeikinêsian*), cf. *Laws* 10, 894B–896B. Plato does in fact seem to have in mind
life rather than cognition.

of change; by saying it is always changed he expresses its vivifying power, for it always gives life.

55   In addition to these opinions there is a fourth which is true: that he is speaking of a human intellect which is identical with that which is in potentiality. For when the intellect which is in potentiality is perfected, it comes to be in actuality. Hence that which is in potentiality and that which is in actuality are one and the same in essence, and differ in being perfect and imperfect. That Aristotle's remarks about the intellect in actuality do not fit either the creative intellect or, in a word, any other intellect which is external to the human soul, is clear from those remarks themselves.

60   In the first place, to raise the question whether the intellect is separate or not would be irrational if he were enquiring about the creative intellect. For could there be any doubt that it might have its being in some body as its subject? But neither is the question a reasonable one to raise about the intellect which is next above the

65   soul and illuminates it. It is rational to ask 'Will it be separated?' neither about this intellect itself, since it is [assumed all along to be] separate, nor about its illumination, since illumination is not separate. And how can it be fitting to say of the creative intellect

46   that it enters from outside and is analogous to art and light? How also can it be called 'psychical'? Again, it can be seen from the

70   definition he gives of all soul in general that he is speaking neither of the creative intellect nor of any other intellect higher than ours: no such intellect would be 'the actuality of an organic body'.[7] And it is clear too from what is said here. He says 'knowledge which is in actuality is identical with the thing [known]; knowledge which is in potentiality is temporally prior in the individual'.[8] By 'know-

75   ledge' he means the intellect which is in actuality, for it is that which he says is identical with the intelligibles, just as sense in actuality is identical with the things perceived; and he says that the intellect in potentiality is temporally prior to that which is in actuality in man. It would be unreasonable to say of that intellect[9] that it is temporally posterior or that it comes into being at all in men or that its illumination is separate and immortal; for an

80   illuminator[10] is destroyed simultaneously with that which is illuminated. It would also be unreasonable, when he has announced the intention of speaking of the soul, to divert his discussion from this plan and think he is talking about that intellect which is divine and transcendent, for that is the business rather of the theologian.

[7] 412b5–6.

[8] 430a19–21.

[9] sc. the creative intellect.

[10] sc. one actually illuminating. Bossier, however, may be right in thinking we should correct to *illustratio*, 'illumination'.

But this[11] could reasonably be said of the creative intellect, which it is for the theologian to discuss.

It may seem that it would not be irrelevant to the present busi- 85
ness to speak about some intellect which is next above us, since his[12] discussion is about all souls. But that what is said is not[13] about this sort of intellect either is plain from the following.

Such an intellect must either be part of ours[14] or not a part but something external and separate from our substance. If it is part 90
of ours, then since he says it is in essence actuality, plainly we have some part which is by nature such as to understand always. That being so, why is it that we do not understand always? For not all human beings operate with intellect, nor do they operate always but only at certain times. They do not operate when they are children or when they are in a stupor[15] or asleep. 95

If someone says that we do understand at all times but we are 47
not conscious that we do, in the first place it is impossible to say this. For it is not possible to understand without being conscious that you understand. Furthermore not even those who have attained the summit of virtue and operate with the intellect achieve 00
this [operation] at all times. If age or passion puts an impediment in the way of consciousness those who are separated from passion ought to be conscious always of the functioning of understanding. But in fact they are not. Such an intellect, then, is not part of ours.

But it is clear that if it is external to us what Aristotle says will 5
not fit it either. He says that the intellect in potentiality is all those things in potentiality which the intellect in actuality is in actuality, and when that which is in potentiality is perfected it comes to be in actuality. 'When', he says, 'it becomes particular things as a knower does it is said to be' intellect 'in actuality'.[16] It is impossible that our intellect should sometimes come to be what the intellect 10
separate from us is. For it to transcend its substance and be included among higher things is an impossibility. For every substance has [only] a certain perfection attending it.[17] Just as a non-rational soul would never come to be of the same dignity as a rational one, so our intellect would never be the equal of those kinds which are 15
above it. Hence Aristotle will not be speaking of any other intellect superior to us.

[11] Presumably that it is separate etc.; but this sentence looks to me like a gloss.
[12] Reading *sibi* with T for *agitur* at 46,87 (Bossier).
[13] Reading *utique* with CV for *itaque* at 46,87 (Bossier).
[14] Or 'of us' likewise for 46,90 and 47,4.
[15] Taking *alienationibus* (literally 'madness') to translate *karois* (margin of T, cf. G 95,21) (Bossier) likewise for 48,23.
[16] 429b5–7.
[17] Conjecturing *assectibilem*, translating *parakolouthêtikon* at 47,12 (Bossier) for *affectibilem* 'which it can attain'.

That those people too are talking nonsense who say that there are two intellects in us, one which is in actuality and one which is potentiality, is clear from the same considerations. If there is in us
20 an intellect which is always in actuality, we ought always to operate intellectually; for it is because it operates that the intellect in actuality is so called. But in fact not even all men operate intellectu-
48 ally; when they are boys they do not, or when asleep or in a stupor. That not one of these three opinions is consistent with Aristotle's
25 words is clear. Nor does he at any other place or time appear to mention any other intellect external to human souls which perfects our intellect or which comes into being at all in us.

From what has been said, then, it appears that the fourth opinion is correct: it is the same intellect which Aristotle says is in poten- tiality and in actuality, and it is transmuted from intellect in poten-
30 tiality to intellect in actuality, and it is led into actuality by another intellect which also is in the human soul, sc. in the soul of the teacher, and which also was once led from potentiality to actuality. We should recognise how what Aristotle says accords with this. Just, he says, as in every natural thing there is something which
35 has the nature of matter and becomes all things and something else which makes all things, so it is in the soul also. If the intellect in potentiality becomes intellect in actuality it should have the nature of matter, and what leads it to actuality is the maker. In the case of natural things the cause which makes is itself first a thing in potentiality and later made to be in actuality. What is potentially
40 a man is led to actuality by that which is a man in actuality, and this latter was itself first in potentiality, and was led to actuality by another man in actuality. Similarly in other cases: a vine gener-
49 ates a vine; the plant receives in itself some material such as happens to be potentially a plant, and makes it a plant in actuality. Therefore the intellect in actuality which perfects the intellect in
45 potentiality in us and leads it to actuality itself, it too was formerly intellect in potentiality and was led into actuality by another thing which was intellect in actuality. The intellect in actuality, then, if it was formerly in potentiality, also belonged to the soul and is of one form with the intellect in potentiality. And indeed[18] he says the intellect in potentiality is the same as the intellect in actuality,
50 differing from it only in time – the knower is prior to the non- knower in time but not in substance – and when he said earlier 'When the intellect becomes particular things',[19] that is, when it receives the forms of perceptible things as happens in the case of one who knows, it becomes intellect 'in actuality', he made it clear

---

[18] The MSS have *quando*, normally meaning 'when' but here, perhaps, translating *hopote kai* introducing further confirmation (Bossier).
[19] 429b5–7, see pp. 16–20.

that what is said to be intellect in actuality is the same as what was formerly in potentiality.

That it is this intellect of ours which he says is not mixed but 55 pure and separate and immortal is clear from what has been said already. He not only said these things about it, but showed them. For he said[20] earlier that it is not mixed with the body either in the way in which bodies are mixed ('for it would have some quality', he says, 'such as hot or cold')[21] nor in the way in which incorporeal 60 things are mixed, since it would need an organ. 'What part the intellect would hold together and how', he says, 'it is difficult even to imagine.'[22] Nowhere would he have said this of any other superior intellect, least of all of the creative intellect. And he has said it is unaffected in many places. 'It would be likeliest to be destroyed by the weakness which comes with old age',[23] and again 'It must be 65 unaffected'[24] and 'the unaffectedness of that which understands is not like the unaffectedness of that which perceives'.[25] And he also says it is separate: 'for that which perceives', he says, 'is not without body, but the intellect is separate.'[26] And in Book Lambda[27] of the work called *Metaphysics*, having said that there are certain pre- 70/50 existing, simple and everlasting forms of things, he goes on to say that we ought to enquire whether there are perhaps some separate and everlasting forms among those which are here. 'In some,' he says, 'there is no reason why there should not be something like this. For we should consider whether anything remains after separation, for instance if the soul is of this kind – not all soul, but the intellect, for perhaps that all soul should remain is impossible.' All 75 these things can fittingly be said only of our intellect. How could he say of some other soul which is above us 'if anything remains after death'? So he says that intellect in potentiality and intellect in actuality are the same in nature and differ only in time, and that intellect in potentiality is led to actuality by another intellect which is in actuality but in a soul, and different only as an indi- 80 vidual, not in substance.

[20] Understanding *dixit* for *cum dixisset* at 49,57; Moerbeke probably read *eipôn gar* for *eipen gar* (Bossier).
[21] 429a25–6.
[22] 411b18–19.
[23] 408b19–20.
[24] 429a15.
[25] 429a29–30.
[26] 429b4–5. *Sensibile*, 'that which is perceived', at 49,67 is presumably an error for *sensitivum*, 'that which perceives'.
[27] Understanding Λ, 'Book Lambda', for *quinto*, 'Book V': T has a marginal correction from V to XI, and if Moerbeke misread Λ for Δ he would take the reference to be to Book V (Bossier). The quotation is Λ, 1070a24–6. Aristotle does not say in Λ (or in Δ) that there are 'pre-existing, simple and everlasting' forms, but Philoponus could have construed Λ, 1069a30–6 as tolerant of such entities.

But just as we say all this to show that Aristotle is not speaking
of any other intellect in actuality, but of ours, so those who contradict what we say put before us other texts by which they have been
85 induced to conjecture that Aristotle is speaking of the divine and
creative intellect. How, they ask, if he were speaking of our intellect, could he say that it makes all things, and understands always,
and is in substance actuality? Our intellect is not in substance
actuality, still less does it make all things; it does not even under-
90 stand always: these things fit the divine and creative intellect. We
reply that they also fit our intellect, and are said about that. Aristotle says that the intellect in actuality makes all things in the
way in which he says the intellect in potentiality becomes all things.
When he says that the intellect in potentiality becomes all things,
51 it is not on the ground that it becomes the heavens, and the angels
95 and God and the rest, but because it receives the forms of all things
and understands everything that such an intellect is naturally capable of understanding. Similarly when he says that the intellect in
actuality makes all things that is not because it produces the substance of all but because it makes the intellect in potentiality come
to be receptive of all.

It cannot, however, be said to make all things even in this way
00 [sc. intelligible] (as Alexander also thinks); by 'all' we must not
understand all intelligibles [sc. without exception]; for there are
some things which are of themselves and by their own nature
intelligible – things which, indeed, are also intellects. It makes all
things, that is, it makes intelligible whatever things are not by
5 their own nature intelligible, I mean material forms. Understanding, then, separates forms[28] which are intelligible in potentiality
from matter and makes them intelligible in actuality.

We do not say this on the ground that Aristotle had no knowledge
of the universal and creative intellect, for he knew both how it
itself has an exalted essence and how it perfects our intellect. But
it perfects our intellect as the Sun is said to generate men: it is a
10 cause at a higher level, not part of the causal chain.

. . . understands always where he says 'it does not sometimes
understand and sometimes not' nor . . .[29] For what does he mean
when he says, 'Knowledge which is in actuality is identical with

---

[28] Moerbeke has *si non* at 51,4 which would translate *ei mê*. I agree with Bossier
that Philoponus wrote *eidê* and translate accordingly. If we keep *si non* we could
translate 'if they are not [actually intelligible] understanding separates things . . .'.
[29] Moerbeke's Greek manuscript was apparently illegible here and our MSS leave
spaces for about ten letters at each end. I suggest that the first space might be filled
Nec dicens and the second *conditorem* (understand as object of some word like *dicit*;
Bossier suggests the Greek *dêlôi*), giving the sense: 'Nor, when he says it understands
always – where he says "it does not sometimes understand, sometimes not" (430a22)
– nor does he here refer to the creative intellect.'

the thing, whereas knowledge which is in potentiality is temporally
prior in the individual?'[30] In one and the same individual the imper-   15
fect precedes the perfect in time. For by nature perfect things pre-   **52**
cede imperfect; that which produces is by nature prior to that which
is produced and that which is perfect to that which is being perfected. 'But overall', he says, 'not even in time.'[31] That is, in a given
individual the imperfect does precede the perfect. But if one looks
at all and at the whole universe, that which is in potentiality does   20
not precede that which is in actuality even in time. In the universe
as a whole there are always both intellect in actuality and intellect
in potentiality. Just, then, as it is not the case that once there were
men only in potentiality, and afterwards there came to be men in
actuality, so there are always intellects in potentiality and intellects in actuality. It is, then, because in the universe as a whole
that which is in potentiality does not have to precede in time that
which is in actuality, that he says it does not sometimes understand   25
and sometimes not – as happens in the individual – but always
understands; for in the universe as a whole there are always intellects in actuality. Hence the words 'it understands always' are
applied[32] to all and to the pool of souls in the whole universe, not
because each person on his own understands always.

And indeed even if he says that the human intellect is in sub-   30
stance actuality[33] he does not depart from the truth. Each thing
derives its characterisation[34] and has its being not from being something in potentiality but from being in actuality what it is by nature
apt to be.[35] For example man has being and substance not in the
suitability according to which man is capable of being, not, say, as   35
semen and menses, but according to the form by virtue of which he
has already come to be man. Actuality is more estimable[36] than
potentiality, and each thing derives its characterisation and has its
being according to what is more estimable in it. Hence though a
man has in himself both rational and non-rational powers he is
characterised as a man not from that which is inferior – I mean his   40
non-rational power, for then he would differ in no way from other   **53**
animals which are non-rational – but from that which is more
honourable – I mean the rational – and we say that the substance

---

[30] 430a19–20.

[31] 431a2–3, cf. 430a21.

[32] The MSS have *non ad omne*, 'are not applied' at 52,27. *Omne*, however, 'all',
picks up 'all' above (52,19) and Philoponus' explanation of the words is that they *do*
apply to all, so I omit the 'not'.

[33] 430a18.

[34] Correcting the MSS *characterizat* ('characterises') to *characterizatur* and
unumquemque to *unumquodque* at 52,31 (Bossier).

[35] cf. 55,6; deleting *actum* and the parentheses at 52,33 (Bossier).

[36] An echo of 430a18–19.

of man is rational. All composites consist[37] of matter and form and each is characterised not according to its matter but according to its form.

45   Saying that intellect is in substance actuality, then, is saying only that by which[38] intellect is characterised and has its substance. Just as everything has its substance chiefly characterised according to that which is highest in it, that is, according to its actuality (for
50   sometimes it is a thing in potentiality, sometimes in actuality) <so the intellect,> like everything else, <has as its characterisation>[39] not potentiality but actuality.

This is clearly implied by Aristotle's very words. He says: 'Intellect is separate and unaffected and not mixed, being in essence actuality. For that which makes is always more estimable than that which is affected, and the source than the matter.'[40] I have
55   called the intellect, he is saying, actuality and not potentiality, because all things get their characterisation from what is more estimable in them. The maker is more estimable than the thing affected (for the thing affected is potentiality and analogous to matter, whereas the maker is actuality, that is, form); so we have characterised the substance of the intellect according to its actu-
60   ality, not its potentiality. Hence he says this not on the ground that pure activity, [[that is, actuality itself,]][41] is the substance of the intellect, as though it functioned always, but because its substance is characterised according to its actuality.

This is how Plato also taught us to think of the human soul. He says:[42] 'We seem to have been seeing it here as people see the sea-
65   god Glaucus':[43] they do not see its substance, but the things which have grown into its appearance from outside. In the same way seeing the soul here with its incrustation of passions, no wonder
54   we doubt its immortality. If we wish to come to recognise that it is immortal we must strip it of the passions, sc. spirit and desire,[44] that surround it and consider it as it is in itself, and the things it
70   seeks and attains. Then we shall know that it is immortal, since it attains completely separate and non-material forms. It would be impossible for it to do that if it had nothing in common with them. For if something is inseparable from body in substance and operation, how will it ever be able to attain to things which are wholly

[37] *compositorum omnium entium* probably translates a Greek genitive absolute.
[38] Understanding *quo* or *secundum quod* for *quod* at 53,46 (Bossier).
[39] Some such words seem to have dropped out at 53,50 (Bossier).
[40] 430a17–19.
[41] Words added, probably, by Moerbeke (Bossier).
[42] Reading *ait* for *aiunt* ('they say') at 53,63 (Bossier).
[43] *Republic* 10, 611C-D
[44] In Greek, *thumos* and *epithumia*, parts of the non-rational soul given us by Providence for terrestrial life (G 6,11–25).

separate? It operates with a subject, and for a body to attain to   75
things wholly separate is impossible. Hence if the soul itself attains
to them, it must be separate from all body. It is a direct consequence
of this that it is immortal. It will not be destroyed like a body, since
it is incorporeal as is evident immediately[45] and also because[46] it
has been shown that even sense cannot be corporeal; nor will it be
destroyed like things which exist in bodies as their subjects, since   80
it has its substance separate from all body. Therefore Plato taught
that the soul's substance is characterised according to its highest
operations, and Aristotle now[47] brings out the consequences in
saying that the intellect is in substance actuality.

430a10 Just as in all nature there is something which is   85
matter for each kind, that which is all of them in potentiality.[48]

The word 'nature' is not used here to signify all natural things
without qualification, for it is not the case with heavenly things
that there is something which is in potentiality and something
which is in actuality. By 'nature' we must understand the nature
which consists of things that are generable and destructible. The   90
sense of the passage is this: in the case of natural things of whatever
kind, for example things which sense, or plants, or inanimate
things, there is on the one hand matter, on the other form (or[49]
what is analogous to matter and form). The matter is in potentiality
all the forms it is natural for it to receive, both in the case of   95
natural things and in that of artifacts. The wood in the case of
house-building is in potentiality all the forms it is natural for it to
receive; similarly in the case of natural things the animal material
is in potentiality all the forms it is natural for it to receive; and
similarly with plants. And there is also in each a cause that makes,   **55**
either art or nature. The same things, he says, 'must exist in the   00
soul too',[50] and there is on the one hand an intellect which is
material or analogous to matter, which is the intellect in potentiality, called 'in potentiality' because it becomes all the forms
which it is natural for it to receive. It becomes them, as we have

---

[45] *ex multo astante*, a puzzling phrase. Bossier thinks it may translate *ek pollou
tou parestotos* or *paristamenou*; *legein ek tou paristamenou* is to say what comes into
one's mind without deliberating.

[46] Adding *et* after *sed* at 54,78 (Bossier).

[47] Bossier suggests that instead of *nunc*, 'now', we should read *huic*, 'the consequences *of this*' at 54,83.

[48] This appears to be a minor lemma, not just a quotation. In the major lemma at
42,87 Moerbeke translates *quod potest omnia illa*; here he has *quod omnia illa
potentia*.

[49] Taking *sed quod proportionale* to translate *alla to ge analogon* (Bossier).

[50] 430a13.

said more than once, inasmuch as it receives their forms and under-
5　stands them. And on the other hand there is an intellect which
makes. This perfects the intellect which is all things in potentiality
and makes it what it is by nature apt to be. It is in the soul, not
in the same individual soul but in a soul of the same form.

Why must it be with the soul as it is with natural things? Because
10　even the soul is not completely[51] unchangeable. It is changed in
respect of actuality[52] even if not in respect of nature, and it is
ordered along with a natural thing, the body. That is why it compre-
hends all natural things, including the heavenly ones. They too are
changed – in respect of place: when the sun is in Aries it is in
potentiality in Taurus – and there is a thing which makes, the
nature that moves them.

15　　**430a15 There is another thing which is cause and maker,
because it makes all things, which is how art is in relation to
the material.[53]**

By 'another' he means other than the matter; in each kind of natural
thing there is, on the one hand, something which is material, on
the other, a cause. What sort of cause? One that makes, he says,
and he gives a model: 'which is how art is in relation to the
20　material.' Art is called a cause in that it makes all things, matter
in that it becomes all. Matter, however, becomes all things according to its natural aptitude, not changing its substance, like wood if
it becomes rotten,[54] but receiving a form; and art and nature make
in that potentiality passes into actuality. From the models, then, it
is clear that he means that intellect in actuality passes into actu-
25　ality from intellect in potentiality. But why does he say, not 'as art
does in relation to the artifact' but 'as art does in relation to the
material'?[55] The one is the completed thing,[56] the other the subject.
56　'One[57] is such in becoming all things, the other in making all.' In

---

[51] Moerbeke's *secundum semel* presumably translates *kathapax*.

[52] i.e. it passes from inactivity to activity.

[53] Here too there are minor changes from the translation in the major lemma.

[54] At 55,21–2 the MSS have *quando fit securis* (though in T *securis* is written in
a lacuna), 'like wood when it becomes an axe'. The difficulty with this is that wood
does not change its substance, i.e. its matter, when it is made into an axe-handle.
If it became an axe-head it might have to become iron, but this is too bizarre a
possibility and I follow Bossier in thinking that the Greek was something like *ginetai
sêpsis*, cf. G 289,9–10.

[55] Reading *quid* for *quod* at 55,25 and punctuating with a question mark after
materiam at 55,26 (Bossier).

[56] Reading *apotelesma* for *hypotelesma* with Mansion at 55,26. Philoponus' point
is that intellect in potentiality is analogous to the material which is made into an
artifact, not to the finished product.

[57] Moerbeke has *hoc*, 'one thing'. Aristotle has 'one intellect'. This sentence is
rather a quotation than (as Verbeke prints it) a lemma.

the soul, he says, there is such an intellect as is analogous to matter
in that it becomes all things and there is one that is analogous to
form and actuality in that it makes all things that [the former] is   30
in potentiality.

Someone might say that there is no need for the intellect in
potentiality in us to be perfected by the intellect in actuality of a
teacher; for we often find out many things by ourselves. The answer
is that even if we do find out things for ourselves, we derive the
principles and the dispositional state from the teacher. When the
intellect in potentiality in us has received a principle, there is no   35
awkwardness in supposing that with regard to some things it perfects itself. For possessing universal accounts it is able to produce
from these the ones it derives from the teacher and others it derives
from itself.[58] Similarly with things that grow in the earth: some
need both the continuous attention of men and the revolution of
the heavens, while others come to be simply by the providence that   40
guides the universe, such as those plants that grow spontaneously.

430a15 . . . like a disposition, like light; for in a way light
makes colours in potentiality to be colours in actuality.

He says that the intellect in actuality is analogous to a disposition;
and from this too it is manifest that he is speaking not of the divine
intellect, but of ours. For he has not said that the divine intellect
is a disposition or analogous to a disposition, but straight off it is
actuality without potentiality, as he puts it in the *de Interpreta-*   45
tione.[59]

Then he gives light as an illustration of a disposition; light, he
says, makes things which are potentially visible actually visible.
(He uses the word 'colours' but means visible things. There are
colours in the dark, but though they are colours in actuality they
are visible only in potentiality.) And in the same way the intellect in   50
actuality leads that which is in potentiality forward into actuality.

From this too it is plain that he is not speaking of the creative
intellect. For light does not provide colours with existence but only   57
with visibility. The creative intellect does not make things in this
way, but gives being itself and substance to the things it makes.
Hence these words better fit our intellect, since it makes things   55
not by producing their substance but by making things which are
intelligible in potentiality intelligible in actuality, as has been said.
If Aristotle were speaking here of the creative intellect it would be

[58] This sentence could, perhaps, be construed: 'possessing universal accounts, sc.
the ones it derives from the teacher, from them it is able to produce others also from
itself.' My translation, however, reflects Philoponus' views on the matter.
[59] *de Int.* 23a23.

more reasonable to compare it to the sun than to light; for as the sun produces light and creates its being, so the creative intellect

60 produces that intellect in actuality by which things intelligible in potentiality are made intelligible in actuality, as things visible in potentiality are made visible in actuality by light.[60]

These words are an object of attention to those who laud what Plato says and try to make Aristotle agree with him.[61] For in the earlier passage[62] it looked[63] as if he was placing forms in the intel-

65 lect potentially according to the first mode of potentiality, comparing the intellect to an uninscribed thing you write on. But if he says here[64] that as light stands to colours, so that which is intellect in actuality stands to that which is in potentiality, and if light does not make colours which did not exist but brings into evidence colours which did not appear, then intellect in actuality does not produce forms which did not exist in the intellect which is in potentiality, but makes manifest forms that were hidden.

70 **430a17 And that intellect is separate and not mixed and unaffected.**

By the word 'that' he does not mean to refer to intellect in actuality in contradistinction to intellect in potentiality; he refers as a whole to that in the soul which from being intellect in potentiality becomes intellect in actuality. Hence it is both at once that he calls separate, as has been said above.

430a18 . . . being in substance actuality.

75 The intellect, he says, which is both at once, which is the same thing differing only in time, as has already been said, has its substance chiefly characterised by its actuality. For everything derives

58 its characterisation from that which is most estimable. When it is in potentiality it is analogous to matter and is affected. When it operates it is form and a thing which rather makes than is affected.

80 Everything is characterised according to form, which is what produces an effect in matter, not according to what is affected, namely matter. Aristotle says, then, that the intellect is in substance actuality not because it is never in potentiality – as some have thought, which is why they have transferred what he says to a different

[60] Philoponus no doubt has in mind Plato's image of the sun in *Republic* 5, 508A–509C.
[61] The MSS *sibi* ought to mean 'themselves' but 'him', sc. Plato, gives a better sense and *sibi* often translates *autôi*, so the Greek could have been *autôi*, not *hautois*.
[62] 429a31–430a2; see 37,8–39,20 above.
[63] Correcting the MSS *videbantur* to *videbatur* at 57,63 (so too Bossier).
[64] Conjecturing *hic* for *hoc* at 57,65 (Bossier).

intellect – but because, like everything else, it has its substance   85
characterised not by what it is in potentiality but by what it is in
actuality. That this is so is shown by the connective 'for' which is
explanatory.[65] As though, at least, he had meant by 'being in substance actuality' that it has its substance characterised [not by
what it is in potentiality][66] but by what it is in actuality, he gives
the explanation of this: 'For that which makes is always more   90
estimable than that which is affected, and the source than the
matter.'[67]

If, then, the substance of each thing should be characterised by
that which is most estimable in it, and that which is in actuality
is more estimable than that which is in potentiality, our intellect
too will have its substance characterised according not to what it   95
is in potentiality but to what it is in actuality. By 'source' he means
either that which is formal or that which makes.[68] Either is possible.
Aristotle could mean the formal if he has regard to that which is
perfected and comes to be in actuality; for it assumes[69] its proper
form when it operates or is actualised. He could mean the principle
which makes if he regards the teacher; for the intellect which is   00
actuality in the teacher stands as maker to the intellect in the pupil
when the latter changes[70] from intellect in potentiality to intellect
in actuality.

430a19 Knowledge which is in actuality is identical with the
thing; knowledge which is in potentiality is temporally prior
in the individual, but overall it is not prior even in time.

By **knowledge which is in actuality** he means the intellect, by   5
the thing, that which is intelligible in actuality. If knowledge in   **59**
actuality is the taking in of intelligible forms, knowledge in actuality will be nothing other than an actualised thing contemplated.
Rightly, then, he says that knowledge in actuality is the same as
the thing, just as he said that sense in actuality[71] is the same as   10
the thing perceived, for sense in actuality is nothing but the taking
in of sensible form.

---

[65] Understanding lines 58,82–7, *Quia igitur . . . causalis ens* as one sentence with
manifestat as its main verb (Bossier).
[66] Bossier suggests that these words should be inserted after *characterizatam* at
58,88 or the 'but' which follows them deleted.
[67] 430a18–19; a quotation and not, as Verbeke, a lemma (Bossier).
[68] i.e. Aristotle may be referring either to the formal or to the efficient cause.
[69] Or, perhaps, 'enjoys': Bossier suggests the Greek may have been *apolauei*.
[70] Moerbeke's *transmutante* (intended by him, perhaps, as an ablative absolute)
probably translates *metaballontos*, intransitive, with the pupil's intellect as subject
(so too Bossier).
[71] Deleting *et* at 59,10 (Bossier).

Knowledge 'which is in potentiality', he says, that is intellect in potentiality, 'is **temporally prior**' to that which is in actuality, not prior in time without qualification, but prior in the same individual
15   man. In that in which there are both, sc. the potentiality and the actuality, the potentiality is prior in time, but overall, he says, it is not prior in time. Things cannot begin from what is imperfect, but by nature there are always in the world both what is in potentiality and what is in actuality. By nature what is in actuality is prior to what is in potentiality, if the actual is what activates the
20   potential, but in time neither is prior without qualification to the other, though what is in potentiality is prior in one and the same individual. No one would say that all those with knowledge perished in the deluge and that [only] the others[72] were saved, or vice versa, for such would be mere fancy; but always in the world as a whole there are both those who know in potentiality and those who perfect these.[73]

25   **430a22 But it does not sometimes understand and sometimes not.**

There are different readings for this passage. Those who say that Aristotle is speaking of the creative intellect accept two negatives. They say that the creative intellect 'does not sometimes understand
30   and sometimes not' but understands always: something which cannot be said of the human intellect since our intellect does not understand always. Those who say that Aristotle is speaking of our intellect delete one of the negatives, sc. [the first] 'not',[74] and read:
60/35 'But it sometimes understands and sometimes not'; when it is in potentiality it does not understand, and when it is in actuality it does.

It is possible, however, while accepting the former reading, to take the words as referring to the human intellect. For if we look at the whole spread of souls and not just at one individual intellect
40   we will no longer say that the human intellect sometimes understands and sometimes does not; we will say it understands always, just as Aristotle said that intellect in potentiality is not prior in time to intellect in actuality.[75]

---

[72] Reading *alii* (in Greek *hoi alloi*) for *aliquando* ('sometime') which makes no sense at 59,22 (Bossier).

[73] Conjecturing *hos*, 'these', for *hoc*, 'this', at 59,24.

[74] The Latin is *scilicet 'non'* which does not make clear which negative is to be deleted; the Greek was probably *oukh*, which would make it clear that it is the first (Bossier).

[75] Philoponus has already suggested this interpretation at 52,19–29. I find it forced and should prefer to excise 'Knowledge which is in actuality . . . even in time' from Aristotle's text (so Ross 1961), and take 'It does not sometimes understand and sometimes not' to refer to the existence of the intellect in separation from the body.

430a22 When separated it is that [alone] which is just what it is;[76] and this alone is immortal and everlasting.

Even, he says, if intellect when it is connected with the body is sometimes in potentiality and sometimes in actuality, when it has 45
been separated it is that alone which is just what it is. What was said to be in substance actuality when it has been separated is that alone[77] which characterises its substance; I mean it is solely actuality and not at all potentiality; and 'this alone', he says, 'is immortal and everlasting'. Returning again to the neuter he says 50
[this] *morion* [[that is, 'part', from *morion*, a part]] for at the beginning he said '[Concerning that] part of the soul'.[78] That is why I said earlier[79] that we ought to note that he refers to our intellect, that is, our rational substance, in the neuter. It is plain and manifest from this too that he is speaking of the human intellect. For 55
he would not have said of the creative and divine intellect that when separated it is that alone which is just what it is, as though the divine intellect were sometimes separate and sometimes not. And 'this alone is immortal and everlasting': how would that be said of the divine intellect? What could he be distinguishing it from, and what doubt could there be of its being everlasting? Plainly he 60
is speaking of the intellective part of the human soul, and distinguishing it[80] from the other portions in that it alone among them is everlasting and immortal. It is evident also from this that Aristotle knew that only the rational soul is immortal and that the other parts of the soul are all mortal.

430a33 But we do not remember because this is unaffected. 65/61
The intellect which is affected is destructible, and without this it understands nothing.[81]

---

[76] See note on 16,14–18. I supply the word 'alone' because the commentary shows Philoponus read it.
[77] Retaining Verbeke's text with some misgivings. Bossier suggests reading: *Quid autem dicebatur esse? Substantia actus. Quando autem . . .* which would translate: 'What was it said to be? In substance actuality. When it has been separated it is that alone etc.' and offers G 7,32 as a parallel construction.
[78] I translate the MSS as best I can; the words in double square brackets should be understood as an addition by Moerbeke. I am inclined, however, to accept Bossier's suggestion that Moerbeke read *morion* for *monon* at 60,50. Aristotle's text has *monon*, not *morion*. If this is right the Greek sentence may have been just 'He returns again to the neuter and says *monon*', and all the rest may be due to Moerbeke.
[79] 6,10.
[80] We might expect *ipsam* instead of the MSS *ipsum*, but Moerbeke is probably translating *auto*, agreeing with *morion*.
[81] It is clear from the commentary that this is how Philoponus understands the sentence. It could, however, be construed (both in Latin and in Greek) 'without this nothing thinks', and Ross (*Aristotle: De Anima*, Oxford, Clarendon Press 1961) takes Aristotle's Greek in this way.

He here brings in the solution to a problem he had raised earlier.
He said 'We must consider why it is that we do not understand
always',[82] and I said that he does not omit a solution, as some have
70   thought, but provides it a good deal later.[83] It is here that he gives
the solution of that problem. Why then, he asks, do we not remember always? Because, he says, even if intellect is unaffected, and
because of that we ought not to forget, still the imagination is
destructible – it is the imagination that he calls 'intellect which is
75   affected' as has been said more than once. Since the imagination is
destructible, and without the imagination either helping or hindering intellect does not understand, it is no wonder that we do not
understand always.

These words **without this it understands nothing** should be
taken with the implicit qualification 'for the most part'. The operations of the intellect are for the most part with imagination and
the operations without it are rare. Rarely indeed, hardly once in
80   the whole life of those who ascend to the highest levels of philosophy, does intellect operate without imagination. Because of this
rarity he says as a universal truth that without imagination intellect understands nothing. It understands some things with imagination's help, for instance in mathematics, for imagination is as it
were the vehicle of intellect here, and it helps in connection with
many other things; and intellect understands other things with
85   hindrance from the imagination, as in speculation about intelligible
62   and divine things.[84] In its contemplation of these intellect is dragged
down by imagination which forms images of shapes and magnitudes
and will not allow them to be grasped as they are. Since, then,
without imagination it understands nothing, and imagination is
destructible and on that account changeable and disposed now one
90   way and now another, because of this intellect does not understand
always. It is yoked to the imagination, but instead of having it
always obedient to its initiative it has it hindering and pulling
against it.[85]

Someone might reasonably raise the following problem. If this is
why intellect does not remember always, that its understanding
does not occur without imagination, which is liable to be affected,
95   and when it is affected it also loses impressions,[86] which is forget-

---

[82] I follow Bossier in treating this as a quotation.

[83] 42,72–4.

[84] The Latin *in intelligibilibus et divinis theoriae* cannot be right. My translation
agrees with Bossier's suggestion that the Greek was *epi tês noêtôn kai tôn theiôn
theôrias*.

[85] Conjecturing *contratrahentem* for the MSS *contrahentem*, 'causing to contract',
at 62,91 (so too Bossier) and taking the Greek verb to be *antispan* (or perhaps
kataspan, 'to pull down').

[86] Or, perhaps, 'and which receives and loses impressions'.

ting:[87] this is a plausible explanation in cases where intellect uses imagination as a tool, as with objects of mathematics or sensible things or things which have their being in sensibles. But where things are altogether separate why does forgetting ensue? If the intellect's operations concerning these things are the ones it has by its own power, and imagination does not help but hinders it, then   00
surely once the intellect has taken in these forms and come to be in receipt of them[88] it should have indelible cognition, since it is unaffected. In the case of sensible forms, on the other hand, it uses imagination as a vehicle, and that is how it gets to know the forms of sensible things. Since the impressions, then, appear from the   5
imagination, and the imagination is affected, no wonder there is forgetting for the intellect. But when it receives separate forms, taking in the cognition of them by its own power and being unaffected, how can it forget?

Perhaps imagination is the cause of this too, but in another way. Just as when it [sc. the intellect] descended the composition with   10
non-rational life, as though imposing sleep or a swoon[89] on it, became the cause of its forgetting everything, so it would not be surprising if here too, diverting it into imagination and generally into life in the body, it should cause it partial forgetting which   **63**
darkens its purity and the clarity of its substance,[90] as happens also   15
in drunkenness and similar circumstances. So here too imagination is the cause of this: taking on alien shapes from sensible things and thereby stupefying the intellect it makes it depart from its proper station and cognition. But perhaps for those who have altogether attained such a good life that non-rational life no longer pulls against the intellect but on the contrary attends upon it like a   20
sensible servant, and who because of this are able to devote themselves to intelligibles without imagining[91] – the reception of intelli-

[87] The ablative *oblivione* probably corresponds to a Greek genitive; I think the literal meaning would be 'which happens when we forget'.

[88] i.e. has come to receive them; or, perhaps, has come to be actual in receiving them.

[89] I take *alienatio* (literally 'madness') here as elsewhere to translate *karos*.

[90] Lines 62,12–63,14 are difficult. *Circumtrahens* appears to be subject of *efficere*, and should therefore be accusative. Following a suggestion of Bossier I translate as if we had *circumtrahentem ipsum ad phantasiam*, understanding *circumtrahentem* as a rendering for *perispôsan*; and I take *complexio irrationalis vitae* as subject of *circumtrahentem* and *oblivionem* as subject of *offuscantem*. Bossier points out that we can take *phantasiam* as subject of both, retain *in se ipsum* and translate: 'if here too imagination, diverting it (*ipsum*) into itself and generally to life in the body, should cause it partial forgetting, darkening its purity etc.'

[91] Lines 63,18–21 are among the hardest in the *de Intellectu*. My translation is guided by the following suggestions by Bossier: (i) *ne forte* at 63,18 translates *mêpote*, 'perhaps'; (ii) *mitra*, 'headband', at 63,18 is Moerbeke's rendering for *euzônian*, and the correct Greek is *euzôian*, 'good life' (translated *vita bona* at 89,97: see Sophonias 128,31); (iii) *contratrahat* should be read for *contrahat* at 63,19 as at 62,91; (iv) we

gibles is now not followed by forgetting because the intellect is no longer anywhere affected by non-rational life and imagination.

430a33 But we do not remember because this is unaffected.
25   **The intellect which is affected is destructible, and without this**
       it understands nothing.

Some people take 'without this it understands nothing' to mean that it understands none of the sensible things here without imagination; they understand as implicit 'no sensible form'. And that is not alien to Aristotle's thought. For later, discussing intellect's
30 functioning in connection with sensible forms, he says: 'Since there is nothing separate, it seems, apart from sensible magnitudes, it is in sensible forms that the intelligibles exist, those that are called "abstract" and those that are properties and affections of sensible things. That is why a person who does not perceive will not learn or understand anything. And when a person contemplates he must
35 at the same time contemplate some image.'[92] In this passage too, then, it is clear that it is intellect's speculation about sensible forms which he says occurs with imagination; he does not say this of intellectual functioning generally.

---

should punctuate with commas after *intellectum* at 63,19 and *illum* at 63,20; (v) *opadon bene scientem* translates *opadon eugnômona* (cf. Hermias *in Phaedrum* 179A); the alternative would be to take *scientem* with *sequi*, 'like a servant that knows well how to attend upon it'; (vi) *adhaerere* at 63,21 translates *prosekhein*.
    [92] 432a3–9. For *aquis* at 63,31 I understand *speciebus*; Moerbeke seems to have read *hudasi* for *eidesi*.

430a26 The understanding of indivisible[1] things occurs in cases where[2] there is no falsity; where there is false and true there is already some composition of concepts.[3]   40

Having said what needed to be said about intellect and completed his exposition[4] of it Aristotle turns now to consideration of the things understood, and shows in what way they are intelligible and how intellect understands them. Besides, he announced the   45
intention of enquiring into three problems about intellect: first, how it differs from sense, secondly if it is separate, and thirdly how it understands. Having spent enough time on the first two problems and shown that intellect is different from sense and that it is separate, he now passes to the third, I mean to what intellect's mode of understanding is and how it understands the intelligibles.   50

I say, then, that it understands both simple and composite things. Simple things are, for example, [mathematical] points and terms of propositions. From these things, themselves incomposite, I mean terms,[5] a proposition is put together. Composite things are like the propositions themselves. But whether the things understood are   55/65
simple or composite, intellect understands them insofar as they are simple, indivisible and one.

The indivisible can occur in five ways. [1] There is indivisibility in terms. The terms of propositions are indivisible, since they are not divided into simpler significant utterances. For in the *de Interpretatione* it was shown that 'the parts of nouns and verbs do not   60
signify anything by themselves'.[6] [2] Again, what is continuous is said to be indivisible inasmuch as it has unity in actuality, even though it is divisible in potentiality; for instance wood which has not been cut, or time. [3] A thing may also be called indivisible in respect of form,[7] form consisting in configuration and form consist-

---

[1] The Latin *indivisibile* is most naturally translated 'indivisible'. The Greek word which Aristotle uses, however, *adiaireton*, can mean either 'indivisible' or 'undivided' and this ambiguity must be kept in mind throughout the following discussion.

[2] So Ross (1961) translates Aristotle. This seems to me preferable to 'is among the cases', though the latter is possible and favoured by Hamlyn.

[3] Aristotle adds 'as constituting one thing'.

[4] The Latin *theoria* here probably transliterates the Greek technical term, on which see pp. 6–7 above.

[5] Punctuating *ex his, dico terminis* at 64,53 (Bossier).

[6] 16a20–1 (nouns); 16b6–7 (verbs).

[7] The Latin is naturally translated so but Philoponus may have written something more like ' "Indivisible" is also said of form'.

65   ing in substance.[8] For[9] the substance of each thing is indivisible; if
      it were divided it would destroy the whole too;[10] and similarly the
      configuration, for the parts are not by nature such that after div-
      ision each can exist on its own. [4] Again, points and instants are
      called 'indivisible' since they have no extension and are not by
      nature such as to be cut in half. [5] Also called 'indivisible' is what
      is truly indivisible, I mean intellectual and divine forms, which
66/70 have no potentiality at all, but exist in actuality without poten-
      tiality, and therefore are not divisible even potentially.
          Intellect, then, says Aristotle, understands each intelligible thing
      according to the indivisibility which belongs to it.[11] For instance [1]
      it understands terms inasmuch as they are simple; and because
75   they are simple it does not understand one part of a term in one
      time and another in another; it understands a term as a whole all
      at once. And it understands propositions too not insofar as they are
      composite but insofar as they signify one thing; it does not under-
      stand the parts one by one as man and pale but as man is pale.[12]
80   And that being so it understands them not only as something indi-
      visible but in an indivisible time. It does not understand man in
      one part of time and pale in another; if it did, it would understand
      them as divided; in the whole time in which it understands, it
      understands the whole [proposition] all at once.
          [2] Again, it understands continua not insofar as they are capable
85   of being divided but insofar as they are in actuality undivided. For
      instance if I understand the Trojan War which took place over such
      a length of time, I do not understand it part by part as something
      divided and composed of many elements, but as something single
      and continuous. Similarly when I understand a line I do not under-
90   stand it as divisible in parts or composed of so many parts but as
      one and continuous. If I understand it part by part I understand it
      not as one line but as several, and I understand each part as a
      single undivided line. Hence I understand the line as something
      undivisible and in an indivisible time. I do not cut the line in my
95   understanding, but understand the whole of it as a single thing all

---

[8] The Latin words I translate 'form', 'configuration' and 'substance' are *species*,
forma and *substantia*; the corresponding Greek words in Sophonias 127,22–3 are
eidos, morphê and *ousia*. Aristotle generally uses *eidos* and *morphê* interchangeably;
but he uses them to cover two different sorts of thing, mathematical forms such as
shapes and the essence of living things. Philoponus' distinction is between these: cf.
G 211,20–3, which refers to *Phys.* 2.2.

[9] Reading *enim* after *uniuscuiusque* at 65,64 with CV (Bossier).

[10] Reading *corrumpit et* with T for *corrumpitur* which would give 'the whole is
destroyed' at 65,65 (Bossier).

[11] Deleting *intelligibilium* ('of the intelligibles') after *ipso* at 66,73 (so too Bossier).

[12] The copula is not in the Latin or Sophonias' Greek but must surely be understood
(its omission is not illicit in either language). Philoponus would not count a phrase
like 'pale man' (cf. 117,12; 69,53–4) as a *protasis* or proposition.

at once, and hence the time too in which it is understood must be indivisible. If it were divisible, the line would be divided along with it; and then I shall be understanding it not as one line but as several.

[3] Similarly with forms: intellect understands them according to   00/**67** their indivisibility. It understands the configuration of a statue as one thing and as the whole which consists of all the parts. When I understand it part by part, the foot or the hand or the eye, I understand not the configuration of the statue but each of the parts, nor[13] do I understand it as a whole and as one unless incidentally. For when we understand each of the parts we could be said to have   5 understood the whole; not, however, in itself or as a single thing, but incidentally.

[4] Points and instants, which are indivisible, it understands in an indivisible way,[14] but since they do not have existence on their own, it understands them by abstraction from what is continuous,[15] and by negation, saying that they do not admit division like conti-   10 nua. And we get to know other things which do not have existence of the primary kind by denial of forms opposite to them, for example evil by denial of good, and crooked by denial of straight. All these are negations, even if they have affirmative names.

[5] As for those things which are truly indivisible, I mean intellectual forms, intellect gets to know them by what is called 'simple   15 intuition' separately from all imagination.

430a26 The understanding of indivisible things occurs in cases where there is no falsity.

He speaks first of the sort of indivisible we find in terms. He says that the understanding of indivisibles occurs in cases in connection with which there cannot be either falsity or truth. Of this kind are simple, incomposite words, I mean terms. If I say 'man' or anything   20 else you please a thousand times, I have not expressed anything either true or false. 'Truth and falsity are to do with composition and division' as is said in the *Categories*.[16] It is in the putting   **68** together of simple things, a putting together which is proper to the

---

[13] Inserting *neque* before *ut* at 67,3. Keeping Verbeke's text we should have to translate: 'not the configuration of the statue, unless incidentally, but each of the parts as a whole and as one.'

[14] Correcting *indivisibile* to *indivisibiliter* following Sophonias 128,1 at 67,8 (so too Bossier). If *indivisibile* were retained it would have to be taken as subject: 'something indivisible understands.'

[15] Sophonias has 'by denial of continuity' which may well be correct but 'abstraction' is not an inappropriate word here.

[16] The words quoted come in *de Int*. 16a12–13 but the doctrine can be found at *Cat*. 2a4–10; see also *Met*. 6, 1027b18–31.

25   intellect, that truth and falsity are thought, for instance when I
      put together 'Socrates' and 'philosopher' or 'unjust': in the first case,
      truth is thought, in the second, falsity. Aristotle likens the putting
      together of simple concepts to what Empedocles says about the
      composition of animals.[17] Empedocles first forms each of the parts
30   of the animal by itself, and then produces animals by the putting
      together of these parts by Friendship. So it is, says Aristotle, with
      concepts which admit of truth and falsity. They are first simple and
      separate from each other, but the intellect puts them together, and
      once they are made in composition into a single thing, truth and
      falsity have an existence. If a person opines that which is present
      in something as present in it, he speaks truly; if what[18] is not
35   present as present, he speaks falsely. Similarly with denials. In
      illustration he gives us 'commensurable' and 'diagonal' and 'incom-
      mensurable' and again 'diagonal'.[19] If I merely say these simple
      things 'commensurable' or 'incommensurable' or 'diagonal', I say
      nothing either true or false. If I put them together and say that the
40   diagonal is commensurable with the side, plainly I say something
      false. If I say it is incommensurable, I speak the truth.
         **The understanding of indivisible things occurs in cases
      where there is no falsity**. He is speaking here of indivisible terms,
      but he should not be understood as saying: 'There is no falsity
45   in terms' as is said in the *Categories*,[20] because simple words in
      themselves contain neither truth nor falsity, but truth and falsity
      are to do with composition and division. For there simple words are
      said to possess neither truth nor falsity, whereas here it is only
      falsity that he removes from terms. When the intellect understands
50   simple terms in themselves, for example, 'man' or 'horse', it is
      capable of attaining to a certain sort of truth, I mean the sort
69   which belongs to substances,[21] but not yet, of itself, to falsity. When
      intellect is functioning naturally and understanding forms, it is
      incapable of falsity. When it understands a man, say, with five
      heads, this sort of thing pertains to imagination, not to intellect.
55   Intellect understands the nature of the intelligible, that is, the
      actual forms of things.

---

      [17] The passage taken in the major lemma is followed (after 'as constituting one
      thing') by 'As Empedocles said "Many sorts of neckless heads arose" and then has
      them put together by Friendship, so these things, having first been separate, are
      put together' (430a28–31). The Empedoclean passage (Diels-Kranz 31 B 57) has no
      very direct bearing on the present topic but Aristotle often quotes it, perhaps because
      he thought it funny.
      [18] Inserting *quod* before *non inest* at 68,34 (Bossier).
      [19] Aristotle actually says only 'for example incommensurable and diagonal'
      (430a31, immediately after the passage quoted in n. 17).
      [20] 2a8–10.
      [21] i.e. genuineness as opposed to spuriousness.

430a31 If it understands things past or future, it does so by
understanding in addition and putting in time.

When intellect puts things together as present, it does not have
any additional thought about time, but puts the things together in
all their nakedness; for example if it puts together 'Alexander'   60
and 'pale' and understands 'Alexander [is] pale'. When, however, it
thinks of what has been or will be (for there are truth and falsity
in connection with these too),[22] it simultaneously understands time:
the Trojan War occurred such and such a time ago. If it says it
occurred yesterday, it speaks falsely; if at the time at which it did
occur, it speaks truly. Similarly with the future: there will be an   65
eclipse at such and such a time.

For what is present, however, it has no additional thought of
time, perhaps because an instant is not a time, and the present is
an instant.[23] This, then, is what he says also in the *de Interpretatione:* 'either absolutely or in relation to time.'[24] Furthermore some
things are always the same while others, which admit of coming to   70
be and destruction, are different at different times. When things
are always the same, the intellect in putting the terms together
has no need to think of time in addition, for instance when it thinks   **70**
the diagonal incommensurable with the side. The diagonal is not
now like that and otherwise at other times; which is why it has no
need to think time in addition. But that Socrates was lingering in   75
the Lyceum is something it is false to say of yesterday, but of the
former time when he was alive it is true.

430b1 For falsity occurs always in composition.

We should reorder and read this with what was said earlier: 'Where
there is false and true there is already some composition of concepts;
for falsity occurs always in composition.' Not as if truth did not   80
occur in composition; he had said that truth and falsity are to do

---

[22] Taking *etenim* to translate *kai gar kai* (Bossier).

[23] Punctuating *tempus, praesens autem nunc. Hoc* at 69,67 (Bossier).

[24] The reference may be to 16a18 where the words quoted appear or to 16b6–18.
In b6ff. Aristotle says that the present tense signifies 'now', the same word which
he uses for an instant, but he does not draw any distinctions. At a18 he does not
mention instants or 'nows' but appears to distinguish between e.g. 'Men laugh' (i.e.
it is natural for them to do so sometimes) and 'Some men are laughing now, laughed
yesterday'. It is possible that Philoponus is confusing this with the distinction
between the atemporal present ('The diagonal is incommensurable with the side')
and the temporal ('Socrates is, now or sometimes, in the Lyceum') or even with the
distinction between 'now' meaning the present instant and 'now' meaning the present
time-stretch (on which see Aristotle, *Phys.* 4.13). Philoponus and Moerbeke follow
Aristotle in using the same word (*nun, nunc*) both as an adverb meaning 'now' and
as a noun meaning 'an instant'.

with composition and division. He will add this a little later.[25] But the point is that in simple forms there is only truth and no falsity at all. How there is truth in simple things, he will show below.[26]

85   **430b2 For if someone says that something white is not white, he puts together 'not white'.**[27]

He had declared that falsity occurs always in composition. In case anyone should object: 'If I say that snow is not white, I have said[28] something false, but this is not a composition so much as a division', he says that these words 'not white' are put together with 'snow'.

90   **430b3 It is also possible, however, to say that all things are division.**

He has said that 'not white' is put together with 'snow' and that 'all things' are composition, even denials (for 'snow is not white' is a denial). This being so he says that just as we have called all things composition, so we can call them all division. For every
95   proposition divides into a subject and a predicate term, and besides,
71   what is composite is composed in any case of divided things; of this nature too are propositions composed of terms. If, therefore, starting from composites we understand simple things, we have division; if starting from divided things we understand a composite, we have composition.

00   **430b4 But anyhow**[29] **it is false or true not only that Cleon is pale but that he was or will be.**

He now repeats what he has said earlier: truth and falsity occur not only in the putting together of terms (e.g. 'Cleon is pale' or 'not
5   pale') but in connection with future and past time when that is put together with the terms; if I state what has not happened as something which has happened or the reverse,[30] or what is future either as not future or as future.

430b5 What in each case makes the unity is intellect.

[25] The reference is probably to 430b26–31 but cf. 431b10–12, 432a11–12.
[26] 430b26–31; see below 86,14–90,32.
[27] Ross reads 'he puts together <white and> not white' but the addition is unnecessary.
[28] Understanding *dixi* for *dixit*, 'he has said', at 70,87 (Bossier). Moerbeke may have read *eipen* for *eipon*.
[29] Correcting *si* to *sed* (Bossier); *sed igitur* would translate Aristotle's *all' oun*.
[30] So the text; but we should perhaps correct to something like 'if I state what has happened either as having happened or as not having happened' (Bossier).

That which puts together the divided things, he says, and gives them unity[31] is intellect. It is not any other part of the soul. For 10 each term has its own substance, but intellect, putting together a plurality of divided substances, makes something unified out of them. For these things a union is adventitious, <not> natural,[32] with divided things being united by intellect. Intellect unites things which in their essence are divided, like pale and man, when it understands 'The man is pale'.

430b6 Since, however, the indivisible is twofold, that which 15
is in potentiality and that which is in actuality, there is no
reason why it should not <understand>[33] what is indivisible
when it understands a length.

He passes to the second thing signified by 'indivisible'. By 'indivisible in potentiality' he means in potentiality[34] as contradistinguished from actuality. Terms are like this. These are indivisible in 20/72
potentiality in that they can compose and make up a single concept, but divided in actuality; and quantities of water in different places are undivided in potentiality, in that they can be mixed and united, but divided in actuality. A continuum, in contrast, like a piece of wood or a stone or a time-stretch, is undivided in actuality but in 25
potentiality divisible ad infinitum. Every magnitude is like that.
Having spoken of that kind of indivisible which is found in terms, he now speaks of the indivisible in length, which is undivided in actuality but divisible in potentiality. And he says that, the indivisible being twofold, when intellect understands a length, there is no reason why it should not understand the length, not insofar as it 30
is divisible in potentiality, but insofar as it is indivisible in actuality. And on this account the time too, however long it may be, in which it understands the length is indivisible (like the length) in actuality, though divisible in potentiality. The construction[35] of the passage is: 'When it understands a length, nothing prevents it from understanding something indivisible, for it is undivided in 35
actuality', and the intellect understands them 'in an indivisible time'.[36]

---

[31] Reading *unificans* for *vivificans*, 'gives them life', at 71,9 (Bossier).
[32] Reading <*non*>*naturalis* for *naturalis* at 71,12. Verbeke's text would have to be translated 'a natural union is adventitious'.
[33] This word is supplied by Verbeke from Aristotle's text.
[34] i.e. that which is undivided in potentiality as contrasted with that which is undivided in actuality. Reading *contradivisam*, translating *antidiêrêmenên* or *antidiairoumenên* (cf. G 29,5, 477,22) for *condivisam* with CV at 71,19 (Bossier).
[35] i.e. the natural order of words; translating *akolouthia* (Bossier).
[36] The passage in fact continues: '(for it is undivided in actuality) and in an undivided time; for the time is divided and undivided in the same way as the length.'

430b10 We cannot say that in each half [sc. of the time] it understands something;[37] for the halves do not exist, if it is not divided, except potentially.

That the understanding of an undivided magnitude occurs in an undivided time is obvious, he says. It is impossible to say that we
40 understand part of the magnitude in this part of the time and part in that. The understanding of a whole is not like this, but even if we remained a whole day in understanding a magnitude or any-
73 thing else as a whole, we should understand the whole in the whole. This happens because the first grasping of concepts is instan-
45 taneous. Forms come to be in matter without taking time, for the form of a house does not come forward before the last tile[38] has been put on. If anything is lacking, it will not have the form of a house. Similarly we do not have a garment before the last sewing has been done, for that which is deficient cannot function as garments do.[39] The same account holds for products of nature. As it is, then, with
50 the generation of forms, so it falls out with understanding: intellect understands them without taking time, in an instant, by its first intuition. When I understand that the three angles of a triangle are equal to two right angles, I do so in an indivisible intuition. If I took time, plainly in each part of the time I should understand
55 some part of the theorem, and it is not possible to say which part I understand in which part of the time. Since, then, the first intuition of the intellect by which it first understands anything occurs without taking time, it follows that even if it should have understanding which is accomplished in a longer time, it understands the whole in the whole time, not insofar as this time is divisible in potentiality but insofar as it is undivided in actuality,
60 as in the illustration provided. It understands something continuous, e.g. a stade, and it will never be possible to say, concerning the time[40] in which it understands the stade, that it understands half the stade in some one part of that time and the other in another. The understanding of the whole occurs in the whole time. And as the time is undivided, so is the understanding which occurs in it.
65   Then because it is possible, when a magnitude is divided, for

---

[37] Aristotle says: 'We cannot say *what* it understands in each half.' The alteration of an accent turns this into 'We cannot say that it understands *something* in each half' and this I think Moerbeke wrote or should have written. The MSS give us: 'We cannot say that he understands each thing something in the half'; I have corrected *utrumque* to *utroque* at 72,36–7.

[38] Reading *tegula* for *regula*, perhaps with T, at 73,46 (Bossier).

[39] Or (taking *operari* to translate *apergazesthai*) 'incomplete [sewing] cannot finish off garments' (Bossier).

[40] We should perhaps understand *temporis* for *tempus* at 73,61 (Bossier).

intellect to understand one part of it one time and another in another, Aristotle says that when intellect divides a length 'and understands each of the parts separately, then it straightway divides the time along with it too'. For as the continuum is divisible in potentiality but undivided in actuality, so is the time. But intel- 70
lect no longer understands each part as part of the whole, but as a continuum and a whole. Hence the time too in which it understands each part is a continuum and undivided. 'And then they are like **74**
lengths.' When we understand each part in a [separate] time, he 75
says, we no longer understand the whole as one length and as a continuum. We understand each part as a whole, and the whole as many lengths and not one, and each as a continuum.[41] And the time too is divided along with it and is not one continuum but several 80
continua. Time is like length in respect of being divisible and indivisible.

430b13 But when [we understand the length] as that which consists of both parts we understand it in a time which embraces both.

That is, if we understand the length as one thing composed of both parts, in line with this the time too is then composite and becomes 85
a single continuous thing consisting of both parts, and like the magnitude is undivided in actuality but divisible in potentiality.

430b14 That, however, which is indivisible not in respect of quantity but in form, it understands in an indivisible time and with an indivisible part of the soul.[42]

The third thing signified by 'indivisible'[43] is that which is indivisible 90
in respect of form, whether configuration or substance.[44] He says that this too is understood[45] by virtue of that in it which is indivisible. For whether you call 'configuration' or 'essence'[46] that in a form which is perfect and the totality of the shape by which intellect understands the totality of the form and its impartitionable account,

---

[41] Punctuating *multas longitudines et non unum, et* at 74,78 (Bossier).

[42] This sentence interrupts the discussion of divisible lines and times and is therefore often transposed to 430b20, the end of that discussion. It is puzzling and I should prefer to excise it altogether as a marginal note by Aristotle, or, more probably, by a later hand. In *Met.* 5, 1016a21, discussing grounds for calling things 'one', Aristotle says that water is one in that it is 'indivisible in form' and presumably members of any species are 'indivisible in form' in a similar way. For a different interpretation (by Themistius) see 78,14–17.

[43] Reading *indivisibilis* with C for *indivisibile* at 74,90 (Bossier).

[44] See n. 8 above.

[45] Punctuating *substantiale. Intelligitur igitur et hoc, ait* at 74,91 (Bossier).

[46] The Greek word will have been *ousia*, translated 'substance' at 74,91.

95   in this is the totality and account of the common substance by
which we are all men. Both the time in which we understand this
and the part of the soul in which we understand it are indivisible.
All things are understood in an indivisible element of time, that is,
75   in an instant, which is something temporal since it is that at which
time is divided. And if[47] sense perceives in something indivisible
00   and in something without parts, [we understand][48] similarly in an
indivisible part of the soul. For it does not, like sense, understand
through a bodily organ, but in the intellect itself. For sense does
indeed judge sensible things in something indivisible, as has been
shown.[49] But perhaps to make clear it is not by a bodily organ that
intellect judges, to oppose this idea, he says 'in an indivisible part
5   of the soul'. For whereas it is because the effect of sensible things
occurs in the body that it is graspable by sense, it is not like that
with intelligible things, that because they work on the body they
are graspable by intellect; the affections produced by intelligible
things are in the impartitionable element of the soul itself – I mean
the intellect – being immediately next to it.[50] He does not claim
10   this, however, as a peculiarity of things indivisible[51] in respect of
form, as if it were peculiar to them to be graspable by an indivisible
element in the soul. This is common to all intelligibles, as it is also
to grasp them in an indivisible time, and understand them not *qua*
divisible but *qua* indivisible. But because he has not said this at
the start, he adds it now.
15   There is also the reading 'in a divisible time and with a divisible
part of the soul'. If that reading is correct, we must again suppose
an allusion to the present instant. Since this is not able to exist by
itself but is always contained in a time-stretch which is divisible,
he says 'in a divisible' to bring out the contrast with immaterial
20   forms which we understand by a simple intuition apart from any
form of time.
An instant can also be called 'divisible' because it is at once an
end and a beginning. Similarly by 'a divisible part of the soul' we
may understand a part divided not spatially but in account, taking
the whole substance of the soul to be divided into various powers,
rational and non-rational.

25   **430b16 Incidentally and not as those things, that by which**

---

[47] Reading *Sique* with T for *Si quae* at 75,99 (Bossier).

[48] I prefer understanding some such words to bracketing *Sique . . . sentit* (75,99–00)
as a gloss (so Bossier).

[49] The reference may be to 426b17–29.

[50] Punctuating *dico autem intellectum, immediate* at 75,8, and taking *approximantia* with *passiones*. *Approximantia* is neuter whereas *passiones* is feminine, but
passiones probably translates *pathê* which is neuter.

[51] Reading *indivisibilibus* with T for *divisibilibus* at 75,9 (Bossier).

we understand and the time in which we understand are divisible, but as indivisible . . .[52]

'That by which' we understand such things, Aristotle says, that is, the part of the soul by which we understand them, and 'the time in which' are indivisible in themselves,[53] for such is the nature of an instant and an intellect or soul. But incidentally they are divisible. Inasmuch as the same instant is an end and a beginning it is divisible, and similarly intellect and soul are divisible. They are 'not divisible as those things', that is, forms in the sense of configuration and in the sense of essence. Those forms are divisible in themselves, not incidentally. A form in the sense of configuration is divided of itself into nose, eye and the other parts, one in the sense of essence is divided into genus and specific differences, and above all[54] it is divisible into different individuals. It has its being in many and there is no single common man, unless by thinking and abstraction from many we understand what is common. The whole meaning, then, is that the time and the intellect, in the way in which the forms which it understands, I mean material forms, are divisible – and they are divisible in themselves – in this respect, sc. in themselves, the time and intellect are indivisible; but in the way in which they are indivisible – they are indivisible incidentally, having a unity which is adventitious and not essential – in this way the intellect and the time are divisible.[55]

30/**76**

35

40

45

430b17 There is in these things something indivisible, though perhaps not separable, which makes the time and the length one.[56]

[52] A difficult Aristotelian text. Philoponus takes it as part of the discussion of things 'indivisible in form', and his interpretation is forced. Modern editors of Aristotle take it to belong to the discussion of divisible extensions but are not agreed on how it should be understood. I side with Ross who takes it thus: 'Incidentally and not as such [i.e. not *as* that which is understood and the time in which it is understood], that which is understood and the time in which it is understood are divisible; but as such they are indivisible.' Ross, I think rightly, amends the MSS *hôi*, 'that by which' intellect understands (preserved by Philoponus) to *ho*, 'that which', and inserts *ekeina*, 'such' or 'those things'. Hamlyn accepts these emendations but translates: 'That which is thought and the time in which it is thought are divided incidentally and not as those things [sc. the half-lengths of 430b11–12] were, though they are undivided as they were.' I think that the Greek word *hêi*, which Hamlyn translates 'as', must mean 'insofar as [they are]', not 'in the same way as': for the latter we should expect *hôsper*. Themistius takes the same view as Ross (see below, 79,35); Philoponus inclines to that of Hamlyn. Moerbeke's word *qua* is a correct translation of *hêi* but has to be understood as meaning 'in the same way as'.
[53] Reading *quo intelligimus, ait, talia, hoc est secundum quam partem* with Bossier, and deleting the *in* before *quo* at 75,27.
[54] Taking *aliterque et* to translate *allôs te kai* (Bossier).
[55] Punctuating 76,39–46 as one sentence and reading *illae* for *ille* at 76,43 (Bossier).
[56] Aristotle's text continues: 'and this is present likewise in every continuum, whether a time or a length.'

He has said that the time in which we understand is indivisible
50   in itself but divisible incidentally. But he has now said of time[57]
something almost unthinkable, since every time is in itself divisible
ad infinitum, as in general is every continuum. Hence he says, as
though in defence: there is something indivisible 'in time and
length' and, in general, 'in every continuum', something existing
55   in them and inseparable from them by virtue of which a continuum
has the property of being a unity. In the case of time this is the
instant, in length the point. These are the common termini to which
each part of the continuum is coupled and by which it is united.
77   And he calls[58] the partless instant in which intellect understands
60   things indivisible in form an instant 'of time' because it is in time
and inseparable from it and unites it. On the same account a point
is called a 'length', not of itself, but because it is inseparable from
length.

There is another way of interpreting these passages. Intellect,
people say, understands forms either as they are in matter or by
65   understanding separately the account of their substance. When
it understands them as material, but with a certain shape and
configuration, it does so using as its instrument the imagining part.
This imagining part of the soul in itself, indeed, is indivisible; it is
not divided either spatially, like continua, or in account. For there
70   are not different accounts of the substance of that which imagines,
nor can there be division into different accounts in the way in which
there is one account of that which nourishes, another of that which
generates or produces growth. In itself, then, it is indivisible,
though incidentally it is divisible. For just as white is said to be
moved incidentally in that the body is moved in which the white
75   is, so imagination will be said to be divisible incidentally in that
the forms which arise in it are divisible either spatially like shapes
or in account like configuration and anything else of that kind.
There is one account of the eye, another of the nose and so on. But
that imagination is indivisible in itself is plain from the fact that
we have memory and the likenesses of theorems do not get confused.
80   For if two theorems were inscribed on the same thing you write on
the likenesses of both are confused. It is by virtue of its indivisibility
that imagination keeps its likenesses unconfused. By means of this
imagination, then, in itself indivisible but incidentally divisible,
85   intellect gets to know material forms. But the abstracted accounts
of them intellect understands by itself without imagination; without
an imprint or magnitude it understands the essential accounts of
these things.

---

[57] Or 'in calling an instant a time he has said'.
[58] Conjecturing *nominat* for *nominant*, 'they call' at 78,58.

Consonant with this interpretation is the reading which says 'in a divisible time and with a divisible part of the soul'. In what way he calls the time in which we understand and the part of the soul 'divisible' he goes on to explain: **incidentally and not in the same way as they**, sc. as the material forms which it understands. Some of these were divisible spatially and can be divided in actuality, such as magnitudes; others can be divided in account, like the form of a plant (there is that which generates, that which produces growth, and that which nourishes); and others are divided in both ways like a configuration, say that of a man. The parts are in different places or[59] have different accounts of their substance. Imagination is not divisible in any of these ways except incidentally, as has been said. Nor is time divisible except potentially and by thinking. For it is a continuum and not broken, but it is our thinking that divides it into years, months, days and hours. For the sun never comes to rest to divide time into parts. But just as though every magnitude is said to be divisible *qua* magnitude, not all magnitudes can actually be divided, but only those which admit of generation and destruction (for the heavenly bodies like the sun will never actually be divided; if they were, they would be destroyed), so time, inasmuch as it is a continuum, is divisible into divisible parts indefinitely, but it is not actually divided since it is not possible for the movement of the heavenly bodies to cease.

The words **but as indivisible** are here explained as we explained them in the earlier interpretation.[60] If, however, we understand by 'time' not what is properly time – so that intellect understands in a time which is continuous and actually undivided – but by 'time' Aristotle means[61] an instant, we have said in what way an instant should be understood to be divisible: it is both a beginning and an end.

430b14 That, however, which is indivisible not in quantity[62] but in form is understood in an indivisible time and with something indivisible of the soul.

Themistius interprets these words as follows.[63] He takes things

---

[59] So T. CVB have *et*, 'and', which may be right, but it would be more accurate to say that the parts differ either in place alone, like eyes, or in place and account, like eye and nose.

[60] The reference is probably to 76,40–6.

[61] For *dicit*, 'he (sc. Aristotle) means', at 78,10, T reads *dicimus*, 'we mean', which Bossier prefers.

[62] Correcting *secundum actum quantum* to *secundum quantum* (so too Bossier) at 78,12.

[63] Philoponus 78,13–80,56 paraphrases Themistius' paraphrase: see Verbeke's edition of Moerbeke's translation of Themistius 247,63–249,98.

15   indivisible in form to be things which cannot be divided in respect
      of form, like man and still more Socrates; for the former is divided
      into individuals, not into species, and the latter is not divided even
      into individuals, being an individual already. But if that is right,
      Aristotle will no longer be saying how we understand things which
      are more general, such as animal or substance; and it would be
79/20   irrational to limit the discussion to individual species. Hence we
      should understand things to be indivisible in form insofar as they
      are forms. A form as such will not be divided. Just as a continuum
      as soon as it is divided no longer remains a continuum, so too a
      form as soon as it is divided is destroyed, as we have already said.
25   **In an indivisible time** means 'in an instant', and **in something
      indivisible of the soul** means 'in an indivisible understanding'.
      For intellect does not know half of Socrates in half a piece of under-
      standing and half in the rest. The concept of a man is not a con-
      tinuum stretching out coextensively with the word 'man', any more
      than the thing signified by this word 'man' extends along with the
30   syllables. The word is divisible, but the thing signified by it is
      indivisible.

      430b16 Incidentally, and not as those things are, they are
      indivisible, etc.

      This is explained [by Themistius] as follows. He takes 'that by
      which we understand' to be a thought or concept. So according to
      him Aristotle is saying that if anyone claims a thought or concept
35   is divisible we should say that it can be said to be divisible not *qua*
      thought but incidentally, <because the name>[64] and the word by
      which intellect brings thoughts out are divisible, and thoughts
      which are indivisible fit words which have parts. Because the words
      which they fit have parts they themselves, though indivisible, are
      said to be divisible incidentally because of the words.
40   Then, having said that though the thoughts themselves are indi-
      visible they are divisible on account of those things in which they
      are, Aristotle adds:

      430b17 For there is in these things too something indivisible
      which makes the time and the length one.

      There are many things which are indivisible of themselves but
      become divisible incidentally because of the things through which
45   they are known. The temporal terminus in which we understand,

      ---

      [64] Supplying *sed inquantum nomen* before *et vox* at 79,35 from Themistius 248,80
      (so too Bossier). As the text stands the plural *divisibilia* at 79,36 is ungrammatical.

I mean the instant, we may say is divisible incidentally because it is incidental to the time of which it is the terminus and we get to know it through that. For if there were not a span, a 'now' in the broad sense,[65] say a year or an hour, we should not understand the partless instant. The cause of this is that in all composite things there is something simple. It is not capable of existing on its own, just as it is not possible to hold the meaning of a word apart from the word or to express it without the word or even, perhaps, to understand it by oneself without fitting it to some speech to oneself. Still, it is this which makes a speech which contains parts partless and a speech which is divisible indivisible. Similarly in length there is the point, in motion the leap, in surface what is without width (sc. the line) and in depth what is without depth: a surface itself makes it one.[66]

430b20 But a point and every division and whatever is indivisible in this way is made clear like a privation.

He expounds the fourth species of indivisible which is connected with points.[67] 'What is indivisible in this way,' as is a point, is understood by a denial. 'Indivisible in this way' are a line, a surface and an instant. A point and an instant, being completely without magnitude, do not admit even division in respect of length. A line does not admit division in respect of width, or a surface in respect of depth. He calls these 'divisions' – he says 'a point and every division' – because divisions of magnitudes are through these. A line is divided at a point, a surface at a line, a body at a surface, and a time-stretch at an instant. Every division is at something indivisible. All these things, he says, intellect understands by pri-

[65] 'Now' signifying the present time stretch: cf. Aristotle, *Phys.* 4.13.
[66] Hamlyn suggests that for Aristotle the indivisible unifier of a length or time-stretch is a form. I think that Philoponus is right to interpret it as a point or instant. If we do not insert the passage about things indivisible in form here the discussion of points follows naturally. The word I translate 'leap' is *kinema*, literally a movement or change. Here, however, I think it signifies an atomic movement, that is, an uninterruptible movement over an indivisible distance in no time at all. Such movements are described by Damascius apud Simplicium *in Phys.* 796,32–797,13, translated and discussed by Sorabji in *Time, Creation and the Continuum* (London and Ithaca N.Y. 1983), 52ff. Damascius calls them 'leaps', using the words *pêdêma* and *halma; kinêma* might well be another term for them.
   Bossier suggests that there was a lacuna after *longitudine* in 80,54, and that the words *signum . . . Superficies* were wrongly transferred from 80,75 below. After *pars nulla est;* there he wants to read *similiter autem, sicut in longitudine signum, et in motu kinema, et in superficie aplates, scilicet linea, et in profunditate quod sine profunditate, scilicet superficies: privatio est. . . .* This may be right, but I find the text intelligible enough as it is.
[67] *signum*, translating the Greek *sêmeion*, which primarily means a sign but which is also used, like *stigmê*, for a point.

vation and denial; for they have no special form which makes them[68]
indivisible and by virtue of which intellect understands them in
themselves, but understanding of them comes by denying of them
the nature of the things they are in. Hence they are defined like

75   this: 'A point is that which has no part.' And what <is extended in
one dimension>[69] can be denied extension in another. <Thus the
definition> of a line is 'length without width' and in the same way

81   we understand surface by denying depth. That which is apt to grasp
a positive state also grasps the lack of it, as Aristotle said when

80   speaking of the senses.[70] If, therefore, we understand <line in this
way>[71] and in general whatever is extended, plainly it is by denial
of dimensions that we understand things which lack them: points
and instants by denial of length, line, since it is divisible, by lack
of width, and similarly surface by lack of depth. Aristotle does

85   well to add 'whatever is indivisible in this way' because what is
indivisible in respect of form is understood of itself.[72]

> **430b21** A similar account holds for other things, for how intel-
> lect gets to know evil or black; it knows them by that which
> is contrary in a way.

'Other things' refers to things which do not have existence of themselves. We get to know evil by the lack and denial of good. For

90   Aristotle does not make evil a form; it is the lack of good. 'Black'
is used for darkness,[73] as in the poet's words 'black death'[74] and 'like
black night'.[75] What is shadowy and murky is called 'black' because
white and black, as objects of sight, pertain the former more to
light and the latter to darkness. Hence things which appear at a
distance and are near to being invisible appear black. Intellect gets

95   to know these things by their **contraries**, that is, by the states of
being and having. A person who has come to know light has come
to know that darkness is the lack of this, and similarly evil is the
lack of good. 'Contrary' here means 'opposite'. Aristotle adds 'in a
way' because by denial of the positive state it gets to know the lack,

---

[68] Understanding *sunt indivisibilia*, translating *estin adiaireta*, for *est indivisibile*
at 80,72 (Bossier).

[69] Words supplied from Bate; likewise <Thus the definition> in the next line.

[70] The reference is probably to 425b20–2.

[71] The MSS show a lacuna of about ten letters. I supply *sic lineam*.

[72] Reading *quod enim ut species indivisibile, secundum se intelligitur* for *quod
enim ut species secundum se indivisibile intelligitur* at 81,85 (Bossier).

[73] G 3 522,23–6 justifies this interpretation by saying that black is a positive
property.

[74] *Iliad* 2.834.

[75] Reading *et nigrae* before *nocti* at 81,91 with CVB and taking the quotation to be
from *Odyssey* 2.606 (Bossier); Verbeke refers to *Iliad* 1.47 where there is no mention
of blackness.

and the lack is not the contrary; or perhaps because cognition by   00
denial is not exact.[76]

430b23 That which knows ought to be in potentiality [what it
knows] and [what we know] should be present in it.[77]

Aristotle has taught us earlier that the knower is in potentiality
what is known. He said that sense is in potentiality what is sensible,
and becomes it in actuality when it gets to know it, inasmuch as it   5/82
receives in itself the forms of sensible things. The same, he says,
ought to hold for the intellect,[78] and the things known by it should
be present in it in potentiality. If it knew lacks directly, intuiting
them of itself[79] and not through denial of the positive properties,
then intellect would be in potentiality what they are, that is, they   10
would exist in it potentially, just as it has in it potentially the forms
of positive things. But if it knows lacks by the denial of forms, how
can we say that it is potentially what the lacks are, and[80] that the
lacks are present in it? Or are they in the intellect, as Alexander
thinks, because intellect is able at times not to function? It is not   15
always working, being bound up with bodily functions and with the
body, as in sleep, drunkenness etc. It gets cognition of the lacks
through not being able to function and through the absence of
functioning. The intellect in potentiality, then, on Alexander's
interpretation, is that which is capable of having cognition of lacks
as well as positive states. For that which is in potentiality is always 20
in a state of lacking what it can be. Whereas that 'intellect which
is in essence actuality' and which is never in potentiality has no
cognition of lacks. For forms are always present in it in actuality.
Such, he says, is the First Cause, which he also says is indestruct-
able. So far Alexander.

That Aristotle is talking throughout of our intellect we have   25
already said more than once. And that it is not true that it knows
lacks when it is not functioning is obvious. It is not when we are
asleep or mad, because it is not functioning, that it knows lacks of
forms, but because the knowledge of contraries or opposites is the
same. Plainly when it knows light it also knows the lack of this;   30
similarly with good and the rest. And how can it be reasonable that
the divine and creative intellect should not know privative states?

[76] In the first interpretation 'in a way' is taken with 'contrary', in the second with
'know'.

[77] A difficult Aristotelian text (which may be why the scribes do not indicate it as
a lemma). The second addition is suggested by Philoponus, see below 84,55–7.

[78] Verbeke misleadingly italicises these words as if they were a quotation.

[79] Taking *ex se* to translate *autothen* (Bossier); if we take *ex se* with *ipsis* we have
the less good sense 'intuiting them of themselves'.

[80] Conjecturing *et* for *in* before *inesse* at 82,13 (Bossier).

Even if[81] it does not have forms of them, still, if we by one piece of
83 knowledge know opposite things, it is reasonable that the divine
35 intellect should know them[82] better than we; as it knows particular
things, though it does not have in itself forms of particular things.

When Aristotle says that intellect is in potentiality what the
intelligibles are, and becomes in actuality what they are when it
40 understands, he does not mean that our intellect should be said to
be those things in substance, as we have observed more than once.
It does not, when it understands God, become God, or when it
understands heaven or earth, become any of these things. But since
the accounts of all things are in the soul, the accounts of the better
things which are superior to it in the form of representations, the
accounts of less good things which are posterior to it as examplars,
45 when it actually produces the accounts which are in it, it actually
becomes what they are either, as I said, in a representative or in
an exemplary way, as we say that the image of Socrates becomes
what Socrates is, or that the accounts in the art of building[83] become
what the house is.

50 There is no need to understand the saying that what is known
ought to be in the knower to mean that things known according to
what they lack must also be[84] in the intellect. Since intellect has
all things in itself (which is why it is said to become all things) it
is by denial of those forms which are in it that it gets to know the
privative states. It is by virtue of the fact that the account of the
55 continuum which is in the soul does not fit a point that it gets to
know a point, and so on. The passage, however, is defective; it would
84 be appropriate to add to 'should be present in it' [what] we know',[85]
for these words are missing.

**430b24 If, however, there is any one of the causes which has
no contrary,[86] it gets to know itself and is separate in actuality.**

60 He expounds the fifth species of indivisible thing, I mean things
indivisible as are intellectual things and divine forms. It is these

[81] Moerbeke's *etenim* at 82,32 presumably translates *kai gar* ('for indeed'), but
Philoponus probably wrote *k'an gar* (Bossier).

[82] Reading *ipsa* with TV for *ipsum* at 83,34 (Bossier).

[83] So the MSS; but following Sophonias 128,18 we should perhaps understand
'accounts in the builder', *domificativo* or *aedificatore*, for 'accounts in the art of
building', *domificativa*.

[84] Conjecturing *ut et oporteat*, translating *hôste dein*, for *et quod oportet* (T) or *ut
quod oporteat* (CV) at 83,50 (Bossier).

[85] Bossier suggests that Moerbeke may have read *gnôrizomen*, 'we know', for
gnôrizomenon, 'thing known'.

[86] At 84,58 the MSS have *talium*, 'of such things', presumably translating *toioutôn*.
The MSS of Aristotle have *tôn aitiôn*, 'of the causes', and though Ross obelises this,
85,1 shows it is what Philoponus read (Bossier).

which are indivisible in the strictest sense. We do not find here
the contrariety of divisibility either in actuality or in potentiality.
Rather, forms like these being intelligible in actuality will be pure
activities[87] and intellects in actuality. For as was said above, what 65
is intelligible in actuality is also intellect. Being at once intellect
and intelligible, it understands itself. Of this nature are all forms
that are separate, sublime and divine. And note that he says here,
not that such forms are in substance actuality, but that they are
pure activity without potentiality.[88] Hence in the place where he
says that intellect is in substance actuality, he was speaking of 70
the whole of our rational substance, I mean both of intellect in
potentiality and of intellect in actuality, the substance of which he
said was characterised not according to its potentiality but according to its actuality. That is why, giving the explanation of this he
says that 'that which acts is always[89] more estimable than that
which is affected, and the source than the matter'.[90] But here he
says nothing of this sort. Plainly, then, our intellect, when removed 75
from being affected and its relationship with the body and assimilated to the intelligibles, will be such as they are in proportion to
its substance and power. For all intellectual functioning is like this.
Sense has its thing known outside itself, which is why it does not
know all the time; but intellect has its object within itself, which 80/85
is why when it is pure it understands always.

Alexander[91] asks here: if intellect and intelligible are relative
terms, how can something be both intellect and intelligible?
Opposites will then be the same thing; for [such] relatives are 85
opposite. Aristotle himself shows in *Physics* 8[92] that in an animal
which is said to be self-moving there is one element which moves
and another which is moved, since it is impossible that the same
thing should both move and be moved. These are things which are
relative and opposed.

In solution of this problem Alexander says that what is intellect 90
in actuality and what is intelligible in actuality are neither relative
nor opposed: they are identical. That which is intellect in potentiality is relative to what is intelligible in potentiality, and these
two are opposed. But when they come to be in actuality they are
no longer opposed; they come to be one thing. It is the same with 95
sense in potentiality and what is sensible, and with knowledge and

---

[87] cf. G 35,1.

[88] This is said not here but at *de Int.* 23a23.

[89] Understanding *semper* for *oportet* at 84,73; Moerbeke presumably read *dei* for
the correct *aei* (Bossier).

[90] 430a18–19.

[91] The reference is probably to Alexander's *de Anima* 86,23–6; Alexander does not,
however, make a problem of the point.

[92] 255a10–20, but the fullest account is *de Motu* 10.

what is knowable. In order that they should come to be in actuality, both opposites must have been made one.[92a] In things which proceed from potentiality to actuality, he says, it is like that. But what is always intellect in actuality is never opposed to what is always intelligible in actuality, but the same as it.

00 No wonder, then, that it understands itself, being both intellect and intelligible. But 'cause' must be understood as creative cause.[93] He said this because[94] he set out to describe intellect's grasp of separate and non-separate forms. A form too is a cause, but it is inseparable in that it is a cause as form, whereas the other is 5 separate and creative of non-separate forms.

Having said this about the things which are indivisible in the 86 strict sense, now, following on, he says how our intellect achieves its reception of these things.

430b26 Saying[95] is saying one thing of another, as is affirmation,[96] and is always true or false. But intellect is not 10 always understanding one thing of another. Intellect of what something is, according to what it was for it to be,[97] is true, and is not understanding one thing of another. But just as seeing of a proper object of sight is always true, but whether or not the white thing is a man, that is not always true, so it is with whatever is without matter.

He has said that there are five ways of being indivisible, and shown 15 that in four cases there is something opposed, something divisible. Terms are said to be indivisible in contradistinction to propositions, a continuum in contrast with discrete quantity like lines which are divided in actuality, and forms are indivisible with respect to the accounts proper to them; for a form in a body is extended along 20 with the body and divided along with the matter. He has also said that if there is something of such a nature as to have no opposite, this is intellect and separate and actuality without potentiality.

[92a] Punctuating *actum, unum ambo opportet* at 85,96.

[93] Lines 85,1–5 are difficult and my translation is conjectural. At 85,1 the MSS have *condictive*, a word I cannot find in the lexicons, thought I have had it suggested to me that it might mean 'conventionally', 'according to convention'. With Bossier, however, I prefer to adopt Mansion's emendation *conditive*, literally 'in a creative way', and understand Philoponus to be saying that it is the creative cause which 'has no contrary'.

[94] Reading *quoniam*, 'because', for *quando*, 'when' at 85,1 (Bossier).

[95] From 87,43 it is clear that this word (*dictio*) is intended to express mental saying.

[96] Modern editors of Aristotle amend to 'denial', I think rightly.

[97] *quod quid erat esse*. This is a literal translation (used also by Aquinas) of *to ti ên einai*. Aristotle uses that phrase as a term of art for essence; its meaning should be 'what it was to be' or, perhaps better, 'what it would be to be'.

Now he proposes to teach us what intellect's way of understanding is in connection with such forms.

He says, then, to be brief, that the functioning of intellect concerning separate forms cannot but attain truth. It does not stand in   25
opposition to falsity because its reception of these forms involves no composition or division. Cognition which involves composition and division, saying that one thing is or is not present in another, admits of being opposite to falsity, when what is not is said to be   30
or *vice versa*. Intellect's cognition, however, of separate forms does not proceed by composition and division but by simple intuition of the forms.

Intellect, then, functions in two ways: by simplicity in reception of simple forms and by composition and division. Aristotle speaks   35/87
first of cognition by composition, which is true or false, that being the more easily grasped; then he makes clear the simple mode through denial of this. He says that there is one sort of cognition by composition. This predicates one thing of another or denies it, and does so not only in openly uttered speech but internally in the   40
mind. We can not only say that snow is white but have a mental disposition[98] to this effect without speaking. A composite speech which is uttered he calls an 'affirmation', a mental one he calls a 'phasis', [[that is, a saying]].[99] Such is cognition which involves composition.

But there is another kind of cognition which is simple and neither   45
predicates one thing of another nor denies it. This is the kind which gets to know forms themselves on their own. When intellect knows by composition, putting a subject together with a predicate or dividing them, it always says either what is true or what is false. When it says that an animal is an animated sensible substance, it attains   50
truth in composition. If, in contrast, it merely understands animate, sensible substance, since it does not understand of what this is the definition, it does not understand anything true or false. If, indeed, animal and to be an animal were identical, this sort of cognition would be true. But they are not the same. In the case of material   55
forms it is impossible for intellect to say what is true without composition. But in the case of immaterial forms, where there is no difference between a thing and being that thing, intellect can say what is true without composition. Such cognition does not have falsity set over against it; it is always true. 'Either intellect attains   88
to them or it does not.'[100] If it does, it grasps them; if it does not, it has no understanding of them at all, so it does not say what is   60
false. That is why Plotinus said of intellect: 'Either intellect makes

[98] Reading *disponi* for *dispositionem* at 87,41 (Bossier).
[99] Words added, probably, by Moerbeke (Bossier).
[100] Plotinus, *Enneads* 1.i.9; compare Aristotle *Met.* 9, 1051a22–1052a11.

contact or it does not, for it is inerrant.'[101] In cases where it predicates one thing of another it can err, affirming what does not belong
65   or denying what belongs. But when it contemplates immaterial
forms, it either attains to them, in which case it always says what
is true, or it does not reach them and so does not err.

Aristotle assimilates the truth of intellect in the case of simple
things to perception of forms. Just as sight is true in the grasping
of colours when it does not put together the colour and the coloured
70   subject[102] (for it does not pertain to sight or sense to know this, but
only to judgement and opinion; it is sufficient for sight to receive
truly the visible form and see what it is); so also intellect is true
in its bare understanding of simple forms. The functioning, then,
of intellect concerning separate forms is partly like and partly
75   unlike that[103] of sense concerning the proper sensibles. Inasmuch
as each achieves truth in reaching the object known, they are alike.
But in that sense knows sensible things in a way which is inferior
to knowledge through inference, and intellect in a way which is
superior, the likeness is imperfect.

80   In what way sense may be called 'true' has been said earlier:
it is because it reaches to sensible things without error. But the
functioning of intellect in connection with separate forms is truth
above all and in the strictest sense, because it knows precisely what
each form is. For in the case of these forms, I said, the thing and
89   what it is to be that thing are the same; which is why intellect does
not go wrong about the putting together of subject and predicate.
85   And this sort of functioning is consonant with the nature of things.
For if[104] there ought to be an affinity between cognition and what
is known and non-material and separate forms, as Aristotle says,[105]
are truth itself, since they are without mixture of any contrary –
whereas of material forms none is either genuine or pure since they
are mixed with what is formless; neither is what is beautiful here
90   genuinely beautiful since it is connected with the ugly, I mean
matter, so that cognition of these things is neither exact nor true
but connected with a contrary; separate forms, on the other hand,
are the very things they are without any composition or relationship
to what is opposite, which is why they are truth itself – this being

---

[101] ibid.

[102] We should perhaps delete *et* after *subiectum* at 88,69 (Bossier).

[103] Bossier wishes to read *operationem* with CVB for *comparationem* at 88,74. The
sense of the sentence will be much the same.

[104] Following Bossier I treat 89,85–95 as a single loosely constructed sentence (as
such it is very typical of Philoponus' style). Among other departures from Verbeke's
punctuation, at 89,88–90 we follow De Corte in reading: *quia mixtae sunt ad informe;
neque pulchrum quod hic est sincere pulchrum* ... for the unintelligible *quia mixtae
sunt ad informe neque pulchrum; quod hic est sincere pulchrum.* ...

[105] Aristotle does not, in fact, use this phrase (*autoalêtheia*) in any surviving work.

so, the cognitive functioning too in connection with these ought to be consonant with this, and capable only of truth with no falsity   95
opposed to it. They say, however, that such functioning comes only to those who have reached the summit of a good life and of knowledge, and rarely even to them. Hence Plotinus says in this connection that whoever shall have functioned in this way will know what he means.[106]

These things which have been said about cognition of non-   00
material forms can also be taken as applying to material forms. When intellect does not put a form together with a subject but understands it on its own (for instance when it understands rational without man or a definition without the subject), then it is true in the way in which sense is true when it is of the proper sensibles, and it is clear that in these cases it can only be true and not false.   5
We are reminded what affirmation and denial are because it is by them that there is the cognition through composition in which we say what is true or false.

430b27 But not all intellect is like this; intellect of what something is, according to what it was for it to be, is true.   10

All cognition which involves composition will always be either true or false, whether it is in the mind or uttered in speech. But not all intellect is always either true or false because not all intellect is   **90**
cognition of something composite. That which knows simple and non-material forms is always true.   15

430b28 That which is of what something is, according to what it was for it to be, is true.

That intellect, Aristotle says, which knows substances according to that, precisely, by which they are substances, is always true; that is, which knows pure and non-material forms, or which knows the forms of material things, according to which they are substances,   20
in themselves. This is because instead of seeing images of them it intuits them of itself; as we understand whiteness by intuition into its essence and not by looking at particular white things.

430b28 And is not understanding one thing of another;

that is, which understands some simple thing, not one thing to be   25
present in another.

'What it was for it to be' always signifies the essence of things;

---

[106] *Enneads* 5.viii.1.

and since 'what it is' signifies substance, and that which consists of the two together, I mean subject and form, is also called 'substance', but the term applies most strictly to that which is simple, to substance in the sense of form, which signifies the simple essence, having said **intellect of what something is** he adds **according to what it was for it to be**, that is, intellect which knows substance in the sense of form.[107]

107 Punctuating with a comma after *essentiam* at 90,30 (Bossier).

CHAPTER 7

431a1 Knowledge which is in actuality is identical with the
thing. Knowledge which is in potentiality is prior in time in   35
the individual, but in general it is not prior even in time; for
all things which come to be are from that which is in actuality.

He has already said this earlier,[1] that intellect in actuality is the
same as the things understood, since that which is intellect in
actuality is also intelligible. Intellect which is in potentiality pre-   40/**91**
cedes that which is in actuality and is prior in time in the same
man, for it is led from potentiality to actuality. But if one looks at
the whole universe, intellect in potentiality is not prior in time to
that which is in actuality. There is always intellect in potentiality,
and hence there must be that which is in actuality to lead what is
in potentiality to actuality; for whatever is in potentiality is made   45
to be in actuality by something in actuality. In the universe, then,
there is always both intellect in potentiality and that in actuality.
In the individual man intellect in potentiality comes before intellect
in actuality but is brought into actuality by some other intellect
in actuality; that of the teacher, for example, or even the divine
intellect.

But though Aristotle has said these things not long before, he   50
now says them again, not only to make them more manifest (for he
now also states the explanation why intellect in potentiality is not
prior to that in actuality) but also because of what he has said last.
He wants to show why intellect sometimes understands with simple
intuitions and sometimes by putting together. The explanation is   55
that intellect is sometimes in actuality but sometimes in potentiality, and in the latter case it knows composite things by composition. Thinking or opining is like this. Aristotle takes knowledge
as an illustration of intellect. Just as knowledge in actuality is
nothing other than the theorems known, so intellect in actuality is   60
the same as the thing understood, either because it receives its
form or because when intellect is wholly in actuality it is[2] also
intelligible.

And further there are two ways in which intellect in actuality
functions. One is syllogistic; this is cognition by composition and   **92**
division; the other is superior to the way of syllogism. In both kinds 65
of functioning intellect is identical with the things understood, as

---

[1] 430a19.
[2] Reading *sit* at 91,61 with T for *sic* (Bossier).

sense is with sensible things. For what else is intellect in actuality but thoughts, [[that is, concepts,]][3] or sense in actuality but things sensed. But much more is that intellectual grasping which is of altogether separate forms identical with the separate forms. For
70 they are not in a subject so that intellect when it understands them has to choose out one element and not another as it does with material forms: here it has forms stripped and without matter.

431a4 That which perceives[4] plainly makes what is potentially
75   sensible actually so. It is not affected or altered; hence this is
       a different species of change.

Aristotle wishes here to lead us into his teaching about the appetitive part of the soul, but it is useful[5] for him to make these preliminary points. That is why, though he has spoken of these matters earlier, he nevertheless takes them up again as useful for his teach-
80 ing about that which is appetitive. He says, then, that to perceive is not to be altered or changed and neither is to understand. It is enough for his purpose to speak of sense because understanding is like perceiving and comes about in the same way, even if it can even less be thought of as being affected, as he has shown a little earlier. He says, then, that that which perceives plainly makes
85 what is potentially sensible actually so, perceiving by that discernment which derives from sensible things.[6] It is not affected, however, in being transmuted from being this in potentiality to actuality, as he has shown in the preceding book.[7] Hence such a transmutation is not a change, alteration or affection. Or if anyone wants to call it 'change', then 'it is another species of change', not one of the natural sorts, and it is describable as change only in an
90 equivocal way.

In some manuscripts 'thing perceived' is read [for 'that which perceives'] and perhaps this reading is better. But it says the same thing, and so the interpretation is the same. The 'thing perceived' makes 'that which perceives in potentiality' a thing which 'actually'

---

[3] Words added, probably, by Moerbeke (Bossier).

[4] From 92,83–4 it appears that we should read *sensitivum*, 'that which perceives', at 92,73 and not *sensibile*, 'that which is perceived', with the MSS. Philoponus notes below that there is the alternative (and, as he rightly says, superior) reading 'that which is perceived'; if we adopt it we must read 'what perceives in potentiality; at 92,73 for 'what is potentially sensible'.

[5] Philoponus does not say why it is useful and modern readers fail to trace a consecutive line of thought running through this chapter.

[6] Perhaps we should understand 'perceiving the differentiating features of the sensible things' (cf. 94,25). The Greek may have been *tês tôn aisthêtôn diaphoras*; Moerbeke often renders a genitive by an ablative.

[7] 417b2–16.

perceives it. Such a transmutation is not an alteration. Hence the thing perceived does not act, nor is the sense or that which perceives affected. It does not take on one property in place of another but 95 functions by virtue of the one it has. Hence it would not be a case of generation either (for generation occurs through things being altered), but 'another species of change'. 'For change is the actuality **93** of something incomplete',[8] whereas sense is an actuality, but not of something incomplete. Just as one who knows but is not function- 00 ing,[9] when he functions does not engage in an incomplete function- ing – which is why such functioning is not a change – so it is with sense and perceiving; and similarly with intellect: what has the positive state is not incomplete, so neither is its actuality change. For the word 'change' is applied to the actuality of that which is incomplete or that which is in potentiality in that[10] it does not yet 5 have its positive state. A complete thing is one that already has the positive state, and its actuality is no longer change. The trans- mutation, however, of the material intellect into intellect which possesses dispositional knowledge is not of this nature; this trans- formation, then, is more like generation.

431a8 Perceiving is like mere saying and understanding. 10
When, however, [the soul perceives] pleasant or distressing, similarly to affirming or denying, it pursues or avoids. And to experience pleasure or distress is to function with the percep- tive mean in relation to the good or bad as such.

Next[11] he adds to what has been said a discussion about appetition 15 and the appetitive power of the soul, in which he brings out certain **94** analogies between the intellective soul and the sensitive and shows that there is impulse and appetition in both. That in accordance with intellect is wish for good things and avoidance of bad, whereas that in accordance with sense is desire of the pleasant and shunning 20 of the distressing; and he says how these things come about in each case. He starts with sense. He has already said how sense is brought into actuality by the things perceived without being altered or affected. Brought into actuality by the things perceived, sometimes it cognises the substance of the perceived things by itself, but some- times it relates it to the animal and judges. For instance when it 25

[8] It seems better to take this as a quotation than as a lemma, and it is not shown as a lemma in the MSS.
[9] Reading *autem* with the MSS for *aut* at 93,00 and punctuating: *autem, cum operetur non imperfectam operationem operatur, propter quod neque motus est talis operatio, sic autem* . . . (Bossier).
[10] Conjecturing *sic* for *sit* at 93,5 (Bossier).
[11] Reading *hinc*, translating *entheuthen*, for *huic* at 93,15 (Bossier).

perceives something hot as hot, it perceives only its differentiating feature and fiery essence.[12] But when it relates this sort of essence to the animal it then judges it not just as sensible but as unpleasant or pleasant, that is, as preservative or destructive of the animal, and it either avoids it as destructive or pursues it as preservative.

30　Perceiving the essence of sensible things, then, by itself is likened to a kind of saying. By 'saying' he here means a term, whereas a little earlier[13] he had used *'phasis'* for the composite, the whole proposition.[14] When, however, sense relates the sensible thing to the animal and perceives what it perceives as pleasant or distressing, that becomes like a composition and an affirmation or denial.

35　Such perceiving is immediately followed by pursuit and avoidance, which belong to the appetitive power. For when, pleased by the sensible thing, it[15] as it were says 'yes' it pursues it; when it is displeased it says 'no' and avoids.[16] That which is appetitive, then, is not different as a subject from the power to perceive but differs

40　only in account, since sense is simple cognition of the sensible as such, whereas appetition is cognition of the sensible as destructive or preservative of the animal. For to experience pleasure or distress, which are operations of that which is appetitive, is nothing else but to perceive something as commensurate or incommensurate with the perceiver. Aristotle calls perceiving 'acting with the perceptive

45　mean' because the senses have been shown to consist in a certain mean and proportion.[17]

'As such', that is, insofar as they are good or bad things of this particular sort. Sense perceives the object not as good or bad absolutely but as good or bad to this animal, i.e. as pleasant or distressing; for what is pleasant to one animal is distressing to another.

50　Further, 'as such' means 'as good or bad'. These things[18] are objects

95　of appetition not as[19] hot or cold or any other sensible quality they may have, for the grasping of those things is sense, not appetition; but appetition is the discriminator of what can give pleasure or distress.

---

[12] Understanding *discretionem solam sentit et igneam essentiam* at 94,25–6 (as Sophonias 136,32–3) for *discretione sola sentiture, et igneae essentiae* (Bossier).

[13] 430b26; see above 87,43.

[14] Punctuating *'phasim' compositum, totam* at 94,32 for *'phasim' compositum totam* (Bossier).

[15] A feminine subject is indicated; probably 'soul' or 'sense' (feminine in Greek) rather than 'the appetitive power'.

[16] Punctuating *negaverit molestata, fugit* for *negaverit, molestata fugit* at 94,38 (Bossier).

[17] See 424a4–5.

[18] Reading *haec* for *hoc* at 94,50 (Bossier).

[19] Understanding *inquantum*, Greek *hêi*, for *aut'*, Greek *ê*, at 95,51 (Bossier).

430a12 [[It is]][20] both avoidance and appetition in actuality.
And that which pursues and that which avoids are different   55
neither from one another nor from that which perceives, but
their being is different.

By 'that which pursues' Aristotle means not desire (for that depends
on[21] imagination) but simply judgment of what gives pleasure and
distress. 'Both avoidance', he says, 'and appetition' – by 'appetition'
he means pursuit of the pleasing, just as avoidance is flight from   60
what is distressing[22] – are different in subject neither from one
another nor from sense. For they are operations of that which
senses since it is that which senses that judges these things [sc. the
pleasant and the distressing]; but they are different in account.
Sense is receptive of the sensible thing itself by itself; appetition is
pursuit of this and avoidance is aversion from it. After 'avoidance
and appetition' he adds 'in actuality'[23] because it is perception of   65
this kind, sc. of the pleasant or distressing, in actuality which is
avoidance and pursuit. Similarly Plotinus says in this connection
that pleasures and distresses are either perceiving or not without
sense.[24]

430a14 For the soul which thinks images are like sensations.
When the soul says or denies good[25] it also avoids or pursues.   70

Having spoken about simple perceiving, which is like saying,[26] and
of that which goes with the pleasant or the distressing, which is
like affirmation, and having spoken also of the pursuit and avoidance which follow upon such perceiving, he passes to that which

[20] Verbeke here inserts *idem*, 'the same', from Aristotle's text, giving us 'Both
avoidance and appetition in actuality are the same'. Nothing in the commentary,
however, suggests that Philoponus had 'the same' and his explanation of 'that in
actuality' suggests rather that he did not have it. There is some uncertainty about
its meaning in Aristotle. Most scholars take Aristotle to be saying that avoidance
and appetition are the same as one another. I think he means they are the same as
the exercise of the sensory mean just described, and Philoponus' commentary reflects
this view if it reflects either.

[21] Or (taking *phantasia* as nominative) 'that is imagination'.

[22] Following Bossier I treat this sentence as a parenthesis.

[23] In the lemma these words are preceded by *qui*, masculine; here we have *quae*,
feminine, corresponding to Aristotle's feminine *hê*. Philoponus evidently takes that
which is said to be 'in actuality' to be perception, which is feminine in Greek
(*aisthêsis*) and masculine in Latin (*sensus*), not avoidance and pursuit.

[24] *Enneads* 4.iv.19.

[25] Verbeke here inserts 'or evil' from Aristotle's text, but neither the commentary
nor the quotation at 98,29 proves that this was in Philoponus' lemma.

[26] The MSS have *puta de dictione* at 95,72 which should mean 'for example about
saying' but that does not make sense. The Greek probably contained *hoion* which
can introduce an example but which will have meant 'like'.

75   thinks rationally and shows how it resembles sense and how, in a
      way,[27] here too there is that which is appetitive.

96   He says, then, that images, which are like imprints from sensible
      things occurring in the imaginative part of the soul, stand to the
      thinking soul as sensations stand to sense. By 'sensations' he means
80   either sensible things or receivings of them. Imagination receives
      impressions of sensible things through sense, just as sense receives
      impressions from sensible things [themselves], and judges[28] them
      as sense does: like sayings when it receives an image simply of
      heat, like affirmations or denials when it receives them in itself as
85   pleasant or distressing to the animal.[29] Intellect sees these forms
      in the imagination, and when it sees the simple imprint of the
      sensible thing it has a simple concept of it, by virtue of which it
      comes to speak truly, but without composition, of the sensible
      things, analogous herein to simple perceiving. When, in contrast,
      it judges one of these things as good or bad for the animal there is
90   then a composite conceiving, analogous to the perceiving of what
      is pleasant or distressing, and from this comes pursuit or avoidance.

      There are pursuit and avoidance of things pleasant and distress-
      ing not only when they are present but also when they are future.
      For when sense has once judged something pleasant or distressing,
      and imagination has received imprints of these, if the same sensible
      thing approaches imagination applies to it the imprints it contains
95   and either pursues it admitting it as pleasant and preservative or
      avoids it as unpleasant and harmful.

      It is on this account,[30] I mean because there are imprints of
      pleasant and distressing things in the imagination, that brute ani-
      mals too appear to experience pleasure or distress in sleep; dogs, for
      instance, wag their tails as though they were imagining something
      pleasant, or start up agitatedly because some distressing image
97/00 comes to them in sleep.

      Intellect too, then, seeing the imprint of fire (as it might be) in[31]
      imagination, and finding from what is impressed in the imagination
      that this has sometimes been harmful, makes a pronouncement
      about the future. If in the past it has been a sign of terrifying
      enemies, when the terrifying thing[32] appears now it says that enem-

      [27] Conjecturing *modo aliquo*, 'in some way', for *in aliquo*, 'in some cases' at 95,75
      (Bossier).
      [28] Understanding *iudicante* for *iudicans* at 96,82 (Bossier).
      [29] Reading *animali* for *anima*, which has poor MSS support, at 96,54 (Bossier);
      retaining *anima* we should translate: 'when the soul receives them in itself as
      pleasant or distressing.'
      [30] Punctuating *unde, dico autem propter* at 96,96 (Bossier).
      [31] Understanding *in* for *quidem* at 97,1; Moerbeke may have read *touto men* for
      touton en (Bossier).
      [32] Bossier suggests plausibly that Moerbeke has confused *phruktos* ('beacon') with
      phriktos ('terrifying'). If so, the Greek was probably: 'If in the past a beacon was a
      sign of enemies, when a beacon. . . .'

ies are going to attack. Brute animals too, when they have encount- 5
ered some evil, a flood[33] or the like, which they have escaped, know
it when it comes again and shun the peril.[34]

430a16 That is why the soul never understands without an
image.

Since he has said that to the thinking soul images are like sensations and that it is because of them that it avoids the bad and
pursues the good, he is right to append this addition. If it is from 10
images that choice of good and avoidance of evil arise, it is impossible that intellect without an image should understand anything.
Not that it is true of all understanding without exception that
it does not occur without an image. But it is true of practical
understandings in which there is good and evil; also of geometrical
(for this too shares in a kind of activity, for[35] it is mixed); and any 15
kind of understanding that is similar.

Alexander[36] tries very hard to prove from this that Aristotle
thinks our intellect is mortal. If intellect never understands without
an image and imagination depends on sense, then if sense is not
immortal, neither is intellect. So[37] it is because Aristotle thinks our 20
intellect is mortal that he says, not simply that 'intellect' but that
'soul' does not understand without an image: he wishes to signify
that the intellective power of our soul is destructible.

So says Alexander. We, however, have said in many places that
Aristotle thinks our intellect is indestructible. And here it is plain
that he is speaking of the thinking soul[38] – he says, 'for the thinking 25
soul images take the place of sensible things'[39] – and he has said **98**
earlier that this is a capacity of[40] the animal as a composite thing.
Furthermore Aristotle is not talking about understanding of

---

[33] *pluviae*, literally 'rain', but here perhaps a flash flood.

[34] The MSS have *effugerit, cognoscit*. Verbeke, following Bate, changes *cognoscit*
to *cognoscunt*; it is better to keep the MSS reading but understand plurals. For
supervenientia I understand a singular.

[35] Or perhaps 'or at least'; *enim* at 97,15 may translate *goun*.

[36] Philoponus expands Alexander. At his *DA* 12,19–22 Alexander says 'Thinking
also, if it does not occur without imagination, will, it too, occur through the body.
And if there can be no activity of the soul separately from the body clearly soul is
something *of* the body and inseparable from it'; this is an echo of Aristotle's *DA* 1,
403a8–10.

[37] Bossier (following T) wishes to take *ergo* at 97,19 with what precedes; if that is
right we should omit 'so' here.

[38] i.e the soul which engages not in pure intellectual intuition but in discursive
thought, *dianoia*.

[39] Aristotle has *aisthêmata*, 'sensations', here; Moerbeke may have mistaken this
for *aisthêta* (Bossier), but see 117,00.

[40] sc. *dianoia*; see G 155,4ff. Bossier thinks we should understand the Greek to
have been 'that the capacity to think belongs to'.

these things[41] but of practical thinking. For it is after saying 'when
30   it says or denies good or bad it also pursues or avoids' (which
manifestly belong to practical intellect) that he adds: 'That is why
the soul never understands without an image.' But if[42] this is practical understanding (for practical conduct is to do with good and evil),
and this is to do with the composite animal, imagination is given
as an endowment for action. But all practical action is particular,
35   and the operations of the soul while it is in the body are particular.
No wonder, then, it does not understand any practical thing without
an image. But it is plain that not even does contemplative understanding always understand with the aid of an image, still less
intellect in actuality which grasps things by simple intuitions with-
40   out reasoning. Intellect does not need an image when it does proofs
in logic, for instance when it proves that the categorical syllogism
has three figures, or shows how many valid moods there are in
each,[43] or proves the conversion of propositions; not to speak of
when it reasons about intelligibles.

431a17 But the air causes the pupil to be of a certain nature,
45   and the pupil something else, and hearing similarly, and the
last thing is one and there is one mean, though its being is
manifold.[44]

99   Aristotle's meaning here is as follows. In vision the air is altered
by colours, it alters the pupil (I mean the eye itself), the pupil
50   something else (say the visual pneuma),[45] but the last thing altered
is one single thing, the power of sight which judges the forms of

[41] i.e. theoretical understanding of them. Bossier suggests understanding *hoc intellectu* for *eorum intellectu* at 98,28, in which case we should translate 'talking not of
this, sc. theoretical or contemplative, intellect, but of practical'.

[42] Retaining Verbeke's *Si autem* at 98,31. Bossier points out that the MSS support
for this is weak, and wishes to delete it and take *hoc est practica intelligentia* with
what precedes. If that is right we should translate: ' " . . . the soul", that is, practical
understanding, "never understands without an image". For practical conduct is to
do with good and evil, and these are to do with the composite animal so that
imagination is given. . . .'

[43] Reading *quot* for *quod* at 98,41 with Bossier, and understanding *in unaquaque
modi* for *in unoquoque modo*; the MSS text would have to be translated 'or shows
that there are apodictic syllogisms in each mode' (or 'mood') which makes no sense.

[44] This appears to be the beginning of a comparative sentence of which the main
clause is missing. Modern scholars mostly take 'the last thing' to be a single organ
or capacity for all modes of perceiving. Philoponus, however, (followed by Sophonias)
takes the 'last thing' to refer to what is basic in each sense, and the single organ or
capacity comes only in the missing second half of the sentence, supplied by Sophonias
(138,9) in the words 'so there is a common terminus serving as a single boundary
and gathering together the different termini'.

[45] Philoponus draws on the theory of 'connate pneuma' (see Aristotle, *de Motu* 10)
according to which our motor and sensory systems work (not, as we believe today,
by electricity but) by expandings and contractings of a kind of gas (*pneuma*).

visible things; and it is the same with hearing and things that perceive; each sense-organ[46] through some affection produced in it serves the power to perceive, and there is a final thing in which the affection ceases in each sense-organ;[46a] it is a single thing without parts, the power to perceive which he also, as often, calls a 'mean'. This power is one and without parts as a subject but many things in account because it is receptive of many affections. Sight, for instance, receives pale, dark and what is between. Just as a point is one and[47] without parts as a subject, but several things in account because it is the terminus of several straight lines (and in being the terminus of several lines it is several termini), so too sense is one and without parts as a subject, but many things in account through being the terminal point and discriminator for many affections. It is affected differently by different things perceived and receives them differently. Following on here he shows that just as that which judges[48] different visible things is one, and similarly with audible things and the rest, so that which differentiates heterogeneous sensibles, e.g. which judges the visible to be different from the audible and the rest, is again one and without parts as a subject but several things in account.

That is the meaning of what is said. This whole passage about the senses seems to be an insertion.[49] For following on 'That is why the soul understands nothing without an image' we have 'That which understands, then, understands forms in images'. This follows upon the earlier words; the intervening remarks about the senses seem not to form part of the continuity. In fact, however, even these remarks are not thrown in with no regard for continuity at all. They are to show that as sense is one, though it is both common and special and receptive of heterogeneous sensibles, so intellect is one and without parts even if it receives different sorts of intelligible in different ways. As sense stands to sensible things so intellect stands to intelligible things, so that conversely, as sensibles stand to intelligibles so sense stands to intellect. Sense is one for many sensibles, but while it is one and without parts as subject

55

60

65

70

100
75

80

---

[46] Understanding *sensiterium* (Greek *aisthêtêrion*) for the MSS *sensitivum* at 99,52 and 54 (Bossier).

[46a] See n. 46.

[47] Reading and conjecturing *unum quidem est <et>* for *unum est quidem* at 99,58 (Bossier).

[48] The Greek *krinein* here translated combines as no English word does the meanings 'to judge' and 'to differentiate'.

[49] I take *intersertus* at 99,69 (like *interiecta* at 100,74) to correspond to *embeblêntai* in Sophonias 138, 27, and construe *de sensibus* with *locus*, cf. 99,72. The MSS have *intersertus esse ei qui de sensibus* which would give us 'This whole passage seems to be an insertion into that which deals with the senses'. We could understand *ex eo qui* for *ei qui*, 'an insertion *from* that which deals with the senses', but I prefer to think that *ei qui* replaces some relatively unimportant lost words.

it is many things in account. Intellect too, then, is one and the same in subject and without parts but many things in account because it has many operations, since it grasps many intelligibles.

431a20 What it is by which we discern how sweet differs from
85　　sour[50] has been said already, but may also be said here: it is one thing, but one as a terminus.

It is a problem, as we said, by means of what the soul discerns and discriminates the features which differentiate sensible things – whether it does this by means of one thing or several, and if by one, then how. Aristotle has already, as he himself observes, spoken
90　　earlier of this, I mean of what is called the 'common sense'.[51]
Here too, however, he says that it is one thing which discerns the differences between the things perceived by the five senses. For if we grasped one with one thing and one with another instead of employing a single thing which is capable of judging all of these there could not sometimes be perception[52] that the object of a different [sense] was different. For it is the same thing being differently
95　　affected which differentiates different objects as different. It, I mean the common sense, is one, he says, as a terminus is one – meaning by a 'terminus' the final terminal point of several lines which meet,
101　such as the centre of a circle at which meet all the straight lines from the circumference. As a subject this is a single point without
00　　parts but in that it is a terminal point of many things it is many. Of this nature too is the kind of terminus called <a 'frontier'>[53] which delimits regions and places while being itself one: it is the common terminus of several things delimited by it. This[54] capacity too, then, being the terminus of the five senses, like [these other] termini is one as a subject but many things in account. Since it is

[50] Aristotle has 'hot', an object of a different sense, in place of 'sour'.

[51] 426b8–427a14. The use of the expression 'the common sense' in this connection by post-Aristotelian writers seems to arise from a misunderstanding of *DA* 3, 425a27. Having said that shape and size are objects common to several senses Aristotle there says that since we already have 'common perception' of them (sc. by sight and touch) there is no need for a further sense specially to perceive them. Readers took him to mean that we do have a further sense specially to perceive them called 'the common sense'. For my own views on this matter and how, according to Aristotle, we in fact differentiate objects proper to different senses, the reader may see my 'Telling the Difference between Sweet and Pale', *Apeiron* 1981.

[52] Reading and punctuating *omnium, sensum aliquando* for *omnium sensuum, aliquando* at 100,93–4 (Bossier).

[53] The MSS show a lacuna here. I follow Bossier's suggestion that Greek text had *methorios*, 'frontier', here. Verbeke adopts Bate's conjecture *limes terrae seu agrorum*, 'boundary of land or fields'.

[54] Conjecturing *haec* for *hic* at 101,3. If we retain *hic* I would translate 'the capacity here too'. Bossier wishes to read *hoc* (with T) for *hic* and take *potentia* as ablative; we should then translate 'This, being in potentiality the terminus of the five senses . . .'.

one in this way there is nothing surprising in its differentiating 5
different and heterogeneous things. Just as sight is one but differentiates the contraries pale and dark so the common sense is one but
differentiates things different in kind, pale and sweet. And the
same is to be said of intellect.

431a22 And these things, being one by analogy and in number,
stand to each other as those do to one another.[55]   10

'These things', he says, that is those that discriminate the different
sorts of sensible, are one in number and have the same relationship
to one another as the sensible they discriminate. The relationship
with pale and dark, things discriminated by sight, have to sweet
and pale, the common sense has to sight and the other senses.   15
Hence conversely: as sight stands to the things discriminated by
sight and each of the special senses to its proper sensibles so the
common sense stands to the common sensibles. In these it is the
mode of relationship, not the relationship itself, which he represents
as following on, since the resemblance between them lies in the   20
similarity of their relationships.[56]

[55] Our MSS have: *Et haec unum proportionalitate et numero quem habent ad
utrumque, ut illa ad invicem.* This corresponds to our MSS of Aristotle but is untranslatable; I have translated as Ross understands Aristotle.

Modern commentators find this passage about the senses difficult and so did
Philoponus. The first problem is about the reference of 'these things' and 'those'.
Philoponus takes 'these' to be the things that discriminate objects of the senses of
every kind and 'those' to be sensible objects, pale, dark, sweet etc. He does not go
on to interpret the lemma in the most obvious way and say 'As pale stands to sweet
so that which discriminates pale stands to that which discriminates sweet'. This
would not, he thinks, be true, since the discriminators are identical, whereas the
qualities are not (104,76–7). Instead he says something more complicated: 'As homogeneous sensibles like pale and dark stand to heterogeneous like pale and sweet,
so discriminators of homogeneous like sight and taste stand to discriminators of
heterogeneous, sc. to the common sense.' 'Hence conversely': as the discriminator of
pale and dark stands to pale and dark, so the discriminator of pale and sweet stands
to pale and sweet. He says 'so the common sense stands to the common sensibles',
but by 'the common sensibles' he must mean not Aristotle's common sensibles, shape,
size, change etc., but the heterogeneous sensibles which are discriminated by the
common sense. The point he is trying to make (cf. Sophonias 138,19–21) is that since
homogeneous sensibles, though many in number, are discriminated by one thing, in
the case of pale and dark by sight, heterogeneous sensibles too should be discriminated by one thing. The commentary is obscure partly because instead of a clear
statement of this point Philoponus finds in Aristotle the misleadingly bald statement
that the discriminators are related in the same way as the objects discriminated.

[56] This sentence is difficult. I understand it as follows: 'In these things [the discriminators and the objects, or perhaps just the latter] it is the mode of relationship [the
discriminator of pale stands to pale as that of sweet to sweet] not the relationship
itself [the discriminators do not stand to one another as pale to sweet] which he
has represented as following on [which he has represented as the same for the
discriminators] since the resemblance between them lies [since they are things the
resemblance between which lies only] in the similarity of their relationships.' This,

431a24 For what difference is there between wondering how
we differentiate <non>⁵⁷ homogeneous things and how we
differentiate contraries like pale and dark?

That is, it is reasonable that if that which differentiates contraries,
102 as sight differentiates pale and dark, is one and the same (this has
25 been shown earlier),⁵⁸ then that which differentiates sensibles of
several kinds should be⁵⁹ one. For heterogeneous sensibles are
indeed no less different from each other than contraries; but if
one considers carefully, one thing will differentiate heterogeneous
objects more easily than contraries.⁶⁰ For heterogeneous qualities
30 can, while contraries cannot, belong to the same thing at the same
time. Having said this he next proposes an analogy consisting in
contraries and things receptive of these and says that, by resemblance with this, one thing as subject is shown to be discriminative
of all sensible things.

431a25 As A, pale, then, is to B, dark, let C be to D [[in the
35 same relation as they]];⁶¹ hence the converse holds too.

What he means is this. As pale stands to dark so that which receives
pale stands to that which receives dark; they stand in the same
relationship to one another. Hence 'the converse holds too': as the
first members of the pairs stand to each other so do the second; as
40 that which receives pale stands to pale, so that which receives dark
stands to dark. The one perceives the one, the other the other.
What comes next, **If, then, C and D are present in one thing**
is as much as to say: but C and D, the things which receive pale
and dark, a plurality of different things, are present in one thing
45 (for one and the same thing is receptive of contraries); it will be

---

however, is somewhat forced, and Bossier may be right that some verb like *manifestat*
governing *modum proportionis, non ipsam proportionem* has dropped out. Restoring
this we could understand: 'In these things [in this passage] he sets out the mode of
relationship [they can be taken 'conversely'] but not the relationship itself; he has
explained later in what ways the resemblance arising from the analogy is to be
taken.'

⁵⁷ Verbeke correctly supplies the negative from Aristotle's text.
⁵⁸ cf. 423a23–5, 426b10–11, 427a5–14.
⁵⁹ Conjecturing *esse* for *est* before *unum* at 102,25 (Bossier).
⁶⁰ Following Bossier I take *enim* at 102,26 to translate *men gar*, introducing a
concessive clause, construe *magis autem* at 102,27 with what follows, and understand
the pleonastic comparative *facilius* to result from confusing *rhaidion* with *rhaion*.
An alternative would be to change round *minus* with *magis*: 'For heterogeneous
sensibles are no more different from one another than contraries but rather less.'
Either way we should understand *sunt* for *est* at 102,26.
⁶¹ The superfluous words 'in the same relation as they' appear in the MSS of
Aristotle but Ross is probably right to bracket them.

one as are the things discriminated.[62] In what way are the contraries one? They are one in a certain respect but not the same in
account.[63] They are one in genus but different in account. Colours   **103**
have one being in kind and so do sensible things;[64] for sensible
things too in as much as they are sensible are of the same kind;
and so therefore are the powers which discriminate them; and even   50
if they are one in subject[65] and are present in a single thing, they
are not also one in account. For it is one thing to receive pale and
another dark.

Having said this and brought out the relationship there is in
contrary sensibles to the sense that receives them, he transfers this
relationship to heterogeneous sensibles and says it is **similarly**   55
with these.[66] As sweet stands to sour[67] so the power which grasps
the former stands to that which grasps the latter. 'Hence conversely': just as in the former case that which grasps the contraries
is one in number but not in account, so it is here. That which
receives several [heterogeneous sensibles] is one in number but not
in account. Indeed, sensible things are all one in genus inasmuch   60
as they are all sensible, but they differ from one another in account
and form. Although what is said here: 'If, then, C and D are present
in one thing, they will be related as are A and B; they will be the
same, but their being will not be the same; and those[68] similarly'
is ungrammatical as it stands,[69] what it signifies is that these things   65
[sc. A and B] being so related . . . ,[70] C and D are one thing in

[62] So the text (we should probably, as Bossier says, read *ut et* for *ut* at 102,45).
The sequence of thought seems uneven, but Philoponus may be saying to himself
'In what way is that in which C and D are present one? According to Aristotle, as
A and B are.'

[63] Punctuating as a statement, not a question (Bossier).

[64] Reading *sensibilia* for *sensibili* at 103,48.

[65] Reading *subiectum* for *substantiam*, 'substance', at 103,50 (Bossier).

[66] Reading *in his* **similiter** at 103,55 for **in his similiter**.

[67] As at 100,84 *amarum*, 'sour' or 'bitter', seems to be a mistake; we should
understand 'pale'.

[68] Understanding *illa* for *illud*, 'that' at 103,64: there is a plural in Aristotle's text
and above at 103,55.

[69] After *akatallilos* at 103,65 the MSS have *id est non ad invicem*, 'that is, not
reciprocally, not to one another'. This is probably an insertion by Moerbeke giving
what he wrongly takes to be the meaning of *akatallilos* – it could mean 'non-
reciprocally' but here it means 'ungrammatically' or 'without coherence' (Bossier).

[70] The MSS indicate a lacuna of about seven letters after *his sic se habentibus* at
103,66. Bossier suggests supplying *non sequitur*. Lines 66–74 can then be repunctu-
ated to give the sense: 'What it signifies is that, these things being so related, it
does not follow, because C and D are one thing in number (for it is admitted that
that which receives pale is one in number with that which receives dark), that if,
then, pale and dark are similarly related they are one in number; for it is manifest
how they differ and are at a remove from one another, since in addition to being
different they are contrary. As it is, then, with these, so too the same account (or
relationship) will hold for a greater multiplicity of sensible things etc.' This reading
makes it easier to understand 104,80–82 (see n. 74 below). Nevertheless I feel it to

number. For it is admitted that that which receives pale is one in
number with that which receives dark. If, then, even pale and dark
70   are related much as if they were one in number (and it is manifest
how they differ and are at a remove from one another, since in
addition to being different they are contrary), as, then, it is with
these,[71] so the same relationship[72] will hold with a greater multiplicity of sensible things and with the powers that receive them:
they too will be in the same relationship; and the converse will hold
similarly. On the one hand sense should not be divided by the
75   multiplicity of sensibles so that there is one sense of one and another
of another; but neither should it follow, because that which per-
104 ceives all the sensibles and discerns their differences is one in
number, that the sensibles too are one in number. Things which
are analogous to one another do not have their mutual resemblance
extending as far as that, but only so far as to let them be taken
conversely, and these things are more fitting for those doing
proofs.[73]
80   The reading, however, does not agree well with what has been
said above.[74] Instead of 'They will be related as A and B' the text
should run 'A and B will not be so related'. He would be showing
by this[75] that the power which discerns the differences of sensibles
insofar as they are many in account is not one as a subject. That
85   what discerns them is one, he derives from the fact already admitted
that that which discerns the differences between contraries is one.
That they differ in account he derives from his showing that the
powers which receive contraries, though they are one in being, are
several in account, just as the things discriminated by them are not

---

be temerarious, and in my translation I have supposed that nothing of crucial
importance has disappeared in the lacuna: *ut unum* or *ut dicitur* would be possible
fillings.

[71] Punctuating *ut igitur in his, eadem ratio et in pluribus* at 103,71–2 for *ut igitur
in his eadem ratio, et in pluribus* (Bossier).

[72] Or 'the same account'.

[73] That is, loose analogies are more useful than exact ones, or perhaps, if Bossier's
reading of 103,66–74 is correct, what Philoponus has just said is more fitting than
the text on which he is commenting.

[74] I must take this as meaning that the text, in saying that the discriminators
will be as the objects are, does not agree with what Aristotle has said before, namely
that they are one in number. Although I think this a possible interpretation, it
makes Philoponus' comment a little clumsy. On Bossier's interpretation of 103,66–74
we can understand it as neater: 'The text does not agree well with what *I* have just
said.' My interpretation, however, unlike Bossier's, would allow us to insert an *ut*
before *et* in Philoponus' proposed reading, making it 'They will not be related as are
A and B', and this seems to me a likelier proposal for him to make than 'A and B
will not be so related'.

[75] i.e. by the text as it stands.

one in account, even though they are one in a certain respect, as 90
he says of the proper sensibles and the common sense in the *de Sensu*.[76]

The present passage, however, relates to intellect. It too, therefore, will be one thing as a subject but several things in account.

431b2 That which understands, then, understands forms in images.

Having interposed some remarks about sense, Aristotle returns to 95
the discussion of intellect. He has already said a little earlier that
the soul never understands without an image and that for the
intellective soul images take the place of sensible things. Now he
says that the intellect which is in potentiality, that is, *dianoia*, [or 00
intellect][77] contemplates the forms of sensible things in imagination.

Just as when the act of perceiving is still present what is to be
pursued or avoided is determined in the imagination, so even when **105**
perceiving is absent intellect determines what is to be pursued or
avoided in the bare images. When perceiving is present, seeing
something frightening[78] in motion and perceiving that it is fire –
because sight sees the colour – seeing also that it is moving by 5
means of the common sense – for it is this that grasps motion – it
recognises that enemies are coming. In the same way when perceiving is absent it often happens that imagination forms the image of
something frightening, and intellect sees it and, understanding it
is likely[79] something of the same kind will occur in reality, takes
thought about the future, putting together future things with present, and what it judges should be pursued it pursues, while what 10
it judges should be avoided it avoids. For instance a person might
preserve in himself an image of a battle once fought against enemies. Looking at this piece of imagination he reasons and takes
thought how the future will best fall out well for him: whether by
battle against the approaching enemy or by diplomacy, and if by
fighting, when, where, with what troops in what numbers. Reaching 15
in advance a decision about one of the things considered in advance,
this in turn he pursues or avoids.

---

[76] 449a2–20.

[77] Words added, probably, by Moerbeke.

[78] Or 'seeing a torch, a signal-fire': Moerbeke may again (see n. 32) be mistranslating Aristotle's *phrukton* (Bossier).

[79] At 105,8 the MSS have *quomodo*, 'in what way it is likely', but Moerbeke probably read *pôs* for *hôs*, 'that' (or for *pôs* unaccentuated, 'understanding in a way') (Bossier).

431b3 And just as what is to be pursued or avoided is determined for him in those things[80] . . .

Just, he says, as when the act of perceiving is present (this addition
must be understood) what is to be pursued or avoided is determined
in the images.

106/20   **431b5** For instance perceiving something frightening to be
fire, he knows by the common sense, seeing it move, that it is
an enemy.

The construction of the passage is: perceiving, for example, that
something frightening is fire, he sees by the common sense that it
is in motion, and knows it to be an enemy.

          431b6 But sometimes it functions on images in the soul or
25   thoughts[81] . . .

He wants to say how the intelligent takes thought about the future.
It deliberates with an eye to images in the soul concerning what is
now happening, and judges of the future. He calls the images
'thoughts' because he also calls imagination 'passive intellect'.

30   **431b8** And when it pronounces something, as in the former
case, pleasant or distressing, so here it avoids or pursues –
and generally in action.[82]

Just as when the sensible thing is present there is something pleasant or distressing in the imagination, and the man then pursues or
avoids it, so when it is absent intellect looks to that which is
pleasant or distressing among the past things in the imagination,
35   from this it deliberates about similar future things, and it chooses
one thing and avoids another. Hence in every action deliberation
proceeds from experience of things which happened earlier. For

[80] Aristotle's text continues, 'so, when perceiving is not present and it [that which
understands] is functioning on images, it is moved'. Philoponus reserves comment
on this for when the thought reappears in the example.

[81] Aristotle continues 'and, as it were seeing, calculates and deliberates about the
future in relation to the present'.

[82] The sentence is slightly elliptical. Aristotle's thought is not so much (as Philoponus seems to think) 'When, in the absence of the object of perception, as in its
presence, intellect pronounces something pleasant or distressing it pursues or avoids'
as 'When, in the absence of the object of perception, intellect pronounces something
good or bad, as in its presence it pronounces something pleasant or distressing, it
pursues or avoids'. The words 'and generally in action' are in the MSS of Aristotle
but they are obscure and Philoponus' interpretation is not satisfying. Ross by emend-
ing *en* to *hen* obtains the sense 'and generally it will do one thing', but why should
Aristotle say that?

even if the same thing had not happened before, we imagine something similar. The words **and generally in action** signify that all intellectual consideration of this kind, I mean deliberating on whether something is good or bad, takes place in action. For practical intellect is concerned with good and evil, as contemplative is with true and false.

40

431b10 And that which does not involve action, the true and the false, belongs to the same genus as the good and the bad. They differ in that the one is absolute, the other relative.

107

Having said of practical intellect that its source of acting and cause is good or evil (for when it understands good it pursues, and when bad, it avoids) he says that to intellect which is not practical but contemplative and the function of which is the distinction of truth and falsity, these things, I mean truth and falsity, function as good and bad. The true is of the same genus as the good and the false as the bad. True and false are good and bad apart from action; but the good which is truth differs from the practically good, and the bad which is falsity from the practically bad, in that the true is absolutely and more universally and by nature good, and the false is bad in the same way. What is good or bad in things to be done, by contrast, is good or bad not absolutely but at certain times and for certain agents. The same things – bathing, walking, exercising etc. – are not to be done at all times or by all people or in relation to all.

45

50

55

431b12 Things which are called 'abstract' it understands as it understands snubnosed; if it understands it as snubnosed, it does not understand it separately, but if it understands it as hollow, and does so in actuality, it understands hollow without flesh.[83]

60

The fourth species of indivisible things included things which are known 'in the abstract' and which do not have existence [on their own]. Of these, however, he has mentioned only the mathematical point, and he wants to discuss the others also and say how here too intellect understands. He calls them 'abstract' because intellect itself separates things which are not separate from matter, and abstracting them, so to speak, from the subject, understands them as they are in themselves. Intellect, he says, understands mathematical forms as it understands snubnosed. Snubnosedness as such, he says, has its being in a nose, and if a person understands

65/**108**

[83] So the MSS of Aristotle; Ross's extensive emendations are unnecessary.

70 it as snubnosed he does not understand it without nose, since snubnosedness is hollowness in the nose. If, however, he understands it
not as snubnosedness but as hollowness there is no need to understand the subject along with it; separating it, so to speak, according
to its hollowness he understands it as he would understand[84] a
straight line as one which 'lies equably with the points in it'[85] (I
75 say 'straight' to mark the contrast with a circle). And that is how
intellect understands objects of mathematics too. They, the circle
and other shapes, have their being in matter; but it abstracts them
from matter and understands the circle or triangle just as it is in
itself, constructing definitions of the forms themselves without the
subjects.

Besides, he wants to make a distinction for us between the func-
80 tioning of intellect concerning separate forms and its functioning
about what are called 'abstract' things; on that account he gives us
teaching about these abstract things and says what the functioning
of intellect concerning them is.

But if it understands it as hollow, and does so in actuality:
this 'in actuality' should be construed either with 'understands' –
85 'If it actually understands hollow it does so without flesh', i.e. without nose – or, as Alexander recommends,[86] with 'hollow': if it understands hollow as that which is in actuality hollow (which is to make
109 it in actuality intelligible), then separating it from flesh and nose
it understands it as it is in itself, and understanding hollow in this
90 way it understands it apart from flesh, although it has its being
with flesh.

431b15 This is how it understands objects of mathematics.
They are not separate, but it understands them as if they were
separate when it understands them.

Objects of mathematics too, Aristotle says, which do not have their
being apart from matter, are understood as separate from matter
95 when intellect understands them. It is said that Alexander reads,
not, 'They are not separate, but it understands them as if they
were separate',[87] but, 'It does not understand them with something
separate, but as if it were understanding with something separate'[88]
so as to say that our intellect is inseparable from the body. I,
however, have not found Alexander offering this reading for this
passage, even though elsewhere he makes out that intellect is insep-

---

[84] Punctuating *ita intelligit velut si . . . circulum); sic et* at 108,73–5 (Bossier).
[85] This is Euclid's definition, *Elements* 1 def. 4.
[86] The reference is lost.
[87] *non separata, ac si utique* [[*non*]] *separata*: the *non* rightly bracketed by Verbeke.
[88] *non separato, ac si utique separato.*

arable, nor is such a reading either reasonable or probable. For 00
Aristotle's purpose is to speak not of the substance of intellect but
of how it is with mathematical forms when it understands them;
and he says that just as snubnosedness is not separate, but intellect
understands it as separate when it understands it as hollowness,
so it understands mathematical forms as separate though they are
not separate in fact. But even if the text were to read 'not with 5
something separate but as if it were separate' the sense will be the
same if we interpret as follows: though the mathematical form
[sc. by means of which it understands][89] is not separate,[90] when it
understands it intuits it as if it were separate.

431b17 In general intellect which is in actuality is the same
as the things understood.

Having said that intellect separates abstract things and objects of 10
mathematics from matter, and understands them as being in themselves forms separate from matter, he adds what he has already
said more than once, that intellect[91] in actuality is forms without
matter. Just as sense in actuality is sensible forms, and knowledge **110**
in actuality is the things known, so intellect in actuality is intelligible forms, both forms which are without matter and abstract 15
forms. By 'things' Aristotle means 'forms', as often. If, then, intellect
is forms no wonder it will understand mathematical forms without
matter in this way, especially if sense receives the forms of sensible
things without matter. In what way he means intellect is the things
understood, he himself explains in clear terms a little later.[92]

431b17 But whether or not it can understand any separate 20
thing if it itself is not separate from magnitude, we shall have
to consider later.

Alexander says[93] that Aristotle is enquiring whether any form
which is wholly separate from all magnitude – as are the intelligible
forms – can be understood by an intellect which is not separate 25
from magnitude but exists in conjunction with it. On this view
the question is how intellect, *though* not separate from body, can
understand separate forms, and whether this is possible at all.

[89] Those who attribute the questionable reading to Alexander understand him to
take 'that with which' we understand to be the part of the soul with which; Philoponus ingeniously suggests we take it as the concept with which.
[90] Punctuating *mathematica specie, quando intelligit, ut* for *mathematica specie
quando intelligit, ut* at 109,6–7 (Bossier).
[91] Understanding *quod* for *quod enim* at 109,11 (Bossier).
[92] In the next chapter.
[93] Verbeke refers us to Alexander's *DA* 88,20–10; I do not, however, find Alexander
saying this there.

It is better, however, to interpret the question like this. Is it
30   possible for intellect, *while* it is still within the animal and has a
relationship to the body and is not yet removed from it, to understand forms which are separate and divine since they are in every
way[94] separate from body? Whether it is understood in this way or
in the former,[95] the very problem assumes that the rational soul
will be separate if it does indeed understand non-material forms;
35   for it is impossible that an intellect should be adapted to non-
material forms if it exists in matter. Hence even if we accept Alexander's interpretation, the passage proceeds very much as a piece
of inquiry.[96] And then Alexander himself admits that the soul
111   understands separate forms, for so does Aristotle himself,[97] and
Plato has taught us about them, clearly because they had under-
40   standing of them; and besides, if we inquire about separate forms
at all it is plainly because we have received understanding of them
that we raise the question. But it is impossible, if the soul is inseparable from body, for it to receive forms which are wholly separate.
For it is reasonable that that which has its being in body should
be unable to grasp non-material things, seeing that sense does not
45   at all attain to cognition of them except insofar as it provokes
intellect to look for accounts abstracted from sensible things;
besides, things which are in a subject are not capable of functioning
apart from the subject. Plainly, then, intellect will be altogether
separable from body.[98]

We shall have to consider later refers to the *Metaphysics*.[99]
50   There he raises these questions about our soul: can it while still in
the body operate about separate and wholly non-material forms?

That Aristotle thinks our intellect is separable we have shown a
thousand times; also that he is not speaking of any intellect but
55   ours.[100] If we accept Alexander's exposition[101] there will be the great-
est inconsistency between what he says here and what he often

[94] Punctuating *species, modis omnibus cum sint* with T for *species modis omnibus,
cum sint* at 110,32 (Bossier).

[95] The interpretation according to which Aristotle seems to imply intellect is never
separate.

[96] A puzzling sentence. I adopt as the best available Bossier's suggestion that *ut
in quaestione* at 110,37 translates *hôs epi zêtêseôs*.

[97] Bossier suggests reading *et* for *ut* before *enim* at 110,38; we could then translate
'for indeed Aristotle himself and Plato have taught us about them', which would be
an improvement. The singular verb *docuit* at 111,39 is awkward for Bossier's reading, but the plural *intelligentes* is awkward for Verbeke's.

[98] Bossier wishes to punctuate from 110,37 to 111,48 as a single sentence and I
follow him in treating it as a single piece of argument.

[99] I have not located any passage in the *Metaphysics* where Aristotle considers
these questions.

[100] Understanding *non alium aliquem* for *non aliud aliquid* at 111,53; Moerbeke
probably read *oukh allo ti* for *oukh allon tina* (Bossier).

[101] Taking *scripturam* at 111,54 to translate *ekthesin* (Bossier).

says about intellect's being separate. He says this same thing in the *Metaphysics* when he says 'We must consider whether after death anything remains, for instance whether the soul is of this nature – not the whole soul but the intellect, for that the whole soul should remain is perhaps impossible'. He is plainly referring to our soul when he says 'after death'. So it is because it has a   60 separate substance even while it is still in the body that our intellect can operate about separate forms. For if it understands even things which are inseparable from matter because it itself separates them, all the more is it capable of understanding things which are separate in themselves.

CHAPTER 8

65   **431b20** Now let us gather together in a summary way what has been said about the soul, and say again . . .[1]

112   He sums up[2] what has been said about the soul and says it is the full tally[3] of all things. Then he proves this and shows in what way precisely the soul is said to be all things that are.

All things that are, he says, divide into intelligibles and sensibles,
70   for of things that are, some are objects of sense and others of intellect. The functioning of the soul concerning intelligible things is knowledge while that concerning sensibles is perceiving. Knowledge in actuality is nothing else but the things known and sense
75   in actuality is nothing but the things perceived. If, then, our soul has these two ways of functioning, the scientific and the perceptive, and if 'knowledge is the things known and sense the things sensed'[4] (and these include all things that we learn) it follows that the soul will be all things.

Having shown in this way that the soul is all things that are, he inquires in what way it is all of them. Either, he says, the soul is the things themselves in respect of their substance, for instance the
80   heavens, the earth, a stone, an angel; or it is their forms. But it cannot be the things themselves in respect of their substance, for 'there is no stone in the soul'[5] – or water either, as Empedocles[6] seems to say. So it must be the forms of them all, that is, the formal accounts of them – which, indeed, is the fact. That is why, when he
85   says that knowledge is the things known, he adds 'in a way' – and similarly with sense – that is, in a fashion <it>[7] has not the substances of all things, but their accounts.

431b23 But how this is, we should inquire.

[1] Aristotle's text continues: 'that the soul is, in a way, all things that are. For things that are, are either sensible or intelligible, and knowledge is in a way the things known and sense the things sensed.' Philoponus' commentary covers the words omitted from the lemma.

[2] Reading *consummat* for *assumit*, 'takes up', at 111,67 (Bossier).

[3] Moerbeke uses the rare, post-classical word *replementum*; the Greek was probably (cf. G 56,28) *plêrôma*, 'full complement'.

[4] 431b22–3.

[5] 431b29.

[6] Empedocles explains cognition by means of effluences: Diels-Kranz 31 B 89, on which see J. Barnes, *The Presocratic Philosophers*, 480–1.

[7] Supplying *ipsam* in place of Verbeke's *entium* at 112,85 and punctuating *aliqualiter – similiter et in sensu – hoc est modo quodam* (Bossier).

That is,[8] how the soul is said to be all things that are, as knowledge is things known and sense is things perceived.

431b24 Knowledge and sense, then, divide along with things.[9]   90

Having said that knowledge is the things known and sense the things perceived, out of thoroughness he adds this. Since knowledge   113
can be either in potentiality or in actuality,[10] he says that know-
ledge in general is divided along with things, knowledge in potentiality going with things known in potentiality, and actual with
actual. For what else is knowledge in actuality but the aggregate   95
of scientific accounts, and sense similarly?

431b26 That in the soul which perceives and that which knows
are these[11] things in potentiality, the one that which is known,
the other that which is perceived . . .[12]

432a1 Hence the soul is like the hand; for the hand is the
instrument of instruments, and intellect is the form of forms,   00
and sense the form of things sensed.

It has been shown that the soul is all things that are, intellect in
actuality the intelligible things and sense in actuality the sensibles;
what else, then, is intellect but the form of forms? The aggregate   5
of intelligible forms makes that intellect which is in actuality, since
knowledge in actuality is nothing other than the things known. (For
the accounts of the things known are knowledge.) Hence intellect is
a form consisting of forms, and similarly sense is the form of sensible things. Just as the hand, which is an instrument of the soul,
is brought to perfection by operation through perceptible tools, the   10
saw, the drill, the tiller and so forth, and becomes the instrument
of instruments, that is, the form of instruments, so intellect stands
with regard to intelligibles and sense with regard to sensibles.
Hence in general the soul so stands to all things that are.

432a3 Since, however, there is no separated thing, as it seems,   114

---

[8] Supplying *est* after *hoc* at 112,88 (Bossier).

[9] Aristotle continues 'the [mental state] in potentiality corresponding to the things
in potentiality, and the [mental state] in actuality to the things in actuality'.

[10] Understanding *actu* for *actus* at 113,93 (Bossier).

[11] Reading *haec sunt* for *hoc habet* at 113,97 with CV and Aristotle (Bossier).

[12] Reading *hoc quidem scibile, hoc autem sensibile* at 113,98 (so Aristotle) for *hoc
quidem scientionale, hoc autem sensitivum*. Aristotle continues: 'They must be either
the things themselves or the forms. They are not the things themselves. It is not
the stone that is in the soul but the form.'

15 over and above perceptible magnitudes, the intelligible things which are called 'abstract' are in sensible forms, as are all properties and affections of sensible things.[13]

Aristotle has shown above that intellect is separate and not mixed, and that its functioning is completely independent of all bodily
20 functioning; it needs no organ for its own peculiar operations, 'for what part intellect might hold together and how', he says, 'it is difficult even to imagine'.[14] Those, however, who have been deprived of senses from birth seem also to lack kinds of knowledge. Thus persons blind from birth can understand nothing about colours, nor
25 can persons without hearing judge of being in or out of tune. Similarly with geometry, astronomy and arithmetic: without sight and hearing, intellect cannot acquire any branch of knowledge. Why, then, did he say that it does not need an organ?[15] He settles this question and gives his exposition in the present passage.[16]
30 Of intelligible things some[17] are actually intelligible and intelligible by their own nature, whereas others are not intelligible by nature or in actuality, but are naturally sensible and are made intelligible. Of this latter nature are those shapes which constitute the subject of the mathematical sciences, motions and the things which attend upon them, and being in and out of tune; all these
35 things and things like them are by nature sensible and have their
115 being in bodies as subjects. Intellect, however, is by nature able to strip them of their subjects and, though they are not naturally intelligible, make them intelligible by their relation to itself.
It is because the things mentioned are sensible by nature, and it
40 is sense which judges of sensibles, just as intellect is the judge of things intelligible by nature, it is because of this that in the absence of sense no knowledge of these things can arise in the soul, but the soul needs sense to receive the imprints of sensible things and pass them on to imagination. Then intellect, looking at the imprints of sensible things in the imagination, finds accounts of them. Hence
45 if there is no sense for a thing, neither is there imagination or

---

[13] Aristotle continues: 'and because of this a person who does not perceive anything cannot learn or understand anything, and when someone contemplates he must at the same time contemplate some image.'

[14] 411b18–19.

[15] Treating this sentence as a question to which 114,18–27 lead up, and reading *igitur* with CV for *enim* at 114,27 (Bossier).

[16] Following Bossier's suggestion that Moerbeke has misread or mistranslated *touto men oun diaitôn tois prokeimenois ektithetai*. If we adhere to the Latin *Hoc igitur propter causam praemissorum exponit* it is probably best to take *hoc igitur propter* as equivalent to *propter hoc igitur* and translate: 'Because of this [difficulty] he sets out the explanation of the things just mentioned.'

[17] Philoponus here begins an explanation which runs down to 115,50. The Latin starts *quando enim* (114,28–9); for *quando* we should probably understand *quoniam*, translating *epei* as in Sophonias (Bossier).

knowledge of it. For Aristotle says that images are like sensibles for the intellect,[18] that is, as sensible things stand to sense, so the images of sensible things stand to intellect. Just, then, as if there were no sensibles, there would be no sensing of them, so if there were no images there would be no understanding of them. And there will be no images if there is no sense, since imagination arises out of sense. 'That,' he says, 'is why one who does not perceive' will never come to be a knower; 'and when someone contemplates' and functions with knowledge, 'he must at the same time contemplate images'; for intellect looks at the image and does its contemplative thinking about that. We here have[19] stated explicitly what he also said earlier: 'But we do not remember, because this is unaffected. The intellect which is affected is destructible, and without this it understands nothing.'[20] He also said before of imagination that 'it does not occur without sense', and that there is 'no judgment' without imagination.[21]

It is plain from what he says here that he is not speaking of every kind of functioning of intellect but only of that which is concerned with sensible and so called abstract things. In connection with things intelligible in this way, I mean things which are by nature sensible and which are made intelligible, intellect needs imagination and imagination does not exist without sense. But for things which are altogether separate, intellect has no need of sense or imagination; on the contrary, imagination even impedes intellectual functioning, as has been said more than once.

But perhaps someone will say: why then is it through sensible things that we are led back[22] to contemplative thinking about those others, whereas without hearing and sight through which, as Plato says,[23] we acquire knowledge of a philosophical kind, it is <not>[24] at all possible to arrive at understanding of divine things?[25] Why, then, do we not say that sense helps intellect to understand these things?

50

55

116
60

116
65

70

---

[18] 432a9.

[19] Reading *habemus* for *habens* at 115,54 with T and de Corte.

[20] 430a23–5.

[21] 427b15–16.

[22] We should understand and perhaps read *reducimur* with C at 116,66 instead of *reducuntur*.

[23] *Timaeus* 47A.

[24] Our MSS have *omnino* at 116,68, 'it is altogether possible'. Although, however, Philoponus has just said that we can continue in a state of contemplating divine things without using sense or imagination, the sequence of thought of the objection seems to require him to say that without sense we cannot arrive at such intellectual operations. I therefore insert a negative, <non> est omnino.

[25] Punctuating with a comma after *speculationem* at 116,67 and a question mark after *devenire* at 116,69 (Bossier).

I reply that to be deprived of sight and hearing is straightaway[26] not to be an animal, much less[27] a man, since such things are monsters rather than men. Each sort of thing is judged by what is highest and perfect in nature, not by what is imperfect or mutilated.

75 But if by looking with the senses at the universe we come to an understanding of God, sense may be said to contribute to this only as one who wakes[28] a sleeping geometer or who removes a blindfold or the wax in the ears of Odysseus' companions contributes to the proper functioning. An impediment is removed only; they do not of

80 themselves contribute to the functioning. In the case of abstract things sense intuits the things themselves and sends them back to imagination, and from there intellect gathers its pieces of knowledge. But when, looking at the world, we come to an understanding of God, neither sense nor imagination intuits the thing understood itself; rather by means of the things which appear they provoke

85 intellect into bringing out the accounts which are [already] in it. For it is impossible, if accounts concerning divine things do not exist within it, that it should arrive at them from sensible things, as has been said more than once. If one has no understanding of a person or has never seen him, even if one meets him one will never recognise him.

117/90   **432a5 Things which are called 'abstract' and all properties and affections of sensible things.**

Shapes and whatever are the subjects of the mathematical sciences are called 'abstract'. By 'properties' and 'affections' he means, for example, colours, states of health and sickness and the like, for that is how he speaks of them; colours are affections, the rest properties.

95 Intellect understands these too. Hence medical science is knowledge of healthy, sick and (as some think) neutral. Health and sickness are to do with balanced mixture and imbalance of the primary qualities hot, cold, dry and wet.

432a10 But without matter . . . [29]

Sensible things involve matter, for sense[30] intuits bodies them-

---

[26] Taking *sponte* to translate *autothen*.

[27] We should probably read *multo magis neque* for *multo utique magis* at 116,72 (Bossier).

[28] Reading *exsomniantem*, translating *exupnizonta*, for *et somniantem* (which makes the sentence ungrammatical) at 116,76 as Verbeke suggests.

[29] Verbeke prints these words as a quotation and 'but images are like sensible things without matter' as a lemma; it seems better to follow the scribes and do the reverse.

[30] Reading *sensus* with T for *sensu* at 117,99.

selves, 'but images are like sensible things without matter',[31] for it   00
[sc. intellect] has within it sensible things stripped of matter. Some
people take 'without matter' with what goes before: 'When someone
contemplates he must contemplate at the same time[32] images but
without matter'. Both [ways of taking the passage] come to the
same thing.

432a10 Imagination is different from saying and denial; for it   5
is the interweaving of concepts[33] that is true or false.

By 'saying' he means affirmation. The passage, then, means:
imagination by itself neither affirms not denies anything. It does
not interweave one thing with another but only receives the   10
impressions of sensible things. Even if it understands a running
man, it does not do so with the running distinguished from the man
but as a single whole, as when it understands pale man. Hence
imagination speaks neither truly nor falsely; truth and falsity arise
in connection with putting together and separating. But when intellect looks at different images and interweaves one with another,   15
then indeed it speaks truly or falsely. For instance imagination has
the imprint of pale and the imprint of Socrates: suppose intellect   **118**
weaves these together and says that Socrates is pale: if what it
declares to exist in him exists in him it speaks truly; if it does not
exist in him he speaks falsely. And similarly in all cases.

432a12 But as for the primary thoughts, [[that is, concepts,]][34]   20
how do they differ from images? Or are not even the others[35]
images, although they do not exist without images?

Aristotle has summarised[36] what was said about the soul and
declared that in a way it is all things that are, since things are
either intelligible or sensible, and the soul understands all of them.   25
But there are two sorts of intelligible, as we have remarked. Some
things are of themselves and by nature intelligible, such as things
separate from matter, while others are made to be intelligible, like

[31] Aristotle's actual words are 'for images are like sensations' (*aisthêmata* not
aisthêta) 'but without matter'.
[32] Reading *simul* after *necesse* at 117,3 with CVB (Bossier).
[33] Here as at *Cat.* 1a16 Aristotle echoes Plato *Sophist* 262D.
[34] The words 'that is, concepts' are not in Aristotle and are probably a note by
Moerbeke since he has simply transliterated Aristotle's words for thoughts, *noêmata*.
[35] Ross (1961) following Themistius reads 'or are not even *these* things [sc. the
primary thoughts] images?' Philoponus' commentary makes it clear that he read
'others'. In point of fact, by 'the primary thoughts' Aristotle probably means not non-
material forms as Philoponus would like to believe but the first thoughts an ordinary
thinker has, or perhaps simply the thoughts which are 'interwoven' in propositions.
[36] Reading *consummatis* for *assumatis* at 118,23 (Bossier).

material forms. Since he has spoken of things which are not [by
nature] intelligible, but are made to be intelligible, now he speaks
of the remainder. These are the things which are properly intelli-
30   gible, and which he calls 'primary intelligibles'.

Since he has said that we do not understand the others without
an image, he enquires about the primary intelligibles: might they
too be images? He then answers by arguing a fortiori.[37] Why, he
says, should <we ask>[38] concerning the primary thoughts if they
35   are images when 'not even the others', I mean those which are
abstract, 'are images, though they do not exist without images?'
Take the thought that every triangle has its three angles equal to
two right angles: how can that be an image, or the thought that
two sides are always[39] greater than the third, or that in a circle
lines from the centre to the circumference are equal, or anything
40   else that is demonstrated? None of these can be made into an
119   imprint by imagination, but such thoughts do not exist without
imagination. There must be an image of a triangle, and intellect
must then gather what attends upon this.

The words 'not without' can be taken in four ways. They can
mean 'as matter', as when we say that a conveyance is 'not without
wood'. They can signify something harmful, as when we say that
45   travelling by sea in bad weather is 'not without danger'. They can
signify something neither beneficial nor harmful but <simply>[40]
attendant, as when we say that he who walks in light is 'not without
a shadow'. Finally, they can be taken instrumentally as in 'fighting
not without a sword'. It is in this [last] way that intellect is said to
understand abstract things 'not without an image': it uses imagination as a conveyance.[41]

50   We ought to know that he says it is one and the same intellect
which understands the primary forms and which understands the
abstract things which it does not understand without an image. He
said, at least, that the soul is in a way all[42] things that are because
it understands sensible things by sense and intelligible by intellect.
55   Of intelligibles some are primary and some secondary and not with-

[37] Our MSS have *ex circumstante* at 118,33, a difficult phrase; I adopt Bossier's
suggestion that it translates something like *ek periousias* or *ek tou periontos*, literally
'from superabundance'.
[38] Inserting *quaerere* after *si phantasmata sunt* at 118,34 (Bossier).
[39] Conjecturing *semper maiora* for *supermaiora* at 118,38 (Bossier).
[40] The MSS show a lacuna of about seven letters.
[41] Contrast G 45,22–46,2 where Philoponus distinguishes three rather different
uses of 'not without' (he omits the use to introduce the material) and says that in
the present passage it is used to introduce not an instrument but an impediment. I
do not think this discrepancy tells against holding that the same person wrote both
passages; it simply shows Philoponus wavering in his interpretation.
[42] Understanding *omnia*, 'all things' for *entia*, 'things'; Moerbeke probably read
onta for *panta*.

out images. Hence if it is one and the same intellect which belongs to the soul and which gets to know things that are separate too, it will be[43] both separate itself and also not other than our intellect, as some people have thought.

---

[43] Understanding *erit* for *ens* after *separatus* at 119,56 (Bossier).

CHAPTER 9

60   **432a15** The soul of animals is defined by two powers, a discriminative power, which is the work of thought and sense, and also a capacity for change in respect of place.

Here ends the commentary of John the Grammarian or Philoponus or the Alexandrian on the chapter concerning the intellect in Aristotle's *de Anima*. The translation was finished on December 17th
65 1268. The rest of the work I did not think it imperative to translate. The reader should be aware that the Greek manuscript of this work had been destroyed in many places by damp so that I was quite unable to read it. In these places I have sometimes left a space, sometimes supplied what is missing from the sense of what is not, and sometimes I have suspected that the text is corrupted with false readings.

I think that he who reads this will have more light than before to help his understanding of Aristotle's text. Whether or not what is said about the active intellect is true, I leave to the reader's good sense.

Corrected carefully.

Textual Emendations

Suggestions by F. Bossier accepted in this translation

2,17. For *ideo* conjecture *nunc*.

2,18. For *ipsorum* understand *ipsius*.

3,51. For *Troiano* understand *Oiliade*.

3,55. For *omnibus* understand *pueris* (Verbeke).

3,59. After *actum* add *iam*.

5,81. Delete *primo*.

5,84. After *quem* add *et ait*.

5,2. Delete *in* after *neque*.

5,3–4. For *sortitum sive partem ipsum esse dicat nostrae animae, et* read *sortitum, siquidem partem ipsum dicat nostrae animae; et.*

6,8–9. For *practica vel agibilia* understand ⟦*practica vel*⟧ *agibilia.*

6,12. After *dixisset* add *intermedia*.

6,19–20. For *relationem. Dico autem 'morion' neutraliter, id est* **partem animae** read *relationem, dico autem 'morion' neutraliter id est partem* **animae**.

6,21. For *quia solam* understand *quam quidem solam*.

7,59. For *sensibilibus et* punctuate *sensibilibus, et*.

9,3. For *si quae* conjecture *sique*.

9,8. For *erit* conjecture *erat*.

11,57. For *si hoc accidet, intellectum* punctuate *si hoc, accidet intellectum*.

11,62–3. For *neque unam harum (palam quia earum quas nata est suscipere, est enim aliquid), palam quia* punctuate *neque unam harum, palam quia earum quas nata est suscipere, est enim aliquid, palam quia*.

13,3. For *id* read *idem*.

13,7. After *organorum* dèlete *et*.

13,11–12, For **anima**, *non ut: per organum neque le quo* conjecture **anima** *non ut per organum habet le quo*.

13,21. For *hoc* conjecture *haec*.

15,57–8. For *in nobis consimiliter, dicimus quod non est quae in materia pulchritudo sincera? Non* read *in nobis? Similiter dicimus quod non est quae in materia pulchritudo sincera; non.*

18,31. For *sensitivis* conjecture *sensiteriis*.

18,34. For *operationes ea* punctuate *operationes, ea*.

19,49–50. For *ad distinctionem et differentiam perfecti intellectus* read *ad distinctionem perfecti et divini intellectus*.

20,90. For *sensus, qui* punctuate *sensus qui*.

21,98. For *actuans, hoc est* punctuate *actuans hoc, est*.

22,23. For *ipsa separata* understand *ipsae separatae*.

23,28. For *Praedicamento* understand *Praedicamentis*.

24,71. For *operationis* read *operans*.

26,23–4. For *reliquit nobis quod 'carni esse' sine materia; non* read *reliquit*

135

nobis subintelligendum quod 'carni esse' sine materia est; quare si hoc quidem cum materia, hoc autem sine materia, non.

27,39. For *hoc* conjecture *haec*, and possibly continue understanding *sensitivo* [[*cognoscitivo*]] *cognoscimus* [['sensitivo' *autem dicit*]], *ex his autem caro, et carnem.*

27,61. For *In abstractione, ait, mathematica, et* punctuate *In abstractione ait mathematica; et.*

28,66. For *omnis* read *omni.*

29,57. For *intelligeret* understand and probably read *intelliget.*

30,18. For *ipsum* understand *idem.*

30,25. For *erunt igitur, quoniam* punctuate *erunt; igitur quoniam.*

31,42. For *dicitur* understand *dicuntur.*

31,45–6. For *accipiens* understand *accipit.*

31,54. After *enim* add *et.*

32,57. After *illa,* add *puta.*

32,66. For *haec* conjecture *hoc.*

33,75. For *sit* conjecture *fit.*

33,95. Delete colon after *veritatem.*

34,10. For *incorporea in subiecto aut corpore* conjecture *incorporeorum in subiecto autem corpore.*

35,30–1. For **aliquis**. *Adhuc enim ait: dubitabit* punctuate **aliquis**; *adhuc enim, ait, dubitabit.*

39,17. For *et cognitione* understand *cognitionis* and see note ad loc.

40,39–40. For *habente. Non exercens autem habitum, hic* read *habente, non exercente autem habitum; hic.*

41,45. Delete *intellectus.*

44,28. For *suppositum* read *superpositum.*

46,80. For *illustrator* possibly conjecture *illustratio.*

46,87. For *agitur* read *sibi.*

46,87. For *itaque* read *utique.*

47,99. For *aliter quia neque* possibly conjecture *aliterque neque.*

47,12. For *affectibilem* conjecture *assectibilem.*

49,57. For *Cum dixisset* understand *Dixit.*

51,4. For *Si non* understand *Species.*

52,27. For *quare non* understand *quare.*

52,31. For *Unumquemque enim characterizat* understand *Unumquodque enim characterizatur.*

52,33. For *actum (actum illud esse quod aptum natum est)* conjecture and punctuate *actum illud esse quod aptum natum est.*

53,46. For *quod* understand *quo* or *secundum quod.*

53,50. After *substantiae* understand *sic et intellectus characterizatur suae substantiae,* and after *non* understand *secundum.*

53,63. For *aiunt* understand *ait.*

54,70–5. For *est, si ... est. Si igitur* punctuate *est. Si enim ... attingat, impossibile autem ... ad haec – quod enim ... impossibile est –, si igitur ....*

55,21–2. For *quando fit securis* understand *quando fit putrefactio.*

55,24–6. For *actum; propter quod autem non dixit 'velut ars ad artificiale sustinuit', sed 'ad materiam', sed hoc quidem hypotelesma* read and punctuate *actum. Propter quid autem non dixit 'velut ars ad artificiale sustinuit', sed ad 'materiam'? Sed hoc quidem apotelesma.*

57,63. For *videbantur* conjecture *videbatur*.

57,65. For *hoc* conjecture *hic*.

58,86–7. For *omnia. Manifestat 'enim' coniunctio causalis ens, ut* punctuate *omnia, manifestat 'enim' coniunctio causalis ens. Ut.*

58,88. After *characterizatum* understand *non secundum id quod potentia*, and for *actu. Huius* punctuate *actu, huius.*

59,10. Delete *et.*

59,22. For *perierunt; salvati sunt autem aliquando aut* conjecture and punctuate *perierunt, salvati sunt autem alii, aut.*

60,50–1. For *dicit utique: morion (idest partem) de morio (idest parte); parte enim* probably understand *dicit utique 'solum'; 'de parte' enim.*

61,85. For *in intelligibilibus et divinis theoriae* understand *in intelligibilium et divinorum theoria.*

62,91. For *contrahentem* conjecture *contratrahentem.*

62,12. For *circumtrahens* understand *circumtrahentem*, and see note ad loc.

63,18. For *mitram* understand *bonam vitam.*

63,19–20. For *contrahat intellectum; immo e contrario, hanc sicut opadon bene scientem sequi ad illum et* read and punctuate *contratrahat intellectum, immo e contrario, hanc sicut opadon bene scientem sequi ad illum, et.*

64,53. For *dico, terminis propositio* punctuate *dico terminis, propositio.*

65,64. After *uniuscuiusque* add *enim.*

65,65. For *corrumpitur* read *corrumpit et.*

66,73. After *ipso* delete *intelligibilium.*

67,8. For *indivisibile* conjecture *indivisibiliter.*

68,34. Before *non inest* add *quod.*

69,67. For *tempus. Praesens autem nunc, hoc* punctuate *tempus, praesens autem nunc. Hoc.*

70,87. For *dixit* understand *dixi.*

71,9. For *vivificans* read *unificans.*

71,19. For *condivisam* read *contradivisam.*

73,46. For *regula* read *tegula.*

73,61. For *tempus* possibly understand *temporis.*

74,78. For *non unum et* punctuate *non unum, et.*

74,90. For *indivisibile* read *indivisibilis.*

74,91. For *substantiale intelligitur. Igitur et hoc ait secundum* punctuate *substantiale. Intelligitur igitur et hoc, ait, secundum.*

75,99. For *Si quae* read *Sique.*

75,9. For *in divisibilibus* read *indivisibilibus.*

75,27. For *In quo intelligimus, ait, talia? Hoc est: secundum* read and punctuate *Quo intelligimus, ait, talia, hoc est secundum.*

76,41–5. For *divisibiles sunt. Sunt autem divisibiles secundum se (secundum hoc intellectus et tempus indivisibiles sunt, hoc est secundum se), secundum quod autem ille indivisibles. Sunt autem indivisibiles secundum accidens, adventiciam habentes unionem et non essentialem. Secundum* read and punctuate *divisibiles sunt, sunt autem divisibiles secundum se, secundum hoc intellectus et tempus indivisibiles sunt, hoc est secundum se, secundum quod autem illae indivisibiles, sunt autem indivisibiles secundum accidens, adventiciam habentes unionem et non essentialem, secundum. . . .*

78,12. After *secundum* delete *actum.*

79,35. Before *et vox* add *sed inquantum nomen.*

80,72. For *est indivisibile* understand *sunt indivisibilia.*

81,85. For *ut species secundum se indivisibile* read *ut species indivisibile, secundum se.*

81,91. Before *nocti* add *et nigrae.*

82,13. For *in* before *inesse* conjecture *et.*

82,32. For *etenim* understand *etsi enim.*

83,34. For *ipsum* read *ipsa.*

83,50. For *et quod oportet* conjecture *ut et oporteat.*

84,56. For *cognoscimus* perhaps understand *cognitum.*

84,58. For *talium* understand *causarum.*

84,73. For *oportet* understand *semper.*

85,1. For *quando* read *quoniam.*

85,1. For *condictive* read *conditive* (Mansion).

87,41. For *dispositionem* conjecture *disponi.*

88,69. Probably delete *et.*

88,74. For *comparationem* possibly read *operationem.*

89,85–95. Punctuate *Si enim ... ad falsum* as one sentence, and put the words *materialium ... sunt* (88–94) between dashes.

90,30. For *essentiam. Cum* punctuate *essentiam, cum.*

91,61. For *sic* read *sit.*

93,99–3. For *aut* at 93,00 read *autem* and punctuate from *sed ut* to *in intellectu* as one sentence.

93,5. For *sit* conjecture *sic.*

93,15. For *huic* read *hinc.*

94,25–6. For *discretione sola sentitur, et igneae essentiae* understand *discretionem solam sentit et igneam essentiam.*

94,32. For *'phasim', compositum totam* punctuate *'phasim' compositum, totam. ...*

94,38. For *negaverit, molestata fugit* punctuate *negaverit molestata, fugit.*

94,50. For *Hoc* conjecture *Haec.*

95,51. For *aut calida* understand *inquantum calida.*

95,59–60. Punctuate *appetitum autem dicit ... contristante* as a parenthesis.

95,75. For *in aliquo* conjecture *modo aliquo.*

96,82. For *iudicans* understand *iudicante.*

96,84. For *anima* read *animali.*

96,96. For *Unde dico autem* punctuate *Unde, dico autem.*

97,1. For *quidem* understand *in.*

98,41. For *quod* conjecture *quot.*

99,52. For *sensitivorum* conjecture *sensiteriorum.*

99,54. For *sensitivo* conjecture *sensiterio.*

99,58. For *unum est quidem* read and conjecture *unum quidem est <et>.*

100,93–4. For *omnium sensuum, aliquando* read and punctuate *omnium, sensum aliquando.*

102,45. For *ut* read *ut et.*

102,46–7. Punctuate *Secundum quid ... eadem sunt* as a statement, not a question.

103,50. For *substantiam* read *subiectum.*

103,71. Before *contraria* add *et.*

103,71–2. For *in his eadem ratio, et in pluribus* punctuate *in his, eadem ratio et in pluribus.*

105,8. For *quomodo* understand *quod.*

108,73–5. For *intelligit. Velut ... circulum), sic* punctuate *intelligit velut ... circulum); sic.*

109,6–7. For *specie quando intelligit, ut* punctuate *specie, quando intelligit, ut.*

109,11. For *quod enim* understand *quod.*

110,32. For *species modis omnibus, cum sint* punctuate *species, modis omnibus cum sint.*

110,37–111, 48. Punctuate *Deinde ... a corpore intellectus* as one sentence.

111,53. For *non aliud aliquid* understand *non alium aliquem.*

111,67. For *assumit* read *consummat.*

112,85–6. For **aliqualiter**. *Similiter et in sensu, hoc est modo quodam <entium> omnium* read and punctuate **aliqualiter** *– similiter et in sensu – hoc est modo quodam <ipsam> omnium.*

112,88. After *hoc* add *<est>.*

113,93. For *actus* read *actu.*

113,98. For *hoc habet* read *haec sunt.*

114,18–28. Punctuate *Quoniam ... non indigere organo* as a single interrogative sentence.

114,27. For *enim* read *igitur.*

114,28. For *hoc igitur propter causam praemissorum exponit* understand *hoc igitur diiudicans per praemissa exponit.*

114,28. For *Quando* conjecture *Quoniam.*

115,54. For *habens* read *habemus.*

116,66. For *reducuntur* understand *reducimur.*

116,67–9. For *speculationem? Sine ... devenire; quomodo* punctuate *speculationem, sine ... devenire? Quomodo.*

116,72. For *multo utique magis* probably read *multo magis neque.*

117,99. For *sensu* read *sensus.*

117,3. After *necesse* add *simul.*

118,23. For *assumatis* read *consummatis.*

118,34. After *phantasmata sunt* add *quaerere.*

118,38. For *supermaiora* conjecture *semper maiora.*

119,56. For *ens* understand *erit.*

Appendix

The Commentators*

The 15,000 pages of the Ancient Greek Commentaries on Aristotle
are the largest corpus of Ancient Greek philosophy that has not
been translated into English or other modern European languages.
The standard edition (*Commentaria in Aristotelem Graeca*, or *CAG*)
was produced by Hermann Diels as general editor under the aus-
pices of the Prussian Academy in Berlin. Arrangements have now
been made to translate at least a large proportion of this corpus,
along with some other Greek and Latin commentaries not included
in the Berlin edition, and some closely related non-commentary
works by the commentators.

The works are not just commentaries on Aristotle, although they
are invaluable in that capacity too. One of the ways of doing philosophy between A.D. 200 and 600, when the most important items
were produced, was by writing commentaries. The works therefore
represent the thought of the Peripatetic and Neoplatonist schools,
as well as expounding Aristotle. Furthermore, they embed fragments from all periods of Ancient Greek philosophical thought:
this is how many of the Presocratic fragments were assembled, for
example. Thus they provide a panorama of every period of Ancient
Greek philosophy.

The philosophy of the period from A.D. 200 to 600 has not yet
been intensively explored by philosophers in English-speaking
countries, yet it is full of interest for physics, metaphysics, logic,
psychology, ethics and religion. The contrast with the study of
the Presocratics is striking. Initially the incomplete Presocratic
fragments might well have seemed less promising, but their interest
is now widely known, thanks to the philological and philosophical
effort that has been concentrated upon them. The incomparably
vaster corpus which preserved so many of those fragments offers at
least as much interest, but is still relatively little known.

The commentaries represent a missing link in the history of
philosophy: the Latin-speaking Middle Ages obtained their knowledge of Aristotle at least partly through the medium of the com-

* Reprinted from the Editor's General Introduction to the series in Christian
Wildberg, *Philoponus Against Aristotle on the Eternity of the World*, London and
Ithaca N.Y., 1987.

mentaries. Without an appreciation of this, mediaeval interpretations of Aristotle will not be understood. Again, the ancient commentaries are the unsuspected source of ideas which have been thought, wrongly, to originate in the later mediaeval period. It has been supposed, for example, that Bonaventure in the thirteenth century invented the ingenious arguments based on the concept of infinity which attempt to prove the Christian view that the universe had a beginning. In fact, Bonaventure is merely repeating arguments devised by the commentator Philoponus 700 years earlier and preserved in the meantime by the Arabs. Bonaventure even uses Philoponus' original examples. Again, the introduction of impetus theory into dynamics, which has been called a scientific revolution, has been held to be an independent invention of the Latin West, even if it was earlier discovered by the Arabs or their predecessors. But recent work has traced a plausible route by which it could have passed from Philoponus, via the Arabs, to the West.

The new availability of the commentaries in the sixteenth century, thanks to printing and to fresh Latin translations, helped to fuel the Renaissance break from Aristotelian science. For the commentators record not only Aristotle's theories, but also rival ones, while Philoponus as a Christian devises rival theories of his own and accordingly is mentioned in Galileo's early works more frequently than Plato.[1]

It is not only for their philosophy that the works are of interest. Historians will find information about the history of schools, their methods of teaching and writing and the practices of an oral tradition.[2] Linguists will find the indexes and translations an aid for studying the development of word meanings, almost wholly

---

[1] See Fritz Zimmermann, 'Philoponus' impetus theory in the Arabic tradition'; Charles Schmitt, 'Philoponus' commentary on Aristotle's *Physics* in the sixteenth century', and Richard Sorabji, 'John Philoponus', in Richard Sorabji (ed.), *Philoponus and the Rejection of Aristotelian Science* (London and Ithaca, N.Y. 1987).

[2] See e.g. Karl Praechter, 'Die griechischen Aristoteleskommentare', *Byzantinische Zeitschrift* 18 (1909), 516–38; M. Plezia, *de Commentariis Isagogicis* (Cracow 1947); M. Richard, '*Apo Phônês*', *Byzantion* 20 (1950), 191–222; E. Evrard, *L'Ecole d'Olympiodore et la composition du commentaire à la physique de Jean Philopon*, Diss. (Liège 1957); L. G. Westerink, *Anonymous Prolegomena to Platonic Philosophy* (Amsterdam 1962) (new revised edition, translated into French, Collection Budé, forthcoming); A.-J. Festugière, 'Modes de composition des commentaires de Proclus', *Museum Helveticum* 20 (1963), 77–100, repr. in his *Études* (1971), 551–74; P. Hadot, 'Les divisions des parties de la philosophie dans l'antiquité', *Museum Helveticum* 36 (1979), 201–23; I. Hadot, 'La division néoplatonicienne des écrits d'Aristote', in J. Wiesner (ed.), *Aristoteles Werk und Wirkung* (Paul Moraux gewidmet), vol. 2 (Berlin 1986); I. Hadot, 'Les introductions aux commentaires exégétiques chez les auteurs néoplatoniciens et les auteurs chrétiens', in M. Tardieu (ed.), *Les règles de l'interprétation* (Paris 1987), 99–119. These topics will be treated, and a bibliography supplied, in a collection of articles on the commentators in general.

uncharted in Liddell and Scott's *Lexicon*, and for checking shifts in grammatical usage.

Given the wide range of interests to which the volumes will appeal, the aim is to produce readable translations, and to avoid so far as possible presupposing any knowledge of Greek. Footnotes will explain points of meaning, give cross-references to other works, and suggest alternative interpretations of the text where the translator does not have a clear preference. The introduction to each volume will include an explanation why the work was chosen for translation: none will be chosen simply because it is there. Two of the Greek texts are currently being re-edited – those of Simplicius *in Physica* and *in de Caelo* – and new readings will be exploited by translators as they become available. Each volume will also contain a list of proposed emendations to the standard text. Indexes will be of more uniform extent as between volumes than is the case with the Berlin edition, and there will be three of them: an English–Greek glossary, a Greek–English index, and a subject index.

The commentaries fall into three main groups. The first group is by authors in the Aristotelian tradition up to the fourth century A.D. This includes the earliest extant commentary, that by Aspasius in the first half of the second century A.D. on the *Nicomachean Ethics*. The anonymous commentary on Books 2, 3, 4 and 5 of the *Nicomachean Ethics*, in *CAG* vol. 20, is derived from Adrastus, a generation later.[3] The commentaries by Alexander of Aphrodisias (appointed to his chair between A.D. 198 and 209) represent the fullest flowering of the Aristotelian tradition. To his successors Alexander was The Commentator *par excellence*. To give but one example (not from a commentary) of his skill at defending and elaborating Aristotle's views, one might refer to his defence of Aristotle's claim that space is finite against the objection that an edge of space is conceptually problematic.[4] Themistius (*fl.* late 340s to 384 or 385) saw himself as the inventor of paraphrase, wrongly thinking that the job of commentary was completed.[5] In fact, the Neoplatonists were to introduce new dimensions into commentary. Themistius' own relation to the Neoplatonist as opposed to the

[3] Anthony Kenny, *The Aristotelian Ethics* (Oxford 1978), 37, n. 3; Paul Moraux, *Der Aristotelismus bei den Griechen*, vol. 2 (Berlin 1984), 323–30.

[4] Alexander, *Quaestiones* 3.12, discussed in my *Matter, Space and Motion* (London and Ithaca, N.Y. 1988). For Alexander see R. W. Sharples, 'Alexander of Aphrodisias: scholasticism and innovation', in W. Haase (ed.), *Aufstieg und Niedergang der römischen Welt*; part 2 *Principat*, vol. 36.2, *Philosophie und Wissenschaften* (1987).

[5] Themistius *in An. Post.* 1,2–12. See H. J. Blumenthal, 'Photius on Themistius (Cod. 74): did Themistius write commentaries on Aristotle?', *Hermes* 107 (1979), 168–82.

Aristotelian tradition is a matter of controversy,[6] but it would be agreed that his commentaries show far less bias than the full-blown Neoplatonist ones. They are also far more informative than the designation 'paraphrase' might suggest, and it has been estimated that Philoponus' *Physics* commentary draws silently on Themistius six hundred times.[7] The pseudo-Alexandrian commentary on *Metaphysics* 6–14, of unknown authorship, has been placed by some in the same group of commentaries as being earlier than the fifth century.[8]

By far the largest group of extant commentaries is that of the Neoplatonists up to the sixth century A.D. Nearly all the major Neoplatonists, apart from Plotinus (the founder of Neoplatonism), wrote commentaries on Aristotle, although those of Iamblichus (*c.* 250 – *c.* 325) survive only in fragments, and those of three Athenians, Plutarchus (died 432), his pupil Proclus (410 – 485) and the Athenian Damascius (*c.* 462 – after 538), are lost.[9] As a result of these losses, most of the extant Neoplatonist commentaries come from the late fifth and the sixth centuries and a good proportion from Alexandria. There are commentaries by Plotinus' disciple and editor Porphyry (232 – 309), by Iamblichus' pupil Dexippus (*c.* 330), by Proclus' teacher Syrianus (died *c.* 437), by Proclus' pupil Ammonius (435/445 – 517/526), by Ammonius' three pupils Philoponus (*c.* 490 to 570s), Simplicius (wrote after 532, probably after 538) and Asclepius (sixth century), by Ammonius' next but one successor

---

[6] For different views, see H. J. Blumenthal, 'Themistius, the last Peripatetic commentator on Aristotle?', in Glen W. Bowersock, Walter Burkert, Michael C. J. Putnam, *Arktouros*, Hellenic Studies Presented to Bernard M. W. Knox (Berlin and N.Y., 1979), 391–400; E. P. Mahoney, 'Themistius and the agent intellect in James of Viterbo and other thirteenth-century philosophers: (Saint Thomas Aquinas, Siger of Brabant and Henry Bate)', *Augustiniana* 23 (1973), 422–67, at 428–31; id., 'Neoplatonism, the Greek commentators and Renaissance Aristotelianism', in D. J. O'Meara (ed.), *Neoplatonism and Christian Thought* (Albany N.Y. 1982), 169–77 and 264–82, esp. n. 1, 264–6; Robert Todd, introduction to translation of Themistius *in DA 3, 4–8*, forthcoming in a collection of translations by Frederick Schroeder and Robert Todd of material in the commentators relating to the intellect.

[7] H. Vitelli, *CAG* 17, p. 992, s.v. Themistius.

[8] The similarities to Syrianus (died *c.* 437) have suggested to some that it predates Syrianus (most recently Leonardo Tarán, review of Paul Moraux, *Der Aristotelismus*, vol. 1, in *Gnomon* 46 (1981), 721–50 at 750), to others that it draws on him (most recently P. Thillet, in the Budé edition of Alexander *de Fato*, p. lvii). Praechter ascribed it to Michael of Ephesus (eleventh or twelfth century), in his review of *CAG* 22.2 in *Göttingische Gelehrte Anzeiger* 168 (1906), 861–907.

[9] The Iamblichus fragments are collected in Greek by Bent Dalsgaard Larsen, *Jamblique de Chalcis, Exégète et Philosophe* (Aarhus 1972), vol. 2. Most are taken from Simplicius, and will accordingly be translated in due course. The evidence on Damascius' commentaries is given in L. G. Westerink, *The Greek Commentaries on Plato's Phaedo*, vol. 2, Damascius (Amsterdam 1977), 11–12; on Proclus' in L. G. Westerink, *Anonymous Prolegomena to Platonic Philosophy* (Amsterdam 1962), xii, n. 22; on Plutarchus' in H. M. Blumenthal, 'Neoplatonic elements in the de Anima commentaries', *Phronesis* 21 (1976), 75.

Olympiodorus (495/505 – after 565), by Elias (*fl.* 541?), by David (second half of the sixth century, or beginning of the seventh) and by Stephanus (took the chair in Constantinople *c.* 610). Further, a commentary on the *Nicomachean Ethics* has been ascribed to Heliodorus of Prusa, an unknown pre-fourteenth-century figure, and there is a commentary by Simplicius' colleague Priscian of Lydia on Aristotle's successor Theophrastus. Of these commentators some of the last were Christians (Philoponus, Elias, David and Stephanus), but they were Christians writing in the Neoplatonist tradition, as was also Boethius who produced a number of commentaries in Latin before his death in 525 or 526.

The third group comes from a much later period in Byzantium. The Berlin edition includes only three out of more than a dozen commentators described in Hunger's *Byzantinisches Handbuch*.[10] The two most important are Eustratius (1050/1060 – *c.* 1120), and Michael of Ephesus. It has been suggested that these two belong to a circle organised by the princess Anna Comnena in the twelfth century, and accordingly the completion of Michael's commentaries has been redated from 1040 to 1138.[11] His commentaries include areas where gaps had been left. Not all of these gap-fillers are extant, but we have commentaries on the neglected biological works, on the *Sophistici Elenchi*, and a small fragment of one on the *Politics*. The lost *Rhetoric* commentary had a few antecedents, but the *Rhetoric* too had been comparatively neglected. Another product of this period may have been the composite commentary on the *Nicomachean Ethics* (*CAG* 20) by various hands, including Eustratius and Michael, along with some earlier commentators, and an improvisation for Book 7. Whereas Michael follows Alexander and the conventional Aristotelian tradition, Eustratius' commentary introduces Platonist, Christian and anti-Islamic elements.[12]

The composite commentary was to be translated into Latin in the next century by Robert Grosseteste in England. But Latin trans-

[10] Herbert Hunger, *Die hochsprachliche profane Literatur der Byzantiner*, vol. 1 (= *Byzantinisches Handbuch*, part 5, vol. 1) (Munich 1978), 25–41. See also B. N. Tatakis, *La Philosophie Byzantine* (Paris 1949).

[11] R. Browning, 'An unpublished funeral oration on Anna Comnena', *Proceedings of the Cambridge Philological Society* n.s. 8 (1962), 1–12, esp. 6–7.

[12] R. Browning, op. cit. H. D. P. Mercken, *The Greek Commentaries of the Nicomachean Ethics of Aristotle in the Latin Translation of Grosseteste, Corpus Latinum Commentariorum in Aristotelem Graecorum* VI 1 (Leiden 1973), ch. 1, 'The compilation of Greek commentaries on Aristotle's Nicomachean Ethics'. Sten Ebbesen, 'Anonymi Aurelianensis I Commentarium in *Sophisticos Elenchos*', *Cahiers de l'Institut Moyen Age Grecque et Latin* 34 (1979), 'Boethius, Jacobus Veneticus, Michael Ephesius and "Alexander" ', pp. v–xiii; id., *Commentators and Commentaries on Aristotle's Sophistici Elenchi*, 3 parts, *Corpus Latinum Commentariorum in Aristotelem Graecorum*, vol. 7 (Leiden 1981); A. Preus, *Aristotle and Michael of Ephesus on the Movement and Progression of Animals* (Hildesheim 1981), introduction

lations of various logical commentaries were made from the Greek still earlier by James of Venice (*fl. c.* 1130), a contemporary of Michael of Ephesus, who may have known him in Constantinople. And later in that century other commentaries and works by commentators were being translated from Arabic versions by Gerard of Cremona (died 1187).[13] So the twelfth century resumed the transmission which had been interrupted at Boethius' death in the sixth century.

The Neoplatonist commentaries of the main group were initiated by Porphyry. His master Plotinus had discussed Aristotle, but in a very independent way, devoting three whole treatises (*Enneads* 6.1–3) to attacking Aristotle's classification of the things in the universe into categories. These categories took no account of Plato's world of Ideas, were inferior to Plato's classifications in the *Sophist* and could anyhow be collapsed, some of them into others. Porphyry replied that Aristotle's categories could apply perfectly well to the world of intelligibles and he took them as in general defensible.[14] He wrote two commentaries on the *Categories*, one lost, and an introduction to it, the *Isagôgê*, as well as commentaries, now lost, on a number of other Aristotelian works. This proved decisive in making Aristotle a necessary subject for Neoplatonist lectures and commentary. Proclus, who was an exceptionally quick student, is said to have taken two years over his Aristotle studies, which were called the Lesser Mysteries, and which preceded the Greater Mysteries of Plato.[15] By the time of Ammonius, the commentaries reflect a teaching curriculum which begins with Porphyry's *Isagôgê* and Aristotle's *Categories*, and is explicitly said to have as its final goal a (mystical) ascent to the supreme Neoplatonist deity, the One.[16] The curriculum would have progressed from Aristotle to

[13] For Grosseteste, see Mercken as in n. 12. For James of Venice, see Ebbesen as in n. 12, and L. Minio-Paluello, 'Jacobus Veneticus Grecus', *Traditio* 8 (1952), 265–304; id., 'Giacomo Veneto e l'Aristotelismo Latino', in Pertusi (ed.), *Venezia e l'Oriente fra tardo Medioevo e Rinascimento* (Florence 1966), 53–74, both reprinted in his *Opuscula* (1972). For Gerard of Cremona, see M. Steinschneider, *Die europäischen Übersetzungen aus dem arabischen bis Mitte des 17. Jahrhunderts* (repr. Graz 1956); E. Gilson, *History of Christian Philosophy in the Middle Ages* (London 1955), 235–6 and more generally 181–246. For the translators in general, see Bernard G. Dod, 'Aristoteles Latinus', in N. Kretzmann, A. Kenny, J. Pinborg (eds). *The Cambridge History of Latin Medieval Philosophy* (Cambridge 1982).

[14] See P. Hadot, 'L'harmonie des philosophies de Plotin et d'Aristote selon Porphyre dans le commentaire de Dexippe sur les Catégories', in *Plotino e il neoplatonismo in Oriente e in Occidente* (Rome 1974), 31–47; A. C. Lloyd, 'Neoplatonic logic and Aristotelian logic', *Phronesis* 1 (1955–6), 58–79 and 146–60.

[15] Marinus, *Life of Proclus* ch. 13, 157,41 (Boissonade).

[16] The introductions to the *Isagôgê* by Ammonius, Elias and David, and to the *Categories* by Ammonius, Simplicius, Philoponus, Olympiodorus and Elias are discussed by L. G. Westerink, *Anonymous Prolegomena* and I. Hadot, 'Les Introductions', see n. 2, above.

Plato, and would have culminated in Plato's *Timaeus* and *Parmenides*. The latter was read as being about the One, and both works were established in this place in the curriculum at least by the time of Iamblichus, if not earlier.[17]

Before Porphyry, it had been undecided how far a Platonist should accept Aristotle's scheme of categories. But now the proposition began to gain force that there was a harmony between Plato and Aristotle on most things.[18] Not for the only time in the history of philosophy, a perfectly crazy proposition proved philosophically fruitful. The views of Plato and of Aristotle had both to be transmuted into a new Neoplatonist philosophy in order to exhibit the supposed harmony. Iamblichus denied that Aristotle contradicted Plato on the theory of Ideas.[19] This was too much for Syrianus and his pupil Proclus. While accepting harmony in many areas,[20] they could see that there was disagreement on this issue and also on the issue of whether God was causally responsible for the existence of the ordered physical cosmos, which Aristotle denied. But even on these issues, Proclus' pupil Ammonius was to claim harmony, and, though the debate was not clear cut,[21] his claim was on the whole to prevail. Aristotle, he maintained, accepted Plato's Ideas,[22] at least in the form of principles (*logoi*) in the divine intellect, and these principles were in turn causally responsible for the beginningless existence of the physical universe. Ammonius wrote a whole book to show that Aristotle's God was thus an efficient cause, and though the book is lost, some of its principal arguments are pre-

---

[17] Proclus *in Alcibiadem 1* p.11 (Creuzer); Westerink, *Anonymous Prolegomena*, ch. 26, 12f. For the Neoplatonist curriculum see Westerink, Festugière, P. Hadot and I. Hadot in n. 2.

[18] See e.g. P. Hadot (1974), as in n. 14 above; H. J. Blumenthal, 'Neoplatonic elements in the de Anima commentaries', *Phronesis* 21 (1976), 64–87; H. A. Davidson, 'The principle that a finite body can contain only finite power', in S. Stein and R. Loewe (eds), *Studies in Jewish Religious and Intellectual History presented to A. Altmann* (Alabama 1979), 75–92; Carlos Steel, 'Proclus et Aristote', Proceedings of the Congrès Proclus held in Paris 1985, J. Pépin and H. D. Saffrey (eds), *Proclus, lecteur et interprète des anciens* (Paris 1987), 213–25; Koenraad Verrycken, *God en Wereld in de Wijsbegeerte van Ioannes Philoponus*, Ph.D., Diss. (Louvain, 1985).

[19] Iamblichus ap. Elian *in Cat.* 123,1–3.

[20] Syrianus *in Metaph.* 80,4–7; Proclus *in Tim.* 1.6,21–7,16.

[21] Asclepius sometimes accepts Syranius' interpretation (*in Metaph.* 433,9–436,6); which is, however, qualified, since Syrianus thinks Aristotle is really committed willy-nilly to much of Plato's view (*in Metaph.* 117,25–118,11; ap. Asclepium *in Metaph.* 433,16; 450,22); Philoponus repents of his early claim that Plato is not the target of Aristotle's attack, and accepts that Plato is rightly attacked for treating ideas as independent entities outside the divine Intellect (*in DA* 37,18–31; *in Phys.* 225,4–226,11; *contra Procl.* 26,24–32,13; *in An. Post.* 242,14–243,25).

[22] Asclepius *in Metaph.* from the voice of (i.e. from the lectures of) Ammonius 69,17–21; 71,28; cf. Zacharias *Ammonius, Patrologia Graeca* vol. 85, col. 952 (Colonna).

served by Simplicius.[23] This tradition helped to make it possible for Aquinas to claim Aristotle's God as a Creator, albeit not in the sense of giving the universe a beginning, but in the sense of being causally responsible for its beginningless existence.[24] Thus what started as a desire to harmonise Aristotle with Plato finished by making Aristotle safe for Christianity. In Simplicius, who goes further than anyone,[25] it is a formally stated duty of the commentator to display the harmony of Plato and Aristotle in most things.[26] Philoponus, who with his independent mind had thought better of his earlier belief in harmony, is castigated by Simplicius for neglecting this duty.[27]

The idea of harmony was extended beyond Plato and Aristotle to Plato and the Presocratics. Plato's pupils Speusippus and Xenocrates saw Plato as being in the Pythagorean tradition.[28] From the third to first centuries B.C., pseudo-Pythagorean writings present Platonic and Aristotelian doctrines as if they were the ideas of Pythagoras and his pupils,[29] and these forgeries were later taken by the Neoplatonists as genuine. Plotinus saw the Presocratics as precursors of his own views,[30] but Iamblichus went far beyond him by writing ten volumes on Pythagorean philosophy.[31] Thereafter Proclus sought to unify the whole of Greek philosophy by presenting it as a continuous clarification of divine revelation,[32] and Simplicius argued for the same general unity in order to rebut Christian charges of contradictions in pagan philosophy.[33]

Later Neoplatonist commentaries tend to reflect their origin in a teaching curriculum:[34] from the time of Philoponus, the discussion is often divided up into lectures, which are subdivided into studies of doctrine and of text. A general account of Aristotle's philosophy

---

[23] Simplicius *in Phys.* 1361,11–1363,12. See H. A. Davidson; Carlos Steel; Koenraad Verrycken in n.18 above.

[24] See Richard Sorabji, *Matter, Space and Motion* (London and Ithaca N.Y. 1988), ch. 15.

[25] See e.g. H. J. Blumenthal in n. 18 above.

[26] Simplicius *in Cat.* 7,23–32.

[27] Simplicius *in Cael.* 84,11–14; 159,2–9. On Philoponus' *volte face* see n. 21 above.

[28] See e.g. Walter Burkert, *Weisheit und Wissenschaft* (Nürnberg 1962), translated as *Lore and Science in Ancient Pythagoreanism* (Cambridge Mass. 1972), 83–96.

[29] See Holger Thesleff, *An Introduction to the Pythagorean writings of the Hellenistic Period* (Åbo 1961); Thomas Alexander Szlezák, *Pseudo-Archytas über die Kategorien*, Peripatoi vol. 4 (Berlin and New York 1972).

[30] Plotinus e.g. 4.8.1; 5.1.8 (10–27): 5.1.9.

[31] See Dominic O'Meara, *Pythagoras Revived: Mathematics and Philosophy in late Antiquity* (Oxford 1989).

[32] See Christian Guérard, 'Parménide d'Elée selon les Néoplatoniciens', forthcoming.

[33] Simplicius *in Phys.* 28,32–29,5; 640,12–18. Such thinkers as Epicurus and the Sceptics, however, were not subject to harmonisation.

[34] See the literature in n. 2 above.

is prefixed to the *Categories* commentaries and divided, according to a formula of Proclus,[35] into ten questions. It is here that commentators explain the eventual purpose of studying Aristotle (ascent to the One) and state (if they do) the requirement of displaying the harmony of Plato and Aristotle. After the ten-point introduction to Aristotle, the *Categories* is given a six-point introduction, whose antecedents go back earlier than Neoplatonism, and which requires the commentator to find a unitary theme or scope (*skopos*) for the treatise. The arrangements for late commentaries on Plato are similar. Since the Plato commentaries form part of a single curriculum they should be studied alongside those on Aristotle. Here the situation is easier, not only because the extant corpus is very much smaller, but also because it has been comparatively well served by French and English translators.[36]

Given the theological motive of the curriculum and the pressure to harmonise Plato with Aristotle, it can be seen how these commentaries are a major source for Neoplatonist ideas. This in turn means that it is not safe to extract from them the fragments of the Presocratics, or of other authors, without making allowance for the Neoplatonist background against which the fragments were originally selected for discussion. For different reasons, analogous warnings apply to fragments preserved by the pre-Neoplatonist commentator Alexander.[37] It will be another advantage of the present translations that they will make it easier to check the distorting effect of a commentator's background.

Although the Neoplatonist commentators conflate the views of Aristotle with those of Neoplatonism, Philoponus alludes to a certain convention when he quotes Plutarchus expressing disapproval of Alexander for expounding his own philosophical doctrines in a commentary on Aristotle.[38] But this does not stop Philoponus from later inserting into his own commentaries on the *Physics* and *Meteorology* his arguments in favour of the Christian view of Creation. Of course, the commentators also wrote independent works of their own, in which their views are expressed independently of

[35] ap. Elian *in Cat.* 107,24–6.

[36] English: Calcidius *in Tim.* (parts by van Winden; den Boeft); Iamblichus fragments (Dillon); Proclus *in Tim.* (Thomas Taylor); Proclus *in Parm.* (Dillon); Proclus *in Parm.*, end of 7th book, from the Latin (Klibansky, Labowsky, Anscombe); Proclus *in Alcib. 1* (O'Neill); Olympiodorus and Damascius *in Phaedonem* (Westerink); Damascius *in Philebum* (Westerink); *Anonymous Prolegomena to Platonic Philosophy* (Westerink). See also extracts in Thomas Taylor, *The Works of Plato*, 5 vols. (1804). French: Proclus *in Tim.* and *in Rempublicam* (Festugière); *in Parm.* (Chaignet); Anon. *in Parm.* (P. Hadot); Damascius *in Parm.* (Chaignet).

[37] For Alexander's treatment of the Stoics, see Robert B. Todd, *Alexander of Aphrodisias on Stoic Physics* (Leiden 1976), 24–9.

[38] Philoponus *in DA* 21,20–3.

the exegesis of Aristotle. Some of these independent works will be included in the present series of translations.

The distorting Neoplatonist context does not prevent the commentaries from being incomparable guides to Aristotle. The introductions to Aristotle's philosophy insist that commentators must have a minutely detailed knowledge of the entire Aristotelian corpus, and this they certainly have. Commentators are also enjoined neither to accept nor reject what Aristotle says too readily, but to consider it in depth and without partiality. The commentaries draw one's attention to hundreds of phrases, sentences and ideas in Aristotle, which one could easily have passed over, however often one read him. The scholar who makes the right allowance for the distorting context will learn far more about Aristotle than he would be likely to on his own.

The relations of Neoplatonist commentators to the Christians were subtle. Porphyry wrote a treatise explicitly against the Christians in 15 books, but an order to burn it was issued in 448, and later Neoplatonists were more circumspect. Among the last commentators in the main group, we have noted several Christians. Of these the most important were Boethius and Philoponus. It was Boethius' programme to transmit Greek learning to Latin-speakers. By the time of his premature death by execution, he had provided Latin translations of Aristotle's logical works, together with commentaries in Latin but in the Neoplatonist style on Porphyry's *Isagôgê* and on Aristotle's *Categories* and *de Interpretatione*, and interpretations of the *Prior* and *Posterior Analytics, Topics* and *Sophistici Elenchi*. The interruption of his work meant that knowledge of Aristotle among Latin-speakers was confined for many centuries to the logical works. Philoponus is important both for his proofs of the Creation and for his progressive replacement of Aristotelian science with rival theories, which were taken up at first by the Arabs and came fully into their own in the West only in the sixteenth century.

Recent work has rejected the idea that in Alexandria the Neoplatonists compromised with Christian monotheism by collapsing the distinction between their two highest deities, the One and the Intellect. Simplicius (who left Alexandria for Athens) and the Alexandrians Ammonius and Asclepius appear to have acknowledged their beliefs quite openly, as later did the Alexandrian Olympiodorus, despite the presence of Christian students in their classes.[39]

---

[39] For Simplicius, see I. Hadot, *Le Problème du Néoplatonisme Alexandrin: Hiéroclès et Simplicius* (Paris 1978); for Ammonius and Asclepius, Koenraad Verrycken, *God en Wereld in de Wijsbegeerte van Ioannes Philoponus*, Ph.D. Diss. (Louvain 1985); for Olympiodorus, L. G. Westerink, *Anonymous Prolegomena to Platonic Philosophy* (Amsterdam 1962).

The teaching of Simplicius in Athens and that of the whole pagan Neoplatonist school there was stopped by the Christian Emperor Justinian in 529. This was the very year in which the Christian Philoponus in Alexandria issued his proofs of Creation against the earlier Athenian Neoplatonist Proclus. Archaeological evidence has been offered that, after their temporary stay in Ctesiphon (in present-day Iraq), the Athenian Neoplatonists did not return to their house in Athens, and further evidence has been offered that Simplicius went to Harrān (Carrhae), in present-day Turkey near the Iraq border.[40] Wherever he went, his commentaries are a treasure house of information about the preceding thousand years of Greek philosophy, information which he painstakingly recorded after the closure in Athens, and which would otherwise have been lost. He had every reason to feel bitter about Christianity, and in fact he sees it and Philoponus, its representative, as irreverent. They deny the divinity of the heavens and prefer the physical relics of dead martyrs.[41] His own commentaries by contrast culminate in devout prayers.

Two collections of articles by various hands have been published, to make the work of the commentators better known. The first is devoted to Philoponus;[42] the second is about the commentators in general, and goes into greater detail on some of the issues briefly mentioned here.[43]

---

[40] Alison Frantz, 'Pagan philosophers in Christian Athens', *Proceedings of the American Philosophical Society* 119 (1975), 29–38; M. Tardieu, 'Témoins orientaux du *Premier Alcibiade* à Harrān et à Nag 'Hammādi', *Journal Asiatique* 274 (1986); id. 'Les calendriers en usage à Harrān d'après les sources arabes et le commentaire de Simplicius à la *Physique* d'Aristote', in I. Hadot (ed.), *Simplicius, sa vie, son oeuvre, sa survie* (Berlin 1987), 40–57; *Coutumes nautiques mésopotamiennes chez Simplicius*, in preparation. The opposing view that Simplicius returned to Athens is most fully argued by Alan Cameron, 'The last days of the Academy at Athens', *Proceedings of the Cambridge Philological Society* 195, n.s. 15 (1969), 7–29.

[41] Simplicius *in Cael.* 26,4–7; 70,16–18; 90,1–18; 370,29–371,4. See on his whole attitude Philippe Hoffmann, 'Simplicius' polemics', in Richard Sorabji (ed.), *Philoponus and the Rejection of Aristotelian Science* (London and Ithaca, N.Y. 1987).

[42] Richard Sorabji (ed.), *Philoponus and the Rejection of Aristotelian Science* (London and Ithaca, N.Y. 1987).

[43] Richard Sorabji (ed.), *Aristotle Transformed: the ancient commentators and their influence* (London and Ithaca, N.Y. 1990). The lists of texts and previous translations of the commentaries included in Wildberg, *Philoponus Against Aristotle on the Eternity of the World* (pp. 12ff.) are not included here. The list of translations should be augmented by: F. L. S. Bridgman, Heliodorus (?) in *Ethica Nicomachea*, London 1807.

I am grateful for comments to Henry Blumenthal, Victor Caston, I. Hadot, Paul Mercken, Alain Segonds, Robert Sharples, Robert Todd, L. G. Westerink and Christian Wildberg.

Indexes

English–Latin Glossary

absolutely: *simpliciter*
abstract, to: *abstrahere*
abstract: *ex abstractione, in abstractione*
abstraction: *ablatio, abstractio*
account: *ratio*
act, to: *agere*
action: *actio*
activates: *activus*
active, not to be: *quiescere*
activity: *actus, operatio*
activity, pure: *autoactus, autoenergeia*
actualise, to: *actuare*
actuality: *actus, endelichia*
adapted, to be: *adaptari*
adjacent, to be: *adiacere*
admixture: *admixtura*
adventitious: *adventicius*
affected, to be: *pati*
affected: *passivus, passibilis*
affection, being affected: *passio*
affected along with, to be: *compati*
affected along with, being: *compassio*
affected in return, to be: *contrapati*
affirm to: *affirmare*
affirmation: *affirmatio*
against, set over against: *contradivisus*
aggregate: *collectio*
air: *aer*
alter, to: *alterare*
alteration: *alteratio*
analagous, to be: *proportionare*
analagous: *proportionalis*
analogy: *analogia*
angel: *angelus*
angelic: *angelicus*
animal: *animal*
answer, final: *absolutio*
apart, to hold: *distendere*
appear, things which: *apparentia*
appear alongside, to: *inapparere*
appearance: *habitus*
appetition: *appetitus*
appetitive: *appetitivus*
arithmetic: *arithmetica*
art: *ars*
artifact: *artificiale*
ash: *cinis*
astronomy: *astronomia*

attack, to: *supervenire*
attain, to: *attingere*
attained, that which can be: *affectibilis*
attend, to: *assequi*
attending: *assectibilis*
audible: *audibilis*
aversion: *aversio*
avoid, to: *fugere*
avoidance: *fuga*
avoided, to be: *fugibilis*
avoids, that which: *fugitivum*

bad: *malus*
balanced mixture: *commensuratio*
bare: *nudus*
beautiful: *pulcher*
beauty: *pulchritudo*
becoming, world of: *generatio*
beginning: *principium*
being, manner of: *habitudo*
bend, to: *incurvare*
bent: *incurvatus*; not bent: *sine curvatione*
best, to be at its best with: *coalescere*
birth: *nativitas*
black: *niger*
bodily: *corporalis*
body: *corpus*
both at once: *simul uterque*
boundary: *terminus*
brain: *cerebrum*
brute (sc. animal): *brutum*
building, art of: *domificativa*
building, house-: *aedificativa*

categorical: *categoricus*
cause: *causa*
change, to: *movere, transmutare*
change: *motus*
changeable: *transmutabilis*; not changeable: *intransmutabilis*
characterize, to: *characterizare*
child: *puer*
choice: *electio*
choose, to: *eligere*
circle: *circulus*
circular: *circularis*

151

divine: *divinus*
divisible: *divisibilis, partibilis*
divisibility: *divisibilitas*
division: *divisio*
done, thing done: *agibile*
doubling over: *duplicatio*
doubt: *dubitatio*
drag over, to: *attrahere*
draw to self, to: *coattrahere*
drunkenness: *ebrietas*
duality: *dualitas*
duplication: *duplatio*
dyer: *tinctor*

eclipse: *eclipsis*
element: *elementum*
embrace, to: *comparare*
end: *finis, terminus*
enfeebled, to become: *marcescere*
enquiry, to conduct an: *percunctari*
equivocal: *aequivocus*
err, to: *peccare*
error: *peccatum*
essence: *essentia*
essential: *essentialis*
established, to be: *subsistere*
esteem, held in, estimable: *honorabilis*
eternal: *aesternus*
everlasting: *perpetuus*
evident, not evident: *immanifestus*
evil: *malum*
exact: *certus*
exalted: *eminens*
excess: *excellentia*
exemplar, as, in an exemplary way:
   exemplariter
exist, exist on its own, to: *subsistere*
exist in, to: *inexistere*
exist in advance, to: *praeexistere*
existence: *existentia, hypostasis*
experience: *experientia*
explanatory conjunction: *conjunctio
   causalis*
exposition: *theoria*
expound, to: *exserere*
extend along with, to: *condistendere*
extended: *distensus*
extension: *distentio*
external: *extrinsecus*
eye: *oculus*

face to face: *nudus*
false: *falsus*
falsely, to speak falsely, say what is
   false: *mentiri*
falsity: *falsitas, mendacium*
fancy, mere fancy: *ficticius*

fiery: *igneus*
fire: *ignis*
flavour: *sapor*
flesh: *caro*
flight: *discessio*
flood: *pluvia*
following on: *consequenter*
forget, to: *oblivisci*
forgetting: *oblivio*
form: *species, ratio*
formal: *formalis*
formless: *informis*
friendship: *amicitia*
function, to: *operari*; not to be
   functioning: *otiari*
function: *opus*
functioning: *operatio*; not functioning:
   otium
functioning of understanding: *motus
   intelligentiae*
functionless: *inoperosus*
future: *futurus*

gather, to: *colligere*
gender: *genus*
generable: *generabilis*
general: *generalis*
generate, to: *generare*
generates, that which: *generativum*
generation: *generatio*
genuine: *sincerus*
genuinely: *sincere*
genus: *genus*
geometer: *geometra*
geometry: *geometria, geometrica*
glass: *vitrum*
God: *Deus*
good: *bonus*
grasp, to: *percipere, comprehendere*
graspable: *perceptibilis*
grasping: *perceptio*
grasps, apt to grasp: *perceptivus*
growth, that which produces:
   augmentativum

hand: *manus*
happen, happened earlier: *praefactum*
harmful: *nocens, nocivus*
health, state of health: *sanitas*
hearing: *auditus*
heart: *cor*
heat: *caliditas*
heavenly: *caelestis*
heavens: *caelum*
help, to: *cooperari*
hidden: *occultus*
hide, to: *occultare*

highest: *summus*
hinder, to: *impedire*
hollow: *curvus*
homeomerous component: *homeomeria*
honourable: *dignus*
human: *humanus, hominis*
human being: *homo*

idea: *idea*
illuminate, to: *illuminare, illustrare*
illumination: *illustratio*
illuminator: *illustrator*
illustration: *exemplum*
image: *imago, idolum, phantasma*
image, to form the image of: *fingere*
imagine, to: *phantasiare*
imagines: *phantasticus*
imagination: *phantasia*
imagination, without imagination: *non phantastice*
immaterial: *immaterialis*
immortal: *immortalis*
immortality: *immortalitas*
impairment, to suffer at the same time: *condetrimentum pati*
impartitionable: *impartibilis*
impede, to: *impedire*
impediment: *impedimentum*
imperfect: *imperfectus*
imply, to: *insinuare*
impression: *impressio*
imprint: *typus*
imprint, make into an imprint: *typificare*
impulse: *impetus*
inanimate: *inanimatus*
incommensurable: *incommensurabilis*
incommensurate: *incommensuratus*
incomposite: *incompositus*
incorporeal: *incorporeus*
indestructible: *incorruptibilis*
indication: *signum*
individual: *individuus, singularis*
indivisible: *indivisibilis*
indivisibility: *indivisibilitas*
inerrant: *impeccabilis*
inevident: *immanifestus*
inference: *syllogismus*
infinite, infinitely many: *infinitus*
infinitum, ad infinitum: *ad infinita, in infinita*
inflection backwards: *inflexio*
inform, to: *informare*
initiative: *motus proprius*
inseparable: *inseparabilis*
insert, to: *inserere*
instant: *nunc*

instrument: *organum*
intellect: *intellectus*
intellective: *intellectivus*
intellectual: *intellectualis*
intellectually: *intellectualiter*
intelligible: *intelligibilis*
interweaving: *complexio*
intuit: *iacere, adiacere, superiacere*
intuition: *adiectio, superiectio*
irradiate, to: *irradiare*
is, what is: *ens*

judge, to: *existimare, iudicare*
judges, thing that: *iudicativum*
judgment: *existimatio, iudicium*

know, get to know, to: *cognoscere, noscere*
knowable: *scibile*
knower, person with knowledge: *sciens*
knowledge: *scientia*
known, thing known: *cognoscibile, scibile*

lack, to: *deficere*
lack: *privatio*
later: *consequenter*
latitude: *latitudo*
leap: *kinema*
learn, to: *addiscere*
learn, thing what we learn: *mathema*
length: *longitudo*
life: *vita*
life, to give: *vivificare*
light: *lumen*
light, to bring to: *elucidare*
likely: *verisimilis*
likeness: *simulacrum*
limit: *finis*
line: *linea, recta*
line, in line with this: *consequenter*
line of thought: *continuatio intentionis*
liver: *epar*
lofty, in a lofty fashion: *eminenter*
look at, to: *intendere*
lower: *demissior*
luminous form, of: *augoeides*

magnitude: *magnitudo*
make, to: *facere*
maker, such as to make, thing that makes: *factivus*
man: *homo*
masculine, in the: *masculine*
material: *materialis*
mathematical: *mathematicus*
matter: *materia*

mean: *medietas*
meaning: *intellectus, intentio,*
  significatum
memory: *memoria*
menses: *menstruum*
mental: *mentalis*
metaphorically: *metaphora, secundum*
  metaphoram
mind: *mens*
mixed: *mixtus, immixtus*
mixture: *mixtum*
model for: *exemplum*
mood (of syllogism): *modus*
moon: *luna*
mortal: *mortalis*
movement: *motus*
moves, that which: *motivum*

natural: *naturalis*
naturally: *naturaliter*
nature: *natura*
nature, by nature such: *natum esse*
negation: *negatio*
neuter: *neuter*
neuter, in the neuter: *neutraliter*
next (adv.): *consequenter*
non-discursive, in a non-discursive way:
  integraliter, intransibiliter
non-rational: *irrationalis*
nose: *naris*
nourishes, that which: *nutritivum*
number: *numerus*

object: *obiectum*
occupied, to be occupied already:
  praeapprehendi
old age: *senectus*
one: *unus*
one, to be at one with: *communicare*
operate, to: *operari*
operation: *operatio*
operative: *operosus*
opines, that which: *opinativum*
opinion: *opinio*
opposite: *oppositus*
opposition, being opposite: *oppositio*
ordered, to be ordered along with:
  coordinari
organ: *organum*
original, originally: *a principio*
outright: *econtra*
outside, from outside: *foris, de foris,*
  extrinsecus
own, on its own: *nudus*

part: *pars, morion, particula*

part, having, containing parts:
  partibilis
participate in, to: *participare*
particular: *partialis, singulus*
partless, without parts: *impartibilis*
pass, to: *transire*
passing: *transitivus*
past: *praeteritum, factum*
past thinkers: *antiqui*
perceive, to: *sentire*
perceived, thing perceived: *sensibile*
perceiving: *sensus*
perceptive, perceives: *sensitivus*
perfect, to: *perficere*
perfect: *perfectus*
perfection: *perfectio*
perfective: *perfectivus*
peril: *dinum*
phasis: *phasis*
philosophy: *philosophia*
pilot: *gubernator*
place: *locus*
plant: *planta*
pleasant: *delectabilis*
pleased, to be, to experience pleasure:
  delectari
pneuma: *spiritus*
point: *punctum, signum*
pool: *susceptaculum*
positive state: *habitus*
possession, get possession of: *obtinere*
possible: *possibilis*
potentiality: *potentia, potentialitas*
power: *potentia*
powerfulness: *efficacia*
practical: *practicus, activus*
practical action: *praxis*
predicate, to: *praedicare*
predicate: *praedicatum*
pre-exist, to: *praevivere*
pre-existent: *praevivus*
preliminary, to make preliminary
  points: *praeaccipere*
present: *praesens*
present, to be present in: *inesse,*
  inexistere
preservative: *salvativus*
primary: *primus*
privation: *privatio*
problem: *dubitatio*
proof: *probatio*
proofs, to do: *demonstrare*
proper: *proprius*
proportion: *proportio*
providence: *providentia*
prudence: *prudentia*
prudent, to be: *prudentiare*

pull against, to: *contratrahere*
pupil (disciple): *discipulus*
pupil (of eye): *pupilla*
pure: *purus, sincerus*
purity: *puritas*
pursue, to: *persequi*
pursuit: *persecutio*
put together, to: *componere*

qualities, to be a thing of qualities: *qualificari*
quality: *qualitas*
quality, having some quality: *qualis*
quantity: *quantum*

ratio: *ratio*
ratiocinates, that which: *ratiocinativum*
rational: *rationalis*
reach, to: *attingere*
reading: *scriptura*
real: *realis*
reason, to: *ratiocinari, syllogizare*
reasoning: *ratiocinatio, syllogismus*
reasons, that which: *ratiocinativum*
receive, to: *suscipere*
reception, receipt, receiving: *receptio, susceptio*
receptive: *receptivus, susceptivus*
recollection: *reminiscentia*
referent: *suppositum*
refute, to: *redarguere*
refutation: *redargutio*
relation, in relation to: *ad*
relationship: *proportio, proportionalitas*
remember, to: *memorari*
removal: *amotio*
removed: *semotus*
reorder, to: *supersalire, supertransire*
representations, in the form of, in a representative way: *eikonice*
respect, in a certain: *secundum quid*
rest, to be at: *quiescere*
right angle: *rectus*
roundness: *peripheria*

say, to: *dicere*
saying: *dictio*
scientific: *scientionalis*
see, to: *videre*
seek, to: *appetere*
self-moving: *motivus per se*
semen: *sperma*
sensation: *sensima*
sense: *sensus*
sense organ: *sensiterium*
sensed, things sensed: *sensata*
senses, which senses: *sensitivus*

sensible: *sensibilis*
separable: *separabilis*
separate, to: *separare*
separate: *separatus*
separately: *separate*
separation: *separatio, segregatio*
servant: *opados*
shape: *figura*
share in, to: *communicare*
sheet: *carta*
show, to show precisely: *dearticulare*
sickness: *aegritudo*
sight: *visus*
sight, of sight: *visivus*
signified: *significatus*
significant: *significativus*
simple: *simplex*
simplicity: *simplicitas*
simply: *simpliciter*
single, of a single form: *uniformis*
sleep: *somnus*
smell: *odor*
snubnosed: *simus*
snubnosedness: *simitas*
soul: *anima*
special sense: *sensus proprius*
speculation: *theoria*
speech: *dictio, prolatio*
spirit: *ira*
spirited, that which is: *irascitivum*
spontaneously: *sponte*
station: *illocatio*
straight: *rectus*
straight off: *autothen*
straightness: *rectitudo*
stretch out coextensively, to: *coextendere*
strip, to: *denudare*
stupefy, to: *obnubilare*
stupor: *alienatio*
subject: *subiectum*
subject, to be a: *subiici*
substance: *substantia*
substance, of one substance with: *homoousios*
substantial: *substantialis*
suitability: *idoneitas*
sum, to sum up: *consummare*
summit: *summum*
sun: sol
supervene on, to: *accidere*
surface: *superficies*
swoon: *alienatio, nubilum*
syllogism: *syllogismus*
syllogistic: *syllogisticus*

tablet: *tabella, tabula*

take, to take in something additional: *coaccipere*
taking in: *acceptio*
tally, full: *replementum*
teacher: *doctor, docens*
teaching: *doctrina*
teaching (adj.): *doctrinativus*
temporal: *temporalis*
term: *terminus*
terminal point: *terminus*
theologian: *theologus*
theorem: *theorema*
thing: *res*
think, to: *meditare, prudentiare*
thinking: *meditatio*
thinks, that which: *meditativum*
thought: *intellectus, intentio, mens, noema*
thought, to take: *consiliari*
thoughtfully: *sententiose*
through: *penes*
throw in, to: *interiacere*
time: *tempus*
time, form of: *species temporalis*
totality: *totalitas*
touches, that which: *tactivum*
trace: *vestigium*
transcend, to: *transilire*
transcendent: *ereptus*
transmutation: *transmutatio*
transmute, to: *transmutare*
triangle: *triangulus, trigonum*
true: *verus*
truth: *veritas*
truth, to achieve truth: *verificari*
truth, attains truth: *verificativus*
truth itself: *autoveritas*
tune, being in: *harmonia*
tune, what is out of: *inharmonizatum*
tune, being out of: *inharmonizatio*
two together, the: *simul utrumque*

ugly: *turpis*
unaffacted: *impassibilis*
unaffectedness: *impassibilitas*
understand, to: *intelligere*
understanding: *intellectus, intelligentia*
understands, that which: *intellectivum*
undivided: *indivisus*
ungrammatically: *akatallilos*
union: *unio*
unite, to: *unire*
universal: *universalis*
universe: *universus, mundus*
unmixed: *immixtus*
unpleasant: *molestus*
unsuitable: *inidoneus*
unthinkable: *inopinabilis*
utterance: *vox*

vain, in: *frustra*
valid: *demonstrativus*
vehicle: *vehiculum*
verb: *verbum*
virtue: *virtus*
visible: *visibilis*
visual: *visivus*
vivifying: *zoogona*

water: *aqua*
wax: *cera*
what it was to be: *quod quid erat esse*
what something is: *quod quid est*
white: *albus*
whole: *totum*
width: *latitudo*
width, that which is without: *aplates*
wish: *voluntas*
word: *vox, nomen*
work: *opus*
working: *motivus*
world: *mundus, omne*
write, thing you write on: *scripturale*
wrong, to go wrong: *errare*

Latin–English Index

The Greek words translated by Moerbeke are given where they are known from Aristotle or may be inferred from texts of Aristotle, Philoponus, Sophonias and others or from marginalia. Page and line references are to the Latin text of Verbeke.

ablatio, *aphairesis*, abstraction: 76,39
absolute, directly: 82,8
absolutio, final answer: 28,85

abstractio, *aphairesis*, abstraction: 15,53; 67,8
   ex abstractione, abstract: 24,75; 109,9; 110,15; 115,60; 116,80

compassio, being affected along with: 20,86

compati, to be affected along with: 17,19

complexio, *krasis*, composition: 12,79.81.84.85; 62,10; 89,93

componere, *suntithenai*, to put together, compose: 68,32.39; 69,57.58.72; 70,85.89.91; 71,96.5.9.11; 72,21; 87,48; 88,68; 89,2

compositio, *sunthesis*, putting together, composition: 64,39; 67,22; 68,23.24.27–9.32.45; 69,59; 70,77.79–81.86.88.92.93; 71,99.3; 86,26.27.30; 87,35.50.55.57; 89,84.7; 91,55.57; 92,64; 94,34; 96,87; 117,13

compositus, *sunthetos*, composite: 22,21.23.25.27; 23,31.32.36.38.41.44.47; 24,72; 25,81.84.93.95–8.00.1.7; 26,11.31.32; 27,44.56.62.64; 28,67.76.77.79–81.86–8.91; 29,93; 34,7.11; 53,43; 64,51.54; 66,77.87; 71,96–8; 74,84.86; 79,49; 87,42; 90,13; 91,57; 94,32; 96,89

comprehendere, to grasp: 98,38

conceptus, *noêma*, concept: 64,40; 68,27.30; 70,79; 72,21; 73,43; 79,28.32.34; 92,67; 96,86.89; 118,20

conceptuum complexio, *sumplokê noêmatôn*, interweaving of concepts: 117,5

concupiscentia, *epithumia*, desire: 54,69; 94,19; 95,57

concupiscitivum, *epithumêtikon*, that which is desirous: 6,30

condetrimentum pati, *sumphthinein*, suffer impairment at the same time, 13,96

condictive, 85,1, read **conditive**, creatively, see note ad loc.

condistendere, to extend along with: 79,29; 86,19

conditor, creator: 13,22; see also **intellectus conditor**

conditivus, creative: 85,4

condividere, to divide along with: 73,69; 74,79; 86,20

congeneus, *homogenês*, homogeneous: 101,21

coniunctio, conjunction: 26,22
  coniunctio causalis, explanatory connective: 58,87

connecti, to be connected: 89,90.91

connexio, connection: 33,90

consequenter, *ephexês, akolouthês*, next, later, in line with this, following on: 39,27; 74,84; 86,6; 99,63.69; 101,19; 102,30

consequentia, *akolouthia*, construction: 72,33; 106,22

consiliari, *bouleuesthai*, to take thought: 105,9.13; 106,26

consummare, *sunkephalaioun*, to sum up: 111,67; 118,23 (see notes)

continuatio intentionis, line of thought: 9,95

continuitas, *sunekheia*, continuity (of exposition): 100,74

continuitas conceptus, concept (not) a continuum: 79,27

continuus, *sunekhês*, continuous: 25,79.82; 27,60; 28,65.66.69.70.77; 65,61; 66,84.88.90; 67,9.10; 72,24; 73,60.69.71.73; 74,77–80.85; 76,52.54.55.57; 77,69; 78,98.4.9; 79,22.23; 83,54; 86,17

contradistinctio, contradistinction: 41,58; 57,71; 86,16

contradivisus, set over against: 74,10; 87,58

contrapati, to be affected in return: 36,56

contrarietas, contrariety: 84,62

contrarius, *enantios*, contrary: 81,87.95.97.99; 82,29; 89,87.92; 101,6.22.23; 102,26.28.29.44.46; 103,53.57.71; 104,85.87

contratrahere, to pull against, 62,91; 63,19; (see notes ad loc.)

contristare, to distress: 95,60

conversio propositionum, *antistrophê protaseôn*, conversion of propositions: 98,42

cooperari, to cooperate with, help: 20,75; 61,75.82.84

coordinari, to be ordered along with: 55,11

copulare, to couple: 76,58

cor, heart: 6,29

corporalis, *sômatikos*, bodily: 35,26; 75,1.3; 82,16; 114,19

corporeus, *sômatikos*, corporeal: 14,26

corpus, *sôma*, body (human): 2,14; 4,69; 11,68; 12,78–80.82.84.85.89.90.93; 13,95–7.99; 16,87; 17,11.16–18.20–2; 18,28.29.37; 20,68.70.72–5.82.83; 23,55; 24,58–60; 32,68; 49,59; 55,11; 60,44; 62,13; 75,5.6; 82,16; 84,76; 98,35; 109,97; 110,27.30; 111,42.48.50.61

74,81.87; 75,13.15.18.21.25;
76,30–3.37.41.42.46.50.52;
77,73.75.76.88.89; 78,91.96.1.5.10;
79,29.31.34–6.39.40.44.46; 80,54;
81,82; 86,15
divisibilitas, divisibility: 65,62; 66,71;
84,62
divisio, *diairesis*, division: 67,10.22;
68,46; 70,81.88.90.94; 71,98;
80,57.63–6.69; 86,26.28.31; 87,35;
92,64; 117,13
divisus, *diairêtheis, diêirêmenos*, 65,65;
66,87; 71,96.98.9.11,13; 72,21.23;
78,2; 86,18
docens, teacher: 58,99
doctor, *didaskalos*, teacher:
10,36.48.31; 56,32.34.37; 58,99;
91,48
doctor extrinsecus, teacher from
outside: 19,46
doctrina, *didaskalia*, teaching: 18,45;
19,47; 92,76.79; 108,81
doctrinativus, see **intellectus
doctrinativus**
domificativa, art of building: 83,47
dualitas, *duas*, duality: 28,72.78
dubitatio, doubt: 60,60
êporêmenon, problem: 29,98; 30,13;
31,38.39; 33,94.95; 35,29; 36,49;
37,78; 40,45; 42,72.94; 43,99;
61,67.71; 85,90; 110,3
duplatio, duplication: 27,62
duplicatio, *diploê*, doubling over, being
doubled over: 23,48; 24,76; 27,55
dyanoia, *dianoia*, dianoia: 19,66;
20,69.71.73.74.76.81; 104,00

ebrietas, drunkenness: 12,94; 39,15;
63,15; 82,17
eclipsis, *ekleipsis*, eclipse: 69,65
econtra, *antikrus*, outright: 4,67 (see
note)
efficacia, *to drastêrion*, powerfulness:
18,30
eikonice, *eikonikôs*, in the form of
representations, in a
representative way: 83,43.45
electio boni, choice of good: 97,10
elementum, *stoikheion*, element: 31,41;
39,8
eligere, to choose: 92,71; 106,35
elucidare, *ekphainein*, to bring to light:
40,37
eminens, exalted, 51,7; see also **causa
eminens**
eminenter, magis eminenter,

eminentiore modo, *kreittonôs*, in
a more lofty fashion: 32,60; 88,78
endelichia, *entelekheia*, actuality:
46,71
ens, what is, being: 13,19; 14,36.37
epar, *hêpar*, liver: 6,30
ereptus, *exêirêmenos*, transcendent:
45,39
errare, to go wrong: 89,84
essentia, *ousia*, essence: 3,54; 6,35;
7,42; 25,93.94; 27,51; 29,93.94;
51,8; 71,13; 74.94; 76,33.36;
90,22.26.30; 94,26.29; see also
actus essentia, unus essentia
essentialis, essential: 76,45; 77,86
evidens, *saphês*, clear: 2,28
excellentia, excess: 32,61
exemplar, original: 119,66
exemplariter, *paradeigmatikos*, as
exemplars, in an exemplary way:
83,44.46
exemplum, *hupodeigma*, illustration,
model for: 26,25; 28,66; 40,30;
55,18.23; 56,47; 68,35; 73,60; 91,58
existentia, existence: 57,52
huparxis, existence (sc. subsistence):
67,8; 81,88; 107,62
existentia principalis, *proêgoumenê
huparxis*, existence of the primary
kind: 67,11
existimare, *hupolambanein*, to judge:
11,66.69.72; 13,11; 96,89
existimatio, *hupolêpsis*, judgment: 1,7;
88,70; 115,58
experientia, experience: 106,36
exserere, *prokheirizesthai*, to expound:
19,56

facere, *poiein*, to make: 5,93; 21,5; 30,7;
42,88; 43,9.11.12; 44,21; 48,35;
50,87.89.92; 51,96.99.2; 53,53;
55,15.19.22; 56,27; 57,53.55.67;
58,90; 71,8; 83,52; 114,31
factivus, *poiêtikos*, maker, such as to
make, that makes: 42,88; 44,21;
53,56.57; 55,5.14.15;
58,79.80.96.99.00; see also **causa
factiva**
factum, *genomenon*, past: 69,56.61;
71,5.6
falsitas, falsity: 68,26.31.33.45.47.48;
69,51.62; 70,83; 107,48.49; 117,13;
120,69
falsus, *pseudês*, false: 33,96; 64,39;
67,17.18.21.22;
68,24.39.40.42.43.46;
70,75.77.79.82.86.87; 71,00.3.4;

119,59; see also *speculativa*
potentia
potentiality (opposed to *actus*,
actuality): 4,61; 8,65; 37,77; 42,79;
43,17; 48,32; 52,36; 53,50.55.57.59;
56,46; 58,83; 59,15; 60,49; 66,70;
71,19; 84,69.72; 85,97; 86,22; 91,41;
113,92
potentia, dunamei, in potentiality:
4,63; 5,90; 8,80.83; 9,94.6.15;
10,18.24.26.29.30; 11,57.58.73;
14,28.33.39; 15,65; 16,73–5;
19,57.59.61.63; 20,78; 34,1;
36,51.69; 37,73; 39.5.7.12.19.27;
40,51; 42,75.77; 43,8.10.11;
44,21.23; 47,7; 48,29.39; 49,43.47;
51,4; 52.20.23.24.32; 53,48;
54,86.88.94.96.97; 55,2.5.23;
56,30.42.48.50; 57,56.60.61.64.78;
58,86.94.95; 59,18–20.23;
60,35.41.45; 65,62; 66,71; 71,15.18;
72,20.22.25.28.30.33.37; 73,58.69;
74,87; 78,97; 81.1.3.4;
82,7.9–12.20.21; 83,37; 84,63;
85,93.95; 91,45.56; 92,73.84.86.92;
93,5; 113,94.97; see also
intellectus potentia, secundum
potentiam
potentia irrationalis, non-rational
power: 2,27; 12,89; 52,39.40; 75,24
potentia prima, potentiality in the
first sense: 33,84.92
potentia primo modo, potentiality
in the first sense: 16,84.88.91
potentia rationalis, rational power:
7,50; 52,39; 75,24
potentia secundum primo,
potentially in the first sense: 14,43
potentia secundum primo modo,
potentially in the first sense:
16,84.88.91
potentia secundum secundam
potentialitatem, potentially in
the second sense of 'potentiality':
19,62
potentia secundum secundario,
potentially in the second sense:
14,40
potentia secundum secundo
modo, potentially in the second
sense: 16,92
potentiae activae, practical powers:
5,7
potentialitas, potentiality: 66,70
potentialitas prima, potentiality in
the first sense, the first sort of

potentiality: 16,94; 38,82; 40,37;
57,64
potentialitas prior, potentiality in
the first sense: 39,4.8
potentialitas secunda, potentiality
in the second sense: 19,62; 39,11
practicus, praktikos, practical: 6,8;
97,13; 98,28.32.35; 107,52.53
praeaccipere, to make preliminary
points: 92,77
praeapprehendi, to be occupied
already: 17,5
praedicare, to predicate: 87,39.45;
88,63
praedicatum, predicate: 87,48; 89,84
praedicatus terminus, predicate term:
70,95
praeexistere, exist in advance, pre-
exist: 16,87; 50,70
praefactum, progegenêmenon, thing
which happened earlier: 106,36
praeiudicare, reach a decision in
advance: 105,16
praemeditatum, thing considered in
advance: 105,15
praesens, parôn, present (sc. of time):
69,66.67; 96,91; 105,9
praeteritum, to parelthon, past: 38,94;
71,5
praevivere, pre-exist: 38,85
praevivus, probiôtos, pre-existent:
38,85.87.91
praxis, praxis, practical action,
conduct: 98,32.34
principium, arkhê, beginning: 75,22;
76,31; 78,11
principium essendi, beginning to
existence: 38,87.92
principle: 4,62; 56,34.35
source: 53,53; 58,90.96; 84,74; 107,45
a principio, original, originally:
13,4; 19,63
privatio, sterêsis, privation, lack:
80,58.70.73.75;
81,78.79.83.89.90.96.98.99;
82,8.12.13.18–20.22.26.28,30.32;
83,51.53
probatio, kataskeuê, proof: 41,55
profunditas, depth: 80,55.56; 81,78.84
profundum, depth: 80,65
prolatio, in prolatione, uttered in
speech: 89,12
proportio, relationship: 101,12.18.19;
102,37; 103,53.54.72
proportionalis, analogos, analogous:
96,87.90
proportionalia, analogies: 94,16

39,18.20; 47,9; 49,50.52; 59,22;
93,00; 115,51
scientia, *epistêmê*, knowledge: 3,57;
4,61; 13,8; 21,95; 41,60.63; 46,74;
58,5; 59,6.8.12; 82,29; 83,33; 85,95;
89,97; 91,58;
112,72.75.84.88.90.91; 113,92–4.7;
114,22.27; 115,41.45.52; 116,82;
117,91
  scientia circum agibilia, knowledge
  concerning things which are done:
  41,59
  scientia mathematica,
  mathematical science: 114,32;
  117,91
  scientia medicinalis, medical
  science: 117,94
  scientia secundum actum,
  knowledge in actuality: 6,14;
  46,73; 51,13; 58,2.5; 59,6.8.9.13;
  90,34; 91,59; 110,13; 112,73;
  113,95.6
  scientia secundum potentiam,
  knowledge in potentiality: 6,15;
  46,73; 51,13; 58,3; 59,12; 90,35
  scientia speculativa, contemplative
  knowledge: 41,53.58
scientionalis, *epistêmonikos*, scientific:
112,75; 113,95
  scientionale, *epistêmonikon*, that
  which knows: 113,97
scintilla, *spinthêr*, burning coal:
20,76–8.80
scriptura, reading: 59,27; 60,36; 75,16;
77,87; 92,91; 109,99.5
  interpretation: 111,54
scripturale, *grammateion*, thing you
write on: 37,74.79; 38,82; 39,4.16;
57,65; 77,80
secundum quid, in a certain respect:
102,46
segregatio, *diakrisis*, separation: 2,20
semotus, removed: 20,85; 84,75; 110,31
senectus, *gêras*, old age: 4,78; 5,83;
49,65
sensata, things sensed: 92,68
sensibilis, *aisthêtos*, sensible (i.e.
perceivable): 63,30; 94,27; 95,51;
113,10; 114,15; 118,24; and see
species sensibilis
  sensibile, *aisthêton*, sensible thing,
  thing perceived: 7,57.59; 8,75.83;
  9,92.97; 10,22.24; 11,60; 14,44;
  15,49.50.53.54.59.60.62.63;
  17,00.12.17.19; 18,28.30; 21,94;
  23,54–6; 24,58.66.67; 25,86;
  31,44.54; 32,61; 33,82; 34,00; 46,76;

49,67; 59,10; 62,97; 63,16.27.32;
75,2.5; 81,4; 85,95; 88,77.80;
92,66.73.84.85.90.92.94;
94,22–4.30.33.37.40; 95,63;
96,78–81.86.87.94; 98,26; 99,63.65;
100,75.78–80,88.91; 101,11;
102,25.26;
103,48.49.53.55.60.61.72.74;
104,76.83.98; 106,32; 111,46;
112,70.72.74.76.89.91;
113,99.1.3.12; 114,17.32.35;
115,39.42,43.46–8.60.61; 116,66.86;
117,89.98.00.1.9; 119,53; see also
species sensibilium
  sensibile commune, *aisthêton*
  koinon, common sensible: 101,17
  sensibile proprium, *aisthêton idion*,
  proper sensible: 88,74; 89,4;
  101,17; 104,90
sensima, *aisthêma*, sensation: 95,69;
96,79; 97,9
sensiterium, *aisthêtêrion*, sense organ:
17,98; cf. 99,52.54
sensitivus, *aisthêtikos*, which senses,
perceptive: 26,33; 27,39; 54,92;
112,75; see also **anima sensitiva**
  sensitivum, *aisthêtikon*, that which
  perceives, senses: 8,70; 10,22;
  12,80; 17,97.3; 18,31; 26,28;
  27,40–2; 36,63; 49,66;
  92,73.83.92.94; 95,56.61.62;
  99,51.52.54 (see note ad loc.); 113,97
  sensitiva medietas, *aisthêtikê*
  mesotês, perceptive mean: 93,13;
  94,44
  sensitiva potentia, *aisthêtikê*
  dunamis, power to perceive: 8,68;
  94,38; 99,53.54
sensus, *aisthêsis*, sense, i.e. ability to
perceive: 2,15.16.21.22.25;
7,49.54.56.59; 8,66.67.83; 9,92.96;
10,24.28.29; 11,60; 12,76.81.85;
13,14.15; 17,98–00.8.11.16;
18,26.27.32; 23,39.43.48.53.54;
24,59.66.68.71.73; 25,85.88.90.2;
26,34; 27,43.44.58; 30,26; 31,44.54;
32,55.60.61; 33,77.79.81.91; 54,79;
59,9.11; 64,45.48; 75,99.1.2.5;
81,79.4; 84,78; 85,95;
88,67.69.74.76.79; 89,4; 92,81.94;
93,99.2; 94,19.21.39.44;
95,52.61.62.66; 96,79.81.82.92;
97,18; 99,61.69.73;
100,75.78–80.92.93; 101,3;
103,53.75; 104,90.95; 110,17;
111,44; 112,76.85.89–91;
113,96.12; 114,22;

Index of Names

Page and line references are to the Latin text of Verbeke.

Subject Index

References in italics are to the pages of the Introduction. Other references are to page and line of Verbeke's Latin text.